Bablake School and the Great War

First Edition 2007

CU01508528

Published by War Memorial Park Publications

ISBN: 978-184426-427-8

Printed by Printondemand-worldwide Ltd

For a copy of this publication e-mail trevor_harkin@hotmail.com

Bablake School

and the

Great War

Trevor Harkin
2007

War Memorial Park Publications

For Dad

(1933 -2006)

Contents

Preface	1
Acknowledgements	2
The Evidence	4
Bablake a Brief Introduction up to 1914	6
Bablake and the Great War	10
The School Magazine	15
Cadet Corps at Bablake	20
Enlisting	26
Roll of Honour	32
The Wounded, the Missing & POW's	35
Died at Home	38
The War at Sea	48
- Battle of Jutland	48
- The Merchant Ships	52
- Protecting the Convoys	53
- Torpedoed	56
The War in the Air	57
Gallipoli	60
Mesopotamia	65
Palestine	67
Italy	68
The Western Front	69
1914	69
1915	70
1916	78
1917	100
1918	116
The Unverified	135
Back from the Dead	137
Medals Won	139
Campaign Medals	147
Post War	149
War Memorial Fund	154
Some Reminiscences	156
Conclusion	158
Appendices	159
Meet the Author	192
Index	193

Preface

Having researched my own family tree, in 2005 I began a project to research the Memorial Plaques in Coventry's War Memorial Park. The WW1 plaques gave few details about those commemorated, purely initials, surname, rank and regiment. Local appeals were made and Terry Patchett, the grandson of Private William Ivens Patchett, came forward. William served with the Warwickshire Yeomanry and on the 8th November 1917 in Palestine the Yeomanry charged a retiring enemy and captured 12 guns and 100 prisoners. Private Patchett was mortally wounded and died on the 14th November 1917.

In addition to providing details about his grandfather, Terry, a former teacher at Bablake from 1964 to 2003, was kind enough to show me the Bablake War Memorial and the *'Roll of Honour'* with 96 names of those who died in the Great War. A cross-check of the 264 plaques in the War Memorial Park and the Bablake fallen showed a match of 23 names. Owing to Terry's enthusiasm, I undertook to research the remaining 73 names.

Several years later, this book is the result.

Trevor Harkin

Acknowledgments

Researching the content of this book would have been impossible without the assistance of Bablake School, in particular Terry Patchett, Robert Dougall, Chris Mellers and the late John Lawrence, who all offered encouragement and information throughout the period of research. I also need to acknowledge the work of Peter Burden, author of *'The Lion and the Stars a History of Bablake School'*, for assistance with the history of the school, prior to and during the Great War.

Researching and compiling this book would not have been possible without the support of my wife, Emma and children Molly and Toby allowing me to indulge in this passion. The Commonwealth War Grave Commission (CWGC) Head Office in particular Maureen Annetts, was fundamental in helping with the complex searches and background information whilst their UK Office assisted with grave location in the UK. The CWGC have also permitted reproduction of the map of the Somme. The work of the equivalent bodies in Australia, New Zealand and Canada also needs to be recognized. Photographs of Herbert Victor Cantrill have been uploaded to the Canadian web page. Information has also been shared with Susan Tall, author of *'Kenilworth and the Great War'*.

The Old Boys joined up with a number of different regiments and thanks need to be expressed to the following curators, regimental museums and other institutions:

Mrs. Lesley Frater from The Fusiliers' Museum of Northumberland, Alastair Massie from the National Army Museum, Jacqueline Minchinton from Northampton County Council, Katharine Higgon from the King's College London Archives, Matthew Buck from Liverpool Museums, Bryan Johnson Curator of the Warwickshire Yeomanry Museum, David Baynham and Stephanie Bennett from the Royal Regiment of Fusiliers (Royal Warwickshire), Mike Marr and Dino Lemonofides, Oxfordshire and Buckinghamshire Light Infantry Museum, Mick Wilkes from the Worcestershire and Sherwood Foresters' Regiment, Celia Green and Martin Everett from the Royal Regiment of Wales Museum, John Taylor of the Shropshire Regimental Museum, Colonel (Retd) IH McCausland of Royal Green Jackets, Dicky Bird, Royal Norfolk Regimental Museum, Elizabeth Stratton, Selwyn College, Cambridge , Alan Readman, West Sussex Records Office, Major (Retd) T. W. Stipling Duke of Cornwall's Light Infantry Museum, William Mullen, The Inniskillings' Museum, Tony Sprason, Lancashire Fusiliers' Museum and Martin Everett, Regimental Museum of the Royal Welsh.

In the research, I came across a number of individuals who are working on projects which have relevance to the Old Boys. In particular, information has been shared with Eric Boden, who is working on a book on the 9th Lancers; Carl Lewis, who concentrates on HMS Strongbow, Martin Edwards and Michael Booker, who maintain www.roll-of-honour.com and Bryn Dolan and John Meyers who maintain www.anzacs.org. I thank them for their input and permission to use pictures and material.

The records maintained by Coventry Local Studies Library and the City Archives have been essential in adding information to the details of the fallen and those who served and their permission to use pictures and photographs is gratefully acknowledged. Information on Captain Harold Meredyth Adcock has been included with the kind permission of the Masters and Fellows of Christ's College, Cambridge and was provided by Colin Higgins. The Regimental Chapel of St. George's in Chichester Cathedral, St. Barbara's Church, Queen's Road Church, Canterbury Cathedral via Caroline Norwood, the Royal Warwicks Club, The Earlsdon Working Mens Club and St. John's Church all supplied information on their memorials.

Neil Clark for access to his pictorial databases on officers who died in the Great War and Kevan Darby for information on the 9th Battalion Royal Warwickshire Regiment. On a more local level thanks to Sheila Adams from *'The Earlsdon Echo'* for printing articles on the Old Boys on St. Barbara's Memorial, Mick Baker for donating an entire series of *'The Great War...I Was There'*, Martin Bird for assistance in enhancing images, Diana Fisher for the indexing work on local servicemen, Tim Parsons and Roynan Buckler for an insight into medal collecting and access to the medals of Acting Sergeant F. A. Buckler and Sub Conductor A. E. Harris. Sue Wilson for assistance with intricacies of Microsoft Word, Nigel Hoare for access to his WW1 books, Alexander Hoare for assistance with promotional materials, Paul Wright from Band Hatton & Co Solicitors and finally Dave Lewis from Culture and Leisure, Coventry City Council.

In several cases I have been contacted directly by the families of the Fallen: Colin Irving, the nephew of Herbert Charles Collingbourne, Rebecca Baker, a relative of Alfred George Middleton, Robert Clarke whose Great Uncle was Victor Leslie Clarke and Roynan Buckler whose Grandfather was Acting Sergeant Francis Albert Buckler. Thanks also to the anonymous relatives of Private Morris for contacting Bablake and leaving memorabilia

To those who remain anonymous but were cajoled into helping by those mentioned above, I also express my thanks.

The Evidence

Throughout this book various resources have been compiled to build a history of the school, those that served and those that fell. Material from the Bablake Archives was fundamental for underpinning this project: The 'Bablake School Magazine' known as *'The Wheatleyan'* and the 'Admission records' were used extensively. The latter records details of six hundred pupils who attended between 1901 and 1911, thirty four records were found relating to the Fallen which provided such details as their father's profession, their elementary school, their dates of birth, period of attendance at Bablake, whether they were day boys, boarders or both in turn, and the profession they entered on leaving.

Many of the school's other records and treasures were destroyed in the air raids of World War 2, fortunately the War Memorial and *'Roll of Honour'* survived. The War Memorial was erected on the 10th February 1921, and is divided into three sections. The left and right sections include the names of seven hundred Old Boys and staff who served in His Majesty's forces and the centre section includes a list of the Fallen and shows ninety six names. The *'Roll of Honour'* records the names of the Fallen and in fifty two cases includes a photograph. Both of these resources played a major part though both of these were lacking in detail.

To supplement the school material, information was obtained from the Commonwealth War Grave Commission. The official cut-off date for a war related death by the Commission is the 31st August 1921, which aligns with *'The Termination of the Present War (Definition) Act'*. Deaths falling after the 31st August 1921 are not formally documented as war related.

Other sources have been consulted: *'Soldiers who died in the Great War'*, *'Canadian Overseas Expeditionary Force Attestation Papers'*, *'The National Archives of Australia'* and the *'City of Coventry: Roll of the Fallen'*. The latter, compiled in 1927, includes the names of 2,600 soldiers who fell and were either born, employed or resided in Coventry. Detail on each entry varies but typically covers name, rank, regiment, former regiment, address, birth details, occupation and in some cases employer. Being educated in Coventry did not qualify for inclusion in the *'Roll of the Fallen'*: research suggests that the names of the Fallen on the War Memorial were provided to the City librarian compiling the Roll and if no further information was received the entry simply read the name and 'Educated at Bablake' as in the case of H. M. Brown.

It is estimated that over 35,000 soldiers from Coventry served during the Great War. Those who attended Bablake strictly speaking were known as the Old Boys however in the context of this book and on the War Memorial, Old Boys refers to staff and former pupils. It is likely that a number of Old Boys died at home some time after the war owing to longer term illnesses such as the effects of wounds received.

The local employee magazines of the time have also been searched for relevant details as well as the local papers, *'The Coventry Graphic'* and *'The Coventry Herald'*. Family information has been obtained from the 1901 census. In some cases siblings could have been born after the point the survey was taken.

In some cases the *'Battalion war diaries'* have been acquired, generally they only name individuals if they were Commissioned Officers. Privates and Non-Commissioned Officers were generally not mentioned; the diaries' entries vary in length dependent on the operations that day. In some cases the date wounds were received has been verified, in the remainder the action the Battalion was involved in on the day or just prior to the date has been included. Museums and local councils have also started their own databases and material has been taken from these sources. In four cases I have been contacted by members of the family and the information was received gratefully. If further details can be supplied about the Old Boys or the school during the Great War please contact me.

It is important to note, however, that the cross- referencing of material has raised anomalies, in particular order of forenames, middle names, rank, spelling, address etc. In these cases I have gone with the majority. Material also came from the National Archives in terms of Medal Index Cards (MIC) and the Registers of Seamen's Services. Searching *'The London Gazette'* provided citations. Each piece of evidence from the above sources adds to the picture of the Old Boys who were to lose their lives and those who served. If the individuals are mentioned on other war memorials throughout the city, I have also noted this but my database is still ongoing and no doubt other material will continue to be added in future editions.

Bablake - A Brief Introduction up to 1914

The exact origins of Bablake School may never be determined, but they certainly pre-date 1560. Evidence shows that the 'Old School' in Hill Street was re-opened in 1560 having been founded by the municipality; forty one boys were in attendance. These boys were going to undertake apprenticeships with various firms in the city, receiving free education, clothing and board whilst at Bablake. The school at this point was heavily reliant on charitable donations.

On April 7th 1563, Thomas Wheatley (a former Mayor) made a generous donation to the school, endowing it with much of his estate. Thomas was an honest man: shortly before his generous donation he had ordered steel wedges from a Company in Spain; on receipt the chest was full of silver ingots, and unable to establish the correct owner, he decided to give the proceeds of the shipment to provide education for the needy of Coventry.

Other local benefactors shortly followed the lead provided by Thomas and made further donations to the school. The original dress of the 'Bablake boy' consisted of a tunic of dark blue cloth, of good quality, extending from the neck nearly to the ankles, and gathered in at the waist with a leathern girdle; a petticoat or a skirt of yellow- coloured material reached to the knees with stockings to match and low shoes with buckles. The headgear was a knitted cap with yellow band and tassel. Linen bands were used as neck ties. The tunic was not monastic in origin, but was the ordinary dress of well-to-do citizens in the 16th century. A former Mayor of Coventry, Richard Southam, wore similar clothing to that of the Bablake boys in 1414.

The school continued to function throughout the 17th and 18th Century and there is little documentary evidence until 1824 when Mr. Henry Mander became the headmaster, supplementing the school's income with an influx of private pupils. In 1837 the dress underwent a change: black cord trousers and grey socks were substituted for the yellow skirt and stockings, and lace-up boots replaced shoes with buckles. Mr. Mander's appointment lasted for 46 years and in 1870 Mr. F. W. Humberstone was appointed as Head.

Aged 24 he beat one hundred and sixty other applicants to the post. He matriculated from King's College, London in 1868 and prior to this was educated at Bancroft's School, a Church of England institution which held services twice daily. Aged 20 he was appointed as an assistant master and organist of Drapers' College, Tottenham. This was a school for the sons of Freemen of the Drapers' Company and was built on the operating principles of Bancroft's. He was not a native of Coventry but was born in Dover in 1846; during his Headmastership he was to play a pivotal role in the shaping of Bablake.

One of Mr. Humberstone's considerations in his new post was to deal with a new proposal to make the school an intermediate institution between the elementary school and the Grammar School, which he managed to delay to 1887. Using his experience gained at Bancroft's and Drapers' College, his Headmastership at Bablake was run on a similar basis, built upon routine, *"A fair proportion of the boys who passed into Bablake were of good natural ability, the sons of self-respecting intelligent artisans"*. In 1872 he introduced the study of Shakespeare with a different play annually, and this work was praised in annual examinations of the school from 1883 to 1887. The inspectors noted *"more than one of the boys recited Shakespeare remarkably well"*. In his adopted city Mr. Humberstone was well known, writing as a musical critic in *'The Coventry Herald'* and as a local historian.

On arrival at the school, boys were asked to provide a specimen of their handwriting, and a further sample was taken when they left, to show the improvement of penmanship in the time spent at Bablake. Samples included that of W. H. Batchelor, who attended from 1879 - 1881 and became Alderman Batchelor, a member of the Education Committee; Mr. A. Pargetter, who served in the Town's Council, and Mr. W. Lord, who was for some years Baths Superintendent at the Council.

On the 28th November 1887, seventeen years after the idea had originally been mooted, the decision was reached to make Bablake an intermediate school and one of the enablers was to build a new school on the Coundon Road site known as 'Crampers Field'. Three other schools would be amalgamated in the move. The new site was already owned by the trustees of the school and they had been obtaining rent off it for many years. The estimated cost of the new build was £16,000.

By 1890 the environment had changed: a Technical Institute opened in Earl Street and the teaching of technical sciences was strongly being encouraged. Bablake had reconstituted itself as an organised science school, when it opened on its new site on October 20th 1890. Mr. Humberstone took up a new position as senior assistant master and Joseph Innis Bates was appointed as headmaster. About this time the tunic, as a form of recognisable dress, was abolished altogether, even though Mr. Humberstone argued that *"the continuity of the school may be recognised by a restoration of quaint and picturesque costume, at least for use on Sundays, speech days and other ceremonial occasions"*.

In 1911 Bablake was to undergo another period of change. The former Head of the school, Mr. Francis William Humberstone retired ending his forty one year association with Bablake to pursue his interests in the history and antiquities of his adopted city. On leaving he received an illuminated address and a case of solid silver, the former from the staff and current scholars, the latter from the Old Boys. In the summer, Joseph Innis Bates also retired, when he ended his appointment as Headmaster which had lasted twenty one years.

A new Head, on a salary of £450 per annum, was appointed, Dr. Frederick Hodson. He had been educated, like Mr. Humberstone, at Bancroft's School and then onto King's College, London but had also achieved a Ph.D. He had seven years' experience as a master, the latter two being spent as a headmaster at King Edward VII Grammar School, Melton Mowbray. Dr. Hodson set about introducing changes, including a house system (roughly split by district), installation of electric light in the buildings and plans, put in place by Mr. Bates, were coming to fruition with the addition of more buildings.

The Bablake headmasters 1870 – 1918

F. W. Humberstone	J. I. Bates	F. Hodson
(1870 - 1890)	(1890 - 1911)	(1911 - 1918)

New masters were being attracted to Bablake and one of these in 1912 was Mr. A. Wilson, who had graduated with an Master of Arts from St. Andrews and had teaching experience both at Brechin High School, Scotland and at the Panchgani Boys High School, India. Mr. Wilson was a keen athlete, played football and had agreed that he would take over the joint management, with Mr. Stones, of the cricket club. He also possessed a good baritone voice, a quality that was a necessity for school concerts.

Traditionally the Mayor of Coventry would come into Bablake and request a day's holiday for the boys. In accordance with this custom the Mayor, Colonel Wyley came in to the school in December 1912 and their holiday was duly granted. In 1913 Mr. G. S. Foster Kemp, a former resident master at Bablake, had started a weekly interchange of letters between boys of the Chinese Public School, Shanghai and his former pupils, whilst closer to home Mr. Jack Parsons, an Old Boy, was scoring his first century for Warwickshire.

With the start of the War approaching the school had been linked with the city's history, in a more or less prominent manner for over three hundred and fifty years, Mr. A. E. W. Mason, a Member of Parliament for Coventry, spoke of an institution *" which is, and always has been, the pride and joy of the citizens"*.

Bablake and the Great War

Many of those who had been pupils or members of staff at Bablake in the years leading up to the declaration of war enlisted. By 1914 some three hundred and twenty pupils were in attendance at Bablake- some thirty six resident boys, the remainder being day boys. 1914 saw the formation of the Cadet Corps, an initiative which had started in 1912. Reports of their activities and ideals are included in the Cadet Corps Chapter; the cadets mirrored the real war, undergoing drill, fire arms training, inspection and promotion within the Corps.

Staff and pupils from the Cadet Corps naturally moved from playing soldier to the real thing and members of the Old Boys club had joined up. First mention of the impact of the war comes in the 1915 January edition of *'The Bablake School Magazine'* where a member of staff, Mr. H. M. Adcock left *"having received a commission as Second Lieutenant in the 10th Battalion, Lancashire Fusiliers"*. His death in action is recorded in the July 1916 edition of the magazine. A member of staff, Mr. Patrick, had initiated drawing up the *'Roll of Honour'* which appeared periodically in *'The Bablake School Magazine'*. This listed the Old Boys names, the year they left Bablake and their unit. By January 1916, two hundred and fifty names were already listed. Sadly four former pupils had already died in action, their deaths denoted by 'killed' after their surnames.

In the school grounds on the 18th June 1916, the Commanding Officer (CO) of the district awarded two Distinguished Conduct Medals (DCM) and inspected all the soldiers then in Coventry, the Bablake & Coventry Cadet Corps, the Boys Brigade, the Scouts and Ambulance Corps. The Mayor made a speech and then all the military units marched past on his conclusion. A month later on the 13th July 1916, one hundred and fifty Bablake boys including fifty cadets attended the Lord Kitchener Memorial Service in St. Michael's Church.

Coventry was a centre of munitions' production and most admirable efforts were made in assisting in the production of shell cases for munitions. Under the supervision of H. L. Allsopp, some of the boys gave up their entire summer and Easter holidays to work in the White & Poppe munitions factory and on occasions worked a twelve hour shift doing 'overtime'; contingents of cadets under Sergeant-Major E. Prattley also attended local war factories to render help.

Nearly eighty boys participated at one time or the other, with no more than fifty present on a given day, nine hundred attendances were reported, typically varying in length from seven to ten hours. The boys were given special consideration: providing sufficient notice they could arrive one hour late or leave at 5.00pm instead of 7.15pm. On arrival at work they were split into squads and given tasks, stopping at noon to 1.00pm for lunch and then 5.15pm to 6.15pm for tea. In conclusion H. L. Allsopp for his article in *'The Bablake School Magazine'* entitled *'War Work in the Holidays'* stated *"we cannot imagine a more interesting or more profitable way of spending one's vacation, to say nothing of the fact that one is doing for the common good"*.

Mr. F. Morgan supervised the manufacture of shell bases in the metal workshop by batches of boys from the upper forms. In addition to the work done during school hours, considerable time had been voluntarily devoted to the work during evenings and on Saturdays. The Reverend Cairns, speaking at an assembly in 1917, spoke warmly of the munitions work done at Bablake and by this point the output of the workshop had been over five thousand shell bases and thirty packaging cases. On several occasions the work had to be abandoned owing to shortage of materials and the rigours of 'overtime' employed.

By December 1918, the metal department had produced 20,000 eighteen-pounder high explosive shell bases, with Bablake being one of the few schools who could work within the engineering tolerances required, the school receiving several congratulatory letters including one from the Inspector of Munitions. The work was also recognised by Alfred Herbert, who awarded seven of the boys special apprenticeships.

Collections from the pupils enabled 'comforts' to be sent to Old Boys at the front and letters received acknowledged how grateful they were to be remembered in such a practical way. The receipt of *'The Bablake School Magazine'* also helped many to feel 'in touch'. One of the school's soccer pitches was taken up and staff supervised enthusiastic pupils growing produce which supplemented the resident boys' diet, which provided another opportunity for the boys to spend their holidays in a patriotic manner though not as profitable. By the end of 1917 the pupils and members of staff had grown approximately five tons of produce.

With many of the masters answering the call to duty and potential candidates also enlisting, the school employed several female teachers including Miss M. D. Birt and Miss P. E. Hanson. Male teachers were also hired and Mr. H. B. Johnson who had graduated with a B.A from Oxford joined the staff for the period of the war. Throughout the war the school endeavoured to carry on as usual; Christmas concerts were still held, the main difference being the attendance of wounded soldiers and patriotic music found its place.

Sports continued during the war; *"No apologies were made for having school football in war time"*. The sports reports took on a new flavour making reference to military terminology: the first football eleven needed *"heavy artillery"*, cricketers need to *"reconnoitre"* the ground and the usual zest had been lost in cricket circles with staff and schoolmates taking part in the *"Great Game"*. Cricket was played on at least one occasion with patients from the Hill Crest VAD Hospital, more regular fixtures being the first year resident boys against the second.

In the summers the annual Sports Days were held as usual. The athletes being witnessed by a large number of parents and friends, great interest was taken by them in the achievement of the boys. The pictures below from *'The Coventry Graphic'* show:
1. Members of the teaching staff who acted as officials
2. Start of the hundred yards flat handicap
3. Holmes winning the high jump
4. Day winning the long jump

Bablake Sports Day

Prize distribution was also affected: the scholars who were entitled to prizes for sporting achievement were instead awarded mementoes from the Great War. Those who completed their studies at Bablake were reminded *"it was not desirable for them to wear their caps and they should also detach their badges"*, this assisted in identifying the current scholars from the Old Boys. The Debating Society also focused on the war with subjects such as *'England would gain nothing from the War'* and *'Conscientious Objectors should be disenfranchised'*.

In April 1918 the school was still practising drills owing to the increased possibility of attacks from hostile aircraft. In the event of such a raid, the pupils had been allotted their respective positions of shelter from flying debris. After a series of practise drills the time taken to take up the correct place of refuge improved considerably. The resident boys noted *"as a break from the usual monotony of resident life, the advent of the air raid gave us ample scope for excitement"*. In one instance the over- zealous members of the indoor fire companies indulged in a *"dust up"*.

Dr. Hodson the headmaster since 1911 became ill in 1917 and subsequently died on the 18th July 1918. Reverend A. R. F. Hyslop was appointed as a temporary replacement during his illness but the task really fell on the shoulders of Mr. Alfred Carter. Neither Reverend Hyslop nor Mr. Carter were offered the position of Headmaster, instead Dr. Hodson was replaced by Dr. Frankland (pictured), who had himself narrowly missed becoming the Headmaster in 1911. Dr. Frankland was tracked down to a school in Cheltenham and offered the position; he initially

refused but was persuaded by negotiation to take up the role, accepting a salary of £800 a year. A *'Report from the University of Birmingham'* dated the 1st November 1918 concluded *"Bablake school will now be able to start again, after the transitional time caused by Dr. Hodson's illness, the new Head-master will find excellent material to hand, and a school machine in good working order. Perhaps if peace really arrives in 1919, he will be able to establish the teaching staff on a permanent basis again, and the feeling of things being temporary will gradually pass away"*.

In the four years of the war 867 Old Boys and staff served, 96 of these fell. The names of 796 Old Boys are recorded on a memorial at the rear of the assembly hall and those who fell in a leather bound *'Roll of Honour'* at the front of the hall. This *'Roll'* contains the names of the fallen, a picture if available and a date or place of death if known. The second page of *'The Roll'* is shown on the following page.

In this book are written the names of those Members of this school who served their King and Country during the wars of 1914-18 and 1939-45

Some there were who served in the Armed Forces of our King, and some in the Auxiliary Services. To some, when war came upon them, it brought swift death or long captivity from which they did not return.

It is for these that this book is placed here by past and present members and friends of the School that the names of those contained herein may be had in remembrance by such as may enter this Hall to pray: that their names may be remembered with honour and thanksgiving and that which we owe to them shall not be forgotten

The School Magazine

'The Bablake School Magazine' was started in 1896 but throughout the war it was fundamental to the communication process for the Old Boys on the front. They were provided with a complimentary copy if they were members of the Old Boys club. The Editor received letters from those at the front and the Old Boys were kept up to date on the fate of their old school chums via the *'Roll of Honour'*.

"You can well imagine how we Old Boys out here like to read 'The School Magazine', for it helps to recall the happy days we spent at Bablake".

An Old Boy in France

The magazine changed from *'The Bablake School Magazine'* to *'The Wheatleyan'* in February 1916. This change was brought about as the blocks used for the cover were worn out and it was thought it was time for a change. To give the magazine an identity it was named *'The Wheatleyan'* in pious memory of Sir Thomas Wheatley, who had made such a generous donation to the school in 1563. Miss Hanson produced the new design incorporating the School's Arms. The cost was four pence and contributions for publication were encouraged: *"If you are an Old Boy in Flanders or Mesopotamia, in munitions shops or on the High Seas write and tell us something about it. We like information which is exclusive to ' The Wheatleyan'; it makes us feel important"*.

Letters from the front were received but not all of these were published. Those that made it to print were from Private William Edwin Clarke of the Royal Army Medical Corps (RAMC), Private Reginald Hegan 7th Battalion Royal Warwickshire Regiment, Bombardier Harold Hegan, Motor Machine Gun Service (MMGS) and Second Lieutenant P. G. Mander 4th West Riding Regiment.

The principal role of the RAMC was the medical evacuation of casualties from the battlefield until their subsequent return to duty. Private Clarke left the school in September 1914 and had previously been a laboratory assistant at Bablake. His letter fully aligns with the role of the RAMC:

"On Good Friday the same night as the Coventry Territorial's received their first baptism of fire, three stretcher squads from each section were detailed to collect the wounded for the first time. Although I belong to the bearer division I did not go out that night, but was fortunate enough to go the following night. We proceeded to a field dressing station and waited there till it was completely dark. Then the bearers set out with the stretchers en route for the regimental aid post.

All around the enemy were sending up star shells which lit the whole place up. As soon as the lights burnt out the crackling of rifle fire was heard in all directions. The wagon was left about a quarter of a mile from the Regimental aid post, the bearers going on. When the star lights went up the ruins of the buildings could be distinctly seen. Most noteworthy were the remains of a church, which had half its square tower blown away. On arriving at the aid post, which was a farmhouse, it was found that there were no wounded to bring in, so we all returned to the wagons and finally to the billets.

There is no need to pay to see flying exhibitions here, as aeroplanes are continually hovering about. Sometimes our scouts fly over the German lines and immediately they are fired upon by the enemy's gunners, the shells bursting all around the machines. Several nights ago an airship dropped several bombs close to where we are billeted, the explosion waking all our fellows, who thought the place was being shelled. Next morning it was found, however, that considering the number of bombs that fell very little damage had been done.

We get plenty of food; the only thing in which we get rather short rations is bread, and we make up for that with biscuits. The menu is as follows: - Breakfast: tea, bacon, bread and jam. Dinner: either bully beef, roast beef or Irish stew. Tea: tea, bread, jam and sometimes butter. Then you can have cheese for supper if you want it. I think it's jolly good fare for active service".

Many of the Old Boys enlisted with the Royal Warwickshire Regiment and Private R. Hegan from the 7th Battalion wrote: *"Since I wrote about a week ago I've had four days turn at another part of the front. Our Company acts as ration carriers to the rest while we are here, and we sleep in dug-outs all day, and go up to the trenches with the grub etc., at night- a very awkward journey. There are plenty of stray bullets flying about, as we are of course behind our own trenches and unprotected. One or two of our chaps have been wounded whilst grub-carrying. When the innumerable star-shells go up we have to stand still until the flare dies down and if we happen to be near the trench, flop we go into the big holes made by the shells and now full of water. It is really pitiful to see the state of the farm-houses round here, all wrecked by shells".* Reginald attended Bablake from 1905 to 1910 and on leaving became a clerk in the cemetery's office.

Bombardier Harold Hegan, in the MMGS wrote a letter to Mr. F. Morgan which was subsequently published in *'The Wheatleyan'*: *"I shall never forget that first visit. We went as far as possible up to the trenches on our vehicles and then distributed our load of guns, ammunition, etc and headed for the lines. Every now and then a flare would go up, and we would all drop to the ground, pause and then up again. This continued until we reached a road running parallel to the lines, when either we were spotted or by chance a machine gun was turned on us. We dropped full length with our loads and for twenty minutes the gun traversed up and down the road, and although many rounds struck objects all around, our prone bodies were left untouched, and finally we rose and entered the communication trench. Here we encountered mud-real mud, and I, personally, lost one of my high rubber boots three times, and several times fell headlong into the mire. At one spot it was impassable with the load I was carrying, and I crawled out of the trench and worked round in the open, rejoining the trench lower down. At last we reached the first line-sixty yards from the Germans and prepared our gun for action".*

Second Lieutenant P. G. Mander after a lapse of some months from the firing line (probably from injury), provided a retrospective look at the attitude of those serving;

"The outstanding feature appears still to be unfailing cheerfulness. Whenever there was anything to be done, no matter how hazardous, there were men to do it in a light-hearted fashion. Exactly why every man lived up to this ideal is difficult to state; in the trenches there was always the chance that he was living his last day, indeed his last minute on this earth and a kind of fatalism was held by most. At the back of every mind was an idea that ran somewhat in the style: If my name happens to be written on a bullet, I shall get it, no matter what I do.

In these circumstances it may not be surprising to learn that for every new job to be done men came up to do it with smiling faces. Men who were exceedingly tired were always ready for another task, with happy expressions on their faces even if their vocabulary left something to be desired from the point of view of the English taught in some schools.

It might appear from these few remarks that the men were unable to conceive what was before them, that they went on with their work without a thought for the consequences; quite the contrary, it was simply an expression of their British pluck and lion- heartedness, and to know that you belong to a nation that has produced such men should make you proud and more than proud.

Of course it is not to be expected that every man possessed the same degree of courage, but throughout all branches of the service that came under my notice, it was easy to discern the same high qualities. In view of this, it is quite possible to understand the readiness of all to make jokes and to see the funny side of things. Those who in the beginning did not possess a sense of humour quickly cultivated one. From a high class joke to a limerick or a pun, passing through comic parodies of popular songs, each had its supporters.
In peace time the best limericks originated in the stock exchange, so it was not my fortune to come across good ones.

The following is quite typical

> *There was an old woman of Ypres*
> *Who was shot in the cheek by some snipers;*
> *And the music she played*
> *Through the holes that they made*
> *Beat the Argyll and Sutherland Pipers*

The songs that were sung behind the lines were favourites brought out from England, or those in evidence at the concert parties a few miles behind the firing line – like the "Fancies" at Poperinghe. "Keep the home fires burning" was kept in the original, but, everyone knows the parody on "Little Grey home in the west." One popular parody was on a song that I imagine has a title "Never mind". Here are two or three of the lines:-

> *If the Sergeant's got the rum, never mind,*
> *Though entitled to a tot*
> *He will drink the blooming lot,*
> > *Etc   never mind.*

Of jokes and tales there was an unending variety. The men were so quick to seize upon anything that was at all promising, and so in conclusion I will recall two or three. Last August at a listening post in the Ypres Salient, the sentry thought he heard some Boche mining, so the information went through the usual chain of responsibility, the corporal, the sergeant, the platoon commander, the officer of the engineers. Later the platoon commander heard the sergeant holding forth to a group of men:" You see it's like this: there are huns in front of us, huns on our right, huns on our left, all firing at us. Huns in aeroplanes above us, trying to drop things on us, and now Huns beneath us trying to blow us up, yet they say in Blighty that we've got the Kaiser tied up in knots. I don't think".

A platoon was in reserve, and a group of men were preparing to fry their breakfast bacon, by the side of the lake that was between them and the firing line. When things were nearly ready a Boche shell dropped into the lake and displaced a fish, which by some peculiar gymnastic feat was able to fall exactly on the frying pan, in its proper place. 'Twas an excellent breakfast dish.

In rest billets there was usually a band to relieve monotony, but when in reserve the only musical instruments available were those easily carried by the men, such as mouth organs, whistles, etc. One evening in a farmhouse billet I went to see how my platoon was faring, and looking in an outhouse found a group of men sitting around a brazier. In the middle was one man on his knees, piously and piteously thanking heaven that there was only one tin whistle in the Company".

Second Lieutenant P. G. Mander later lost his brother, Captain Alfred Ernest Mander who fell in action at Passchendaele. These letters are very poignant and show some insight into the roles performed by the Old Boys; contributions were also received from those who would later lose their lives, Lance-Sergeant Henry Smith Craven and Captain Harold Meredyth Adcock. On the School Magazines' 21st Anniversary readers were reminded that if *"The Wheatleyan is to carry out its proper function as official organ of Bablake School it must be duly upheld by contributions to its composition…it will never be said that Bablake boys are indifferent as to the welfare of their magazine"*. The magazine had grown in size to 32 pages and despite increases in production costs the magazine remained at the same price.

On August the 1st 1919 a regular column in *'The Coventry Graphic'* entitled *'The Week's Causerie'* reviewed and compared publications available in the city. The main focus was on the July issue of the *'Employees Quarterly'* published by the Siddeley Deasy Co. Ltd and *'The Wheatleyan'* published in connection with Bablake School. On the Siddeley Deasy Co. Ltd publication they stated it is *"an excellent number and is an acquisition to the journalistic works of the city. Edited by the social secretary (Mr. W. W. Cheshire), it is a distinct credit to all concerned, and gives a full account of the various activities undertaken by the employees of the firm. Many interesting articles are contained therein, whilst the illustrations are very good indeed. Many of the local firms now have magazines in which to record their activities, but I have not seen one to excel the present number of the Employee quarterly"*.

The Editor was also pleased to see that *"'The Wheatleyan' published in connection with Bablake School continues to flourish and that the future is brimful of hope. The current issue is full of interesting articles and it serves as a splendid connection linking between past and present Bablake Scholars. In addition to an editorial there are school notes, resident boys notes, a report on the Old Boys club, reports of the school sports, Cadet Corps and cricket team, and nicely written articles on 'The humour of everyday life', 'The Royal Flying Corps' (by an Old Boy), 'A trip to Blighty' and a third article on 'Bablake historical'"*.

They concluded that *"altogether ' The Wheatleyan' makes a very fine read"*, and that *"there are still one or two very large firms in the city that should do a bit more for their employees in this respect, as nothing but good can result from such ventures and it is surprising to see some of the younger and enterprising firms showing the older confreres what can be done in the way of social relaxation when tackled in a business like manner"*.

Cadet Corps at Bablake

At the end of 1912 enquiries had been made to the Government with a view to starting a Cadet Corps; the proposal was accepted though the government would not fund every aspect of the Corps. This offered every boy the chance of learning something of military work at the least possible expense and with no interruption in his life work. Quite quickly forty boys came forward submitting their names to Mr. Frank Core the Gymnastics Instructor. Each member was required to contribute five shillings towards the cost of accoutrement to be followed by a small annual subscription and expected to attend the regular training. The majority of boys in residence were also in the Cadet Corps. Two half holidays were granted to cadets who attended regularly the Saturday and Monday parades.

By July 1913 a rifle range had been completed and its use began in September after it had been inspected by representatives of the leading rifle associations. Old Boys were solicited to join the Old Boys' club, which enabled them to not only use the rifle range, but provided membership of the swimming club and copies of *'The Wheatleyan'*. Several Old Boys offered their services to the club, having proved themselves as good shots.

In May 1914 the Corps saw a big advance under the management of Cadet Second Lieutenant H. M. Adcock, having about one Company of twenty two cadets. Friendly competitions were held between the Cadet Corps and the rifle club and the married and single members of staff, which promoted the Corps. With the 1914 summer term approaching, it was anticipated, with arms, uniforms, fine weather and enthusiasm, the number could be raised to one hundred. Requests were made particularly to the boys from Stoke and Foleshill (two of the four Houses) to join the ranks.

As an initial fundraising event a play was staged: *'Knight of the Burning Pestle'*. The proceeds were over nine pounds and this enabled the Corps to start its work. Over the coming years more appeals were made. A donation towards the cost of rifles was generously met by the Governors of the School in 1914. An appeal in 1915 was made to raise hundred pounds with the letter on the following page to Governors and parents. A further appeal was made in December 1916, this appeal compared the Cadet Battalion to the Officers Training Corps (OTC) stressing *"cadets are relatively less able to bear the expense of providing uniforms and equipment than are members of the OTC"*. The Corps was especially indebted to the Governors and to the Tomson's trust who had given it liberal support, which assisted in the cadets going to camp at Stoneleigh.

Bablake School Cadet Company
(A Company 3rd Cadet Battalion, Royal Warwickshire Regiment)
Bablake School
Coventry July 1915

APPEAL FOR FUNDS

Dear Sir (Madam),
We beg leave to ask your interest in, and support for, the work of this Company. Founded in March 1914, the Corps numbered last summer just over thirty cadets. A detachment was then sent to camp, the Company was recognised as efficient, and received the War Office Grant. Last September the number increased to over one hundred.

The Company now forms part of the 3rd Cadet Battalion, which has been recently recognised to date from the formation of the Bablake School Company, and is made up of contingents from nine Warwickshire secondary schools. The Battalion approximates in its constitution and objectives to the Officers' Training Corps (OTC); but it gets only nominal Government support, and cadets are relatively less able to provide all their own equipment, than are members of the OTC. It becomes, however, increasingly clear that Secondary Schools must fill the gaps in the ranks of the country's officers in the field; and the work of such companies as ours is receiving increased attention on all hands.

The camp has been well laid out, the general arrangements are thorough and the health of the boys is excellent. The two chief financial problems which now confront the Corps are (a) the sending of a contingent of sixty cadets to Battalion camp at Stoneleigh in the latter half of August; (b) the enlarging of the Company next autumn to include as many members as can be secured. The number of boys qualified by age to become cadets is nearly three hundred. Camp arrangements are specially expensive and difficult this year, because the war office material (bell tents, cooking utensils etc) which can be had in peace time on loan, is now unavailable.

To meet the needs thus indicated it is hoped to raise a sum of not less then £100;– Friends of the school who usually subscribe to the sports fund will remember that this year they have not been called upon for help in that direction; and it is felt that the Cadet Company's appeal may thus be somewhat the more confidently made.

F. Hodson *Headmaster*
A. Wilson, *Cadet Lieutenant Commanding*

In 1915 the interest in the Cadet Corps increased owing to the war and it was expressed that in the present crisis every boy should make a *"very special effort to become a Cadet, and thus prepare himself to assist in the defence of his country"*. The cadets in July 1915 had one hundred and ten members but when school began in September 1915 this number had fallen to eighty nine. Two of the cadet-scouts seemed so keen that a local press photographer could not resist the temptation of snap shooting them busy with their map.

'The Wheatleyan' editorial for May 1915 stated *"there is this lingering doubt that the war will not be finished for some time yet, and that the generation now uprising will be called upon to finish it. Train therefore and be ready in case you are needed. At any rate the training will not do you any harm"*. A list of subscriptions was published in the same issue; amongst those donating were Colonel Wyley £5. 5s and Mr. Humberstone 10s. 6d. and various councillors had donated over £8.

Recruiting efforts by Mr. Core increased the number and by the end of January 1916 there were 178 cadets on the books. The total number of cadets enrolled since the formation of the Company was 246. In December 1916 the Corps had 4 officers, 22 Non Commissioned Officer's (NCO) and over 140 cadets. The summers at camp were spent with the boys involved in Company drill, field work, judging distances and fire control. In 1914 camp was held with the 1st Battalion Royal Warwickshire Regiment at Castle Park, the cadets being route marched to Warwick. The cost was one shilling a day, and a reminder issued prior to the camp that *"it is the finest life in the world for anyone who does not mind hard work and has a sense of humour"*. Camps took place in the succeeding summers at Stoneleigh.

The practical methods employed at camp

The importance of these camps was recognised, and attendees were regularly inspected. In August 1915, the reporter of *'The Coventry Herald'* paid a number a number of visits to the Bablake boys at Camp. His article was entitled *'Bablake Boys Under Canvas – Soldiers in the making'* and he stated that *"The visitor is given to understand before he has been in conversation with the Bablake boys for half a minute that Bablake Company is 'the' Company. When the 3rd Battalion was formed Bablake became the premier 'A' Company...when one gets past the sentry the first line of tents encountered is the Bablake line...they also take first place in the waiting list at dinner-time"*.

The writer explores how much food that the Bablake boys eat and that any fears the parents have about their offspring's health is unnecessary, on more serious ground *"when one remembers that many Old Boys of Bablake are now serving their country in the trenches, it was good to be able to feel that the present scholars of this historic school are preparing themselves. ..should the call come, Bablake boys would go forward into action with the same fine spirit as now marks their life in summer camp"*.

In 1916 the camp was inspected by Lord Norton, who was accompanied by Major Hall Edwards, a second inspection by Lord Leigh and finally by Colonel Lewis. Dignitaries also attended throughout the two weeks' camp and witnessed sham fighting and field work. These included current and previous members of staff, the Governors and the Mayor and Mayoress of Coventry.

The Officers and Lads of the Cadet Corps practising attack

As the Corps developed, the cadets were organised into three strong platoons. Owing to a shortage of carbines, the Corps only having thirty, squad drills with arms were only taken by half platoons at a time. Numbers 1, 2 and 3 platoons were commanded by Lieutenant Atkinson, Mr. Core and Lieutenant Browne respectively.

The Cadet Corps was given credit in *'The Coventry Graphic'* of September 17th 1915. Leonard Jones, son of Mr. H. Jones, 23 Avondale Road, Earlsdon, Coventry, joined the Australian Expeditionary forces (Signalling Corps) in May 1915 and in two months passed three tests gaining three hundred per cents. The medals and certificates for this achievement were sent to his home. This was an exceptionally good record considering Mr. L. Jones' short time in training and *"there is no doubt the ground work in drill at Bablake School expedited his subsequent proficiency"*. He was at the time of writing at the Dardanelles.

Captain William Smith Wilson, Highland Light Infantry who left the school after four years in 1909 and was formerly with the Nottinghamshire and Derby Regiment felt compelled to write an article for *'The Wheatleyan'* entitled *'The Officer Spirit'*. It was biased towards those members of the Bablake School Cadet Corps who would be in the future taking up commission in HM Forces and the great importance of one's work as an officer singling out Knowledge and Character as traits required to be successful. His article covered four pages and paragraphs have been extracted below:

"You will be responsible for the successful leading of your men in battle; you will be responsible for their safety as far as can be secured in gaining success in battle; you will be responsible for their health, for their comfort, for their good behaviour and discipline. Finally, you will be responsible for maintaining the honour of England and for doing all you can to ensure the security of England
.

KNOWLEDGE It is not a heaven –sent gift-it is the outcome of study, hard work, thought. It is an absolute necessity to one as an officer. It is the foundation of your own character, for without it you cannot gain self- confidence. If you have no confidence in yourself, your men will have no confidence in you either.

CHA...   ... in order to inspire your
men ...   ... your example, and their
endur...
And ...   ... over his men. Where the
office...   ... ould appear to be instant
death...   ... if they believe in him and
he kee...

Alwa...   ... rfulness, but at the same
time ...   ... ohen things go wrong; a
word ...   ... r a smile when pointing
out a ...   ... ind that of your men and
maint...   ... our chief duties is to be
always...   ... n. You must always be
thinkii...   ... at to think is one of the
great ...   ... officer try and carry out
these p...   ... s on the junior officer.

(handwritten note: Core, Frank. p. 20, 22, 24, 26, 145, 151, 166)

Do not forget that the men are your comrades, and that the British soldier can and does appreciate what courage, honour, patriotism, and self sacrifice mean. Talk to the men you will some day command on these great qualities, both in lectures and to individuals personally. You will always find a ready response which will one day stand you in good stead, and what is more important, will stand England and the Empire in good stead".

In 1920 the Corps was six years old having been founded in March 1914 by Captain Adcock. 'The Wheatleyan' stated that "He along with several of its members did their full share for their country's sake. What fitting memorial to them that we, who remain, should carry on the Corps worthily".

Enlisting

With the outbreak of war, many of the Old Boys enlisted in August 1914, even those not previously associated with the Cadet Corps. Typically they would enlist with a regiment near their home; many of the Old Boys for this reason were with the Royal Warwickshire Regiment or the Warwickshire Yeomanry. At the start of the war, the Royal Warwickshire Regiment had eight Battalions, by the end of the war this had grown to twenty five.

The numbering of the Battalions is significant as this indicates a regular battalion, a reserve Battalion or a territorial Battalion. The reserve Battalion consisted of men who had served seven years with the regular Battalion but would remain on the reserve list for a further five years, when war broke out they were called upon. The *'City of Coventry: Roll of the Fallen'* states the date of enlisting and does not distinguish between those who were in the territorial Battalions prior to the war and the civilians who answered the 'call to arms'. Those in the territorial Battalions were part-time volunteers and attended training sessions weekly and an annual camp. Many of the Old Boys were in the 7th Battalion, Royal Warwickshire Regiment a territorial force with men from Coventry and the surrounding area. As the war continued the men of the reserve and territorial Battalions were mobilised making it necessary to precede the Battalion number with a numerical prefix.

Old Boys who had returned to their parents or moved away from the city enlisted with other regiments. The initial 'Call to Arms' was very successful and men trying to enlist in Coventry were forced to queue for many hours, some giving up and returning the following day. Those who could not wait walked to recruitment centres in local towns and villages to enlist.

Members of the Cadet Corps were amongst the first to take up positions in the army, one of them being the driving force behind the Corps Mr. Adcock. His duties in the Corps were taken up by Mr. Wilson and Mr. Atkinson, who received their cadet commissions as Second Lieutenants. Mr. Wilson subsequently gave up the command of the Company on receiving a commission in the Gordon Highlanders. These losses to the Corps were inevitable; Dr. Hodson the headmaster succeeded Lieutenant Wilson to command the Company.

Other Commanding Officers would enlist: Mr. Core joined the Machine Gun Corps (MGC), and Mr. Lawrence left to become a signaller in the Royal Field Artillery (RFA), his duties being taken over by Mr. Cooke. The table on the following page shows the cadets who went on to join the Forces.

The Cadets who joined the Forces

Name	Rank In Corps	Rank and Regiment where known
Mr. H. M. Adcock (Staff)	2nd Lieutenant	Captain, Lancashire Fusiliers
Mr. G. Atkinson (Staff)	2nd Lieutenant	Pioneer, Royal Engineers
Mr. A. Wilson (Staff)	2nd Lieutenant	Lieutenant, Gordon Highlanders
Adams, W. G	Lance-Corporal	Hampshire Regiment
Aveline, R.N.S.	Sergeant	7th London Regiment
Banning, C.	Cadet	King's Own Lancashire Regiments
Brown, W.	Lance-Corporal	Gloucestershire Regiment
Clarke, A. W.	Cadet (Bugler)	HMS 'Indus V'
Cox, F.	Cadet	2nd Lieutenant, Royal Warwicks
Grew. W. E.	Lance-Corporal	2nd Lieutenant, Royal Warwicks
Harker, G. H.	Cadet	2nd Lieutenant, Manchester Regiment
Harris, A. E.	Cadet	Kings Royal Rifle Brigade
Hart, S. B.	Cadet	Royal Navy
Hegan, W. G	Sergeant	Officers Cadet Battalion, Royal Flying Corps
Hiorns, E. A.	Cadet	HMS 'Indus V'
Horsley, H. G.	Company Sergeant Major	Cadet, Royal Flying Corps
Jackson, T.	Corporal	Grenadier Guards
King, H.	Corporal	Corporal, Royal Engineers
Moore, H.	Corporal	Honourable Artillery Company
Nauen, R.	Corporal	Training Reserve Battalion
Oliver, T.	Lance-Corporal	Gloucestershire Regiment
Olorenshaw, J. T.	Company Sergeant Major	2nd Lieutenant, Royal Flying Corps
Parkes, G.	Company Sergeant Major	Royal Military Academy, Woolwich
Prattley, E. C.	Company Sergeant Major	2nd Lieutenant, Norfolk Regiment
Prattley, R.G.	Sergeant	HMS Indus V
Rees, H.	Cadet	Wiltshire Regiment
Roxburgh, C.	Lance-Corporal	Gloucestershire Regiment
Roberts, W. A.	Lance-Corporal	2nd Lieutenant, Royal Flying Corps
Sharpe, F.	Company Quarter Master Sergeant	Army Service Corps, Motor Transport
Sage, E.	Cadet	Royal Warwicks
Tipler, A.	Corporal	Royal Fusiliers (29th)
Tunstall, H.	Corporal	
Ward, B.	Lance-Corporal	2nd Lieutenant, Dublin Fusiliers
Wilson, H.	Lance-Corporal	Gordon Highlanders
Windridge, A.	Lance-Corporal	Cadet, Air Service

Those who enlisted were not only mentioned in *'The Wheatleyan'*, but in some cases mentioned in *'The Coventry Graphic'* and *'The Coventry Herald'*, none more so than a Governor of the school, Alderman W. H. Batchelor. Despite being over the recognised military age Alderman Batchelor (shown below) enlisted with Councillor Bannington. Both were Old Boys and joined the 7th Battalion Royal Warwickshire Regiment as Privates.

'The Coventry Graphic' reported that *"Alderman Batchelor was an old volunteer being a sergeant in the 2nd Battalion Royal Warwickshire Regiment and would have made a very useful soldier by reason of his previous training. He was well known locally and was noted for being a progressive member of the City council and was unstinting in the support which he gave to movements which he believed to be in the interest of the City. By their patriotism Alderman Batchelor and Councillor Bannington had set noble examples".*

In 1914 three brothers who all attended Bablake were chosen as a fine patriotic example of young men, their response to the call of duty being covered by both *'The Wheatleyan'* and *'The Coventry Graphic'*. They were the three sons of Mr. C. H. Fletcher of West Orchard, Coventry. Mr. Reginald Fletcher was with the Warwickshire, Royal Horse Artillery (RHA), Mr. Claude Henry Fletcher left England and was with the 10th Middlesex Regiment and Mr. Chas Leonard Fletcher was with the Warwickshire Yeomanry.

The Fletcher Brothers

All three brothers were associated with Holy Trinity Church; Chas and Claude had done valuable work in connection with the Church Scouts, the former as a schoolmaster, the latter as a standard bearer. Reginald Fletcher was seriously injured at the beginning of 1916, as a result of shelling. In this incident Gunner Herbert Charles Collingbourne also an Old Boy was mortally wounded.

After enlisting many of the Old Boys would serve alongside each other, some officers even found their old school pals part of the Company they were commanding. The photograph below shows a party of Coventry Territorials that was taken by an enterprising French photographer who was still carrying out his business in a town in the fighting area. The men were photographed just as they came from the trenches and shells were falling all around the place while they posed for the camera. The photograph was sent to Mr. S. O. Beaumont, 55 Albany Road, Coventry, the father of S. A. Beaumont and appeared in *'The Coventry Graphic'*. The list of Cadets who joined the Forces also shows that Old Boys served together on HMS Indus V and in some cases served under Second Lieutenants who had been educated at King Henry VIII School.

Photographed 'Fresh from the Front'

Back Row (left to right) Private F. R. Smith, Lance - Corporal F. Matts, Private H. Pearson and Private P. Redfern
Front Row: Privates J. W. Burton, S. A. Beaumont and J. A. Hattrell

Of those shown four were Old Boys, Lance-Corporal Matts, Privates Redfern, Burton and F. R. Smith. Two of the four would die before the end of the war, Lance-Corporal Matts and Private John Weston Burton.

Some of the Old Boys were slightly under age when they enlisted. One of these was Francis William Colledge who was born in 1896 and completed his education at Bablake leaving in 1912. In common with many other men he added a few months to his age and joined the 3rd Battalion, Royal Warwickshire Regiment as a Private in 1914. He became a physical exercise instructor and was promoted to the rank of sergeant, this saw him posted to the Isle of Wight and he returned there at the end of the war having served in France.

Old Boys who emigrated also enlisted, twelve served with the Australian contingent and nineteen with the Canadians. One member of the Australians, Corporal Alfred Bailey was killed in action and two of the Canadians were killed, Private Herbert Victor Cantrill and Private John Samuel Harris. Reviewing the details available from each country's archives provides some insight into names appearing on the War Memorial.

F. W. Barker is Frederick William Barker who left the school in 1901 and enlisted with the Australians on the 26th February 1915. He previously worked for E. J. Peirson & Sons as an accountant in Coventry and had served for three years with the Warwickshire Yeomanry. Despite this he did not see active service: he was declared medically unfit on the 20th March 1916: an appendicitis operation in 1912 had left him with a weakness in his abdominal muscles which resulted in him losing two stone in a period less then twelve months.

One of the Canadians was T. E. Cox. His attestation papers for the Canadian Overseas Expeditionary Force show this was Thomas Edwin Cox and he declared his oath and willingness to serve Overseas on the 26th November 1918 aged 36. A married man he originally came from Luton and had been a serving member of the Canadian Royal Garrison Artillery for over four years, this was presumably in a capacity that did not require him to work overseas.

The son of the former headmaster John Percival Humberstone also enlisted with the Canadians on the 19th July 1915 aged 26, and named his father F. W. Humberstone who lived at 3, Chester Street as his next of kin. A Coventry address was also listed by Francis Edwin Player whose mother lived at 67 Middleton Road. He was 28 years old and had previously served for three years with the 2nd Battalion, Warwickshire Regiment, Volunteers.

Roll of Honour

As many of the Old Boys were joining His Majesty's forces Mr. D. H. Patrick, a member of staff, seized the initiative and started to compile a *'Roll of Honour'*, which showed the number on the Roll, name, date of leaving the school and unit. The first issue at the beginning of 1915 contained two hundred and fifty one

names, of which four had already been killed in action. These were Sergeant H. J. Barker, Sergeant E. Barker, Private J. Rossiter and Sergeant Aston. Subsequent issues started the numbering where the previous issues had ended. The next issue contained an additional sixty two names and subsequent issues bought the number up to five hundred and nine. Throughout the war, various fund- raising events, including a very successful concert, were organised to send presents to the Old Boys serving in the forces. Mr. Patrick and Mr. Pearson ensured the money was put to its proper use, sending each member an illuminated card, a copy of the *'Roll of Honour'* and a packet of cigarettes. Numerous letters received from the Old Boys show these were gratefully received.

It was soon necessary to issue another *'Roll of Honour'*. Those whose names appeared on the new Roll received a copy and the remainder were sold at 3d each to defray expenses whilst the balance was devoted to one of the charitable organisations to which the school subscribed.

'The Wheatleyan' editorial made numerous references to the *'Roll of Honour'* using it to exemplify how *"forward Our Boys are when men's work is necessary"* and followed this in a later edition with *"Those brave fellows from Bablake who are now fighting with our forces have received a little that is due to them – a place of honour for their names in the school. We hope sincerely that the list may remain there for many years to come, so that, when the piping times of peace once more return, the Bablake boys of that day may point out the many names with pride, telling fond parents and relations that our school sent its full quota of men"*.

Visitors to the school also made reference to the Roll. In May 1915 a lecture delivered by Mr. Stanley Lamb of the British and Foreign Sailors' Society congratulated the school on the number of Old Boys whose names appeared on the *'Roll of Honour'* but regretted the scarcity of sailors amongst them, due, he supposed, to the inland position. Despite this he managed to solicit £9 17s 0d to his cause.

The *'Roll of Honour'* was not necessarily aligned with promotions or changes in regiment. The name of H. C. Woodward appears on the war memorial and he also featured in *'The Coventry Herald'* on the 25th June 1915 under the headline ' *Bablake Old Boy's Promotion'*. The article stated *"Harry Collins Woodward recently returned from France promoted Lieutenant RNAS whilst on active service in France. Only son of the late Mr. William Woodward of the City and Mrs. Woodward of 9 Melville Road"*. He obtained a commission as Sub-Lieutenant in the Royal Naval Volunteer Reserve in December 1914 and was shortly afterwards attached to the No. 2 Squadron Armoured car Division under command of the Duke of Westminster and left with the Squadron for France early in February 1915. He received his early education at Bablake before going to Elmfield College, Yorkshire. Prior to obtaining his commission he was for ten years connected with the firm of Vickers Ltd at the Wolsey Tool & Motor Works, Birmingham.

In December 1916 at a school assembly, Alderman W. Lee (Chairman of Governors) in his introductory remarks referred to a large number of Old Boys who were now serving their country. The *'Roll of Honour'* at this point numbered over four hundred and fifty, of whom fifty had commissions and eighteen had already laid down their lives.

Unfortunately Mr. D. H. Patrick, having initiated the compilation, did not live to see the *'Roll of Honour'* completed: he became seriously ill and pluckily attended school until compelled by his illness to desist. He died on March the 18th 1918 aged 54, whilst Head of the lower school. Mr. Patrick was himself an Old Boy and his funeral two days after his death was attended by members of staff and boys.

During any reference to the *'Roll of Honour'*, deepest sympathy was expressed to the parents, families and relatives of the fallen. In addition best wishes were extended to those who were at the front, or were expecting to go soon.

In 1919 two lists were issued in *'The Wheatleyan'*, one containing the list of the Fallen totalling 78 names, the other a list of those who served showing 608 names giving a total of 686. Now many years later, using all the sources, two new lists have been compiled. An alphabetical list of the Fallen is shown in Appendix A, whilst Appendix C shows a list of those who served. The final combined number is 867 men either served or fell, 71 names more than previously published.

In comparison, the *'Roll of Honour'* for King Henry VIII showed some 250 Old Coventrians and staff served, with 38 dying before the war's end. The Bablake numbers are more comparable to Kenilworth, from the outbreak of hostilities 836 men served with 90 of these making the supreme sacrifice.

The Wounded, the Missing & POWs

It was inevitable with battles raging on various fronts that a number of Old Boys would be injured; in some cases those concerned were mentioned in *'The Wheatleyan'* or the local papers. The list is not extensive but serves to show how the injuries to the Old Boys were reported. Soldiers who recovered from their wounds rejoined their units; occasionally the need was such that on recovery they were sent to a different unit or Battalion to increase the effective Battalion strength for units that had suffered heavy losses. Some of the men were wounded numerous times but still had to rejoin the fighting.

In May 1915 *'The Coventry Graphic'* had received news that Private C. H. Elkington, who joined the 18th Hussars at the outbreak of war, had been severely wounded and was in a hospital at Boulogne. Private Elkington was wounded at the beginning of May, receiving injuries to the head.

In June 1915 injuries to Corporal F. W. Payne and Private Joseph Storer were reported in *'The Coventry Graphic'* and *'The Coventry Herald'* respectively.

Corporal Payne was in the King's Royal Rifles and his injury was reported as follows:

"After being in the thick of the fighting since the early days of the war, Corporal F. W. Payne, has been severely wounded and is at present in the Edmonton Military Hospital. Corporal Payne joined the army some years ago, and saw service in India. He took part in several battles in France and Flanders and while in charge of a machine gun near Ypres was badly wounded in the side and left arm after being shot".

Under the headline *'Coventry Soldier Wounded',' The Coventry Herald'* reported that Private Joseph Storer of the 1/7th Battalion Royal Warwickshire Regiment was believed to be the first Coventry Corporation official to be wounded on active

service in the war. A resident of 13 Much Park Street, prior to the war he was employed in the Cemetery Superintendent's office. The news of his injury was received by his family via unofficial channels: his comrade Private Oswald Lanes wrote them a letter stating *"Joe had the misfortune to get wounded in his left arm just below the shoulder. I do not think it is at all serious, in fact he was joking to me about ten minutes afterwards and asking me if I was not jealous of him. It happened quite suddenly. I heard a loud report as if someone had thrown a stone at a tin box which was close by and then he said "Oh I am hit in the shoulder". We soon had his things off and bound up his arm, and* then he was all smiles and began smoking cigarettes. I cooked him breakfast which he ate in a way which showed that his wound had not affected his appetite. We carried him off to the hospital and left him in the hands of the doctor; I believe he is going on all right".*

In late July 1916 many casualties were reported in *'The Wheatleyan'* owing to the opening of the Battle of the Somme, or as reported in *'The Coventry Graphic'*, *'The Great Offensive'* on the western front. The list of wounded included Captain F. L. Morgan, Corporal Harold King, Second Lieutenant Imber, Second Lieutenant A. E. Mander, Second Lieutenant A. J. Adams, Second Lieutenant F. Mills, Private F. Mortlock, Private G. W. Cosby and Private J. Connolly.

'The Coventry Herald' announced in May 1917 that Mr. and Mrs. Alfred Tipler of 1, Carmelite Road, Coventry had received news that their youngest son Private Arthur Frederick Tipler aged 17 of the Royal Fusiliers was wounded. He had left the school in 1915 and enlisted in early 1916 with the Public School Battalion. He was previously employed by the Humber Works and had spent five years at Bablake.

Charles Harper 42nd Battalion, Australian Infantry was 27 years old when he was shot on the 6th June 1917 and suffered wounds to his left arm and chest. Private Harper was returned to England on the 10th June 1917 for convalescence and then to Australia on the 10th September 1917. Prior to emigrating he had served three years with the Warwickshire Territorials.

In December 1917, injuries to more Old Boys were announced but not the extent of the wounds: Second Lieutenant E. C. Prattley, Norfolk Regiment who left in 1916, J. Blackwell and W. Blackwell Royal Naval Air Service (RNAS) who both left in 1901, Harry Blythe Nicholls, RAMC who left in 1911, J. Starley Royal Engineers

(RE) who left in 1909 and finally to member of Staff Second Lieutenant, K. E. Wootton of the Rifle Brigade.

'*The Wheatleyan*' stated that Second Lieutenant Norman W. Hitchens had been seriously wounded, Second Lieutenant John Newman had been wounded for the third time and Second Lieutenant R. E. Moore had been wounded four times and mentioned in despatches. Also announced was a serious wound to Mr. Frank H. Pearson, a former master, while on his country's service, "*It is with deep regret that we announce the news of Mr. Frank H. Pearson's serious wound. The popularity and respect in which Mr. Pearson was held while at school can be easily seen by the intense anxiety which the news of his misfortune caused among all who knew him. However, having successfully undergone a painful trial, we must wish him a speedy and complete recovery, and express our condolence with Mrs. Pearson for the trouble which has overtaken her*".

Private George Arthur Beesley, 55th Battalion, Australian Imperial Force was wounded in action on the 25th May 1918. Official notification of his injury, a severe shrapnel wound to the left thigh, was received by his father in June 1918 and reported in '*The Coventry Herald*' . George left Bablake in 1902 and went to Australia in 1910 on account of ill health; being in Australia must have improved his condition and he enlisted in June 1917. He had been at the front for one month prior to his injury and was discharged on the 14th November 1919.

'*The Wheatleyan*' printed details on W. W. Day, Yeoman of the Signals on HMS Woolwich who left Bablake in 1900. He was rescued by the Germans and was placed in a prisoner of war camp, "*we must see that, if possible, he is not left without those necessaries which according to all accounts prisoners in Germany so grievously lack*". Old Boys also died whilst a prisoner of war. The parents of John Olorenshaw received a telegram from him stating "*Have been interned in Holland, quite well, writing later, unwounded*". Misinformation was prevalent: those reported as missing occasionally were reported safe, but in the majority of cases the point of going missing was listed as the date of death.

Died at Home

It is important to realise that the Old Boys of Bablake did not just die fighting bravely on various Fronts: some of the men were classified as 'died at home'. This means they are buried in a location in the UK. These deaths are attributable to the war as the men were on active service and died as a result of being injured, illnesses, en route back to the UK or as in the case of Second Lieutenant Herbert Nelson a flying accident. Eight Old Boys are buried in cemeteries throughout the UK, six have graves in Coventry, five in London Road Cemetery and one in Windmill Road. Cadet Morley and Lieutenant Roberts are buried outside the boundaries of Coventry in Bath and Derbyshire respectively.

The relatives of the deceased chose between having a private memorial or a war grave headstone. Made from Portland stone the CWGC headstones are instantly recognisable and inscribed with the insignia of the Fallen's regiment. Situated in London Road Cemetery is a Cross of Sacrifice and the inscription reads *"To the honoured memory of those sailors and soldiers who gave their lives for their country in the Great War 1914-1918 and who lie buried in this Cemetery"*.

Sergeant **Harry Aston**, 9th Lancers was born to Julie Beatrice and John Aston. He was the eldest of three brothers with Frank being born 4th December 1893 and Arthur born in 1898. (There is no evidence to suggest these were Bablake boys, and it would have been common for only one family member to attend). The name of H. Aston appears as one of the fallen on the school memorial.

At the outbreak of war the 9th Lancers' depot was Tidworth, Wiltshire, also shared with the 4th Dragoon Guards and 18th Hussars. The 9th Lancers left England for the front on the 14th August, and along with the other two regiments made up the 2nd Cavalry Brigade under General de Lisle. They sailed from Southampton to Boulogne on His Majesty's Transport (HMT) Welshman and HMT Armenian.

The brigade were in reserve on Sunday August 23rd but were soon called into action. About 7.30am on the 24th the 5th Division were in urgent need of support and the cavalry went into action. On arrival near the village of Audregnies, the cavalry dismounted and opened fire on the enemy. This failed to stop the advances and the General ordered a charge on the flanks of the approaching enemy. The 9th Lancers were to lead with the 4th Dragoon Guards and 18th Hussars in support.

The cavalry mounted and made a good advance over the first five to six hundred yards. Unfortunately the ground had been insufficiently reconnoitred and the charge came across two lines of barbed wire which they could not cross and had to gallop along. Men and horses fell in all directions as the enemy threw all its resources at the advancing charge, which drew the rifle and shell fire away from the 5th Division. The remnant of the charge managed to find temporary shelter behind a house but this was quickly shelled and permanent refuge found under a railway embankment near Doubon.

With all senior officers killed or wounded, command fell to Captain Francis Grenfell, who had sustained shrapnel injuries to both his legs, and a wound to his hand: two fingers shot off. Also finding refuge under the embankment was a team of gunners from the 119th Battery of the RFA who had been blasted out of their position by shellfire. Captain Grenfell decided that the guns needed to be saved and went out alone to find a method of reclaiming them. Volunteers were called for. Leaving the horses in relative safety, the guns were trundled to safety with the Germans fast approaching.

For this action Captain Grenfell was awarded the Victoria Cross (VC) but subsequently lost his life on the 24th March 1915 in a sustained gas attack. Over four hundred men started the charge with an initial roll call of only seventy two; a further two hundred turned up over the progressing hours. Eye witness accounts confirm the charge took place but suggest this was not a deliberate act but as a result of confusion where several men were sent out to reconnoitre the ground and were mistakenly followed by the remainder.

On the 7th September the Cavalry covered a German retreat and this gave the opportunity for a further charge. Though fewer in number the Brigade had the better of the Cavalry battles. On occasion the enemy were found on open ground, and in this instance the Lancers were able to use swords on the enemy's infantry. With the onset of trench warfare the cavalry's occupation disappeared and they were generally employed like the infantry in the trenches. Sergeant Harry Aston passed safely through Cavalry battles in which the 9th Lancers were active but was invalided home after receiving injuries from a horse. Julia and John Aston must have attended to their son's needs until his eventual death on the 25th November 1914 aged 24. Sergeant Harry Aston was buried with his younger brother Arthur (who had died 13th January 1908, aged 10).

Sergeant Aston's Private Memorial

Sergeant Harry Aston's name, along with the other 9th Lancers is commemorated on a stone tablet in the cloisters of South Walk, Canterbury Cathedral; the names are surmounted by the crossed lances as per the regimental insignia. The role Harry played in the action is not known but this shows what was expected of the 9th Lancers. They still celebrate Mons Day annually on the 23rd August, which celebrates the last day the regiments charged with the Lance.

Julia and John Aston's remaining son Frank had been working as a construction estimator's clerk before enlisting as a gunner with the RFA in November 1916, just two years after his brother's death. Frank was killed following a gas attack on 2nd July 1918; he is buried in Tourgeville Military Cemetery. Julia and John lived into their 80's and died in the 1950's over thirty years after the death of their last son.

Private **Samuel Husselby Garrett** of the 2/7th Battalion, Royal Warwickshire Regiment was accidentally drowned whilst bathing near Chelmsford aged 17. He was born the 1st April 1898 at Vicarage Hill near Rugby and at the time of his death resided at 18 Broomfield Road, Coventry. His name incorrectly appears on the school memorial as H. S. Garratt although reference is made in *'The Wheatleyan'* to the death of S. H. Garrett, Royal Warwickshire Regiment. An employee of British Thompson Houston Co. Ltd his name appears correctly on the memorial in the Royal Warwicks Club with twelve other employees. He has a private memorial and was the son of George and Eliza Garrett.

The Private Memorial of S. H. Garrett

Private **James Connolly** 20th Battalion, Royal Fusiliers (City of London Regiment) is the third casualty to be buried in London Road; he died of his wounds at home on the 7th May 1917 aged 19. Born 16th June 1897, at Heywood, Lancashire he resided at 13, Carmelite Road, Coventry with his parents, Michael a motor fitter and Helen Connolly. His early education started at St. Mary's R. C. Elementary School; entering Bablake on the 28th October 1907 in Form 1, he stayed until the 6th Form and left on the 1st August 1912 with a Bablake minor scholarship. The final two years were spent as a boarder on a scholarship granted by the Governors of Bablake. After leaving school he became a turner in a motor engineering works and enlisted in August 1915.

The first casualty from Bablake to be buried in 1918 at London Road Cemetery was Lance Corporal **Cecil Sidwell,** the brother of Private Wilfred Hibbert Sidwell (refer to Western Front, 25th March 1917). Cecil was in the 1/1st Warwickshire Yeomanry and married to Marion Grace Sidwell of 7 Wren Street, Coventry.

Cecil was born on the 22nd December 1889, at Hook Norton, Oxon and enlisted in October 1914. Corporal Sidwell had contracted tuberculosis while serving

overseas and died on board the hospital ship 'Kalyan' while being transported back to Southampton. He died at sea near the Scilly Islands aged 27 on the 30th January 1918. His remains were brought back to his native city and he was buried in London Road with military honours on Thursday the 7th February 1918, the school prefects attending his funeral. He was the second son Mr and Mrs S. Sidwell had lost in the service of their country. Although his grave has the reference Square 53, Grave 97 it could not be found and its location is not marked on the Commonwealth War Grave Commission map of the cemetery.

Second Lieutenant **Herbert Nelson,** Royal Flying Corps (RFC), died on 19th March 1918. Born the 28th January 1895 at 2 Brook Street he resided at 136 Earlsdon Avenue and was employed as a draughtsman in a motor works. Herbert died from injuries received during a return flight from Coventry over the Home Counties; his plane came down near Hemel Hempstead. Herbert attended Spon Street Elementary and was at Bablake from 27th August 1906 Form 3C, to the 23rd July 1909 Form 5A. On leaving he entered employment in the Rudge Whitworth drawing office, joined as a cadet, and then received his commission as Second Lieutenant in the RFC. In the 1901 census the Nelsons lived two doors away from the Imber family; both families would suffer losses during the Great War. Herbert was the middle son of Mr. William and Mrs. Elizabeth Nelson, one of the departmental managers of the Rudge-Whitworth Works. His brothers Hugh, the eldest, and Horace, the youngest,

were also in the forces, and both attended Bablake, Horace from 13th January 1908 to the 20th July 1912.

Prior to the war in 1912, Hugh Nelson the eldest brother was already performing heroics. *'The Scotsman'* of Monday May 5th 1912 contained the following *"Yesterday morning an exciting incident which might have terminated with loss of life but for the courageous act of an unknown man was witnessed from the Middle Pier, Granton. Two men were coming ashore from a small boat from a steam launch at anchor in the East harbour, when both men were thrown into the water in consequence of the boat filling and sinking shortly after leaving the launch. One of the men succeeded in reaching and supporting himself at the side of the launch, though unable to pull himself up to deck level, while the other man, who could not swim, was left helpless in the water. He would undoubtedly have been drowned but for the prompt and courageous rescue by a naval artificer-who fortunately happened to be on the pier at the time and witnessed the accident. Springing to a steam drifter alongside the Pharos berth, he promptly divested himself of jacket and vest, swam out to the drowning man, whom he held up till a small boat came to their assistance and brought them ashore.*

The name of the ship of the rescuer is unknown, as after the accident and consequent excitement he quietly slipped away to the boat that was to convey him to his vessel, at present anchored off the harbour. It has since transpired that the rescuer was Hugh Nelson. The occurrence took place on Sunday morning at Granton a few miles from Edinburgh where HMS St. George, to which Mr. Nelson is attached, was on a short visit". Mr. Hugh Nelson was presented with a Vellum Certificate.

Further accounts and photographs from the family appeared in *'The Rudge Record'* where their father was an Assistant Works Manager in the Coventry works and affectionately known as 'Admiral':

"Hugh Nelson served with the Royal Navy for over 10 years. In 1913 he became a pilot attached to the seaplanes in the Royal Naval Air Service (RNAS) having been promoted from an engine room artificer. Since the start of the war, he served in France, Belgium and the Dardanelles. One photograph shows British aeroplanes ready to leave on the coast raid, February 12th 1915, and the other a damaged aeroplane which came down in the neighbourhood of Poperinghe. The centre photograph shows Mr. H. Nelson at Dunkerque

at Christmas, 1914, after a period of hard work which left him no time to shave. He was twice mentioned in despatches and previously an assistant to a gentlemen's outfitters".

Photographs of Hugh Nelson

Horace Nelson left the school in 1912, joined the forces as soon as he became of age as a Private in the Royal Fusiliers, Public Schools' Battalion. He was then commissioned as a Second Lieutenant in the RFC and transferred to the Infantry. Hugh and Horace pictured either side of Herbert survived the war. To differentiate the brothers all forenames were included on the school memorial.

On the 1st April 1918 The Royal Air Force (RAF) was formed by amalgamating the RFC and RNAS and Second Lieutenant **William John Salmons MM** 65th Squadron, was amongst the first casualties. He was accidentally killed whilst flying, 22nd April 1918 age 21. Born the 27th of April 1896, at 13, Gulson Road, he resided at 26 Norfolk Street with his mother Annie Maria and sister Florence. He started his education at St. Mark's Elementary before spending two years at Bablake from 31st August 1908 to the 22nd July 1910. His 1909 commendation certificate is shown on the following page.

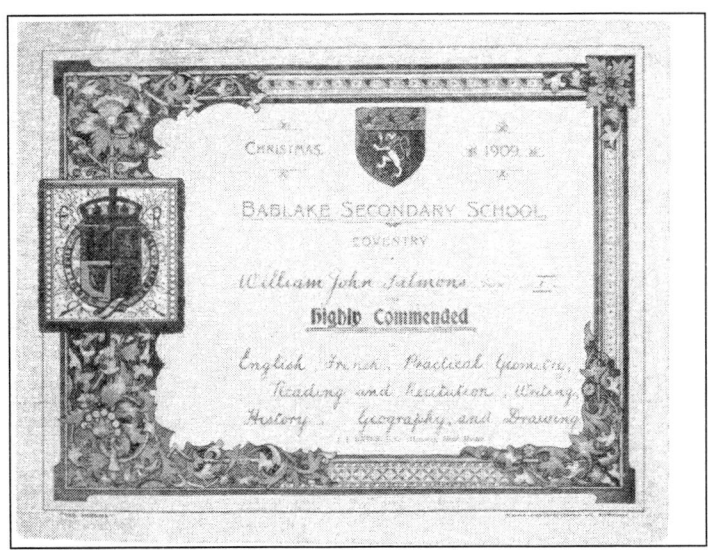

1909 Commendation

William had two occupations on leaving school, initially as a baker then an auctioneer's clerk. He enlisted in September 1914 and was awarded the Military Medal (MM) in November 1916 as Private 2651 with the Royal Warwickshire Regiment for excellent work in sniping, observing and collecting trench intelligence. He was commissioned as a temporary Second Lieutenant with the RFC on the 26th September 1917 and as a Second Lieutenant on the 12th April 1918.

On his death he was buried in London Road Cemetery with his father, also William, a gold watch base maker who died in November 1897, and his sister Doris, who died in infancy on March 23rd 1899.

William's name appears incorrectly on a plaque in the Methodist Central Hall as W. J. Salmon and correctly as W. J. Salmons on a stained glass panel in St. John's church.

Despite emigrating Private **Herbert Victor Cantrill** of the Canadian Army Service Corps (CASC) is buried in Windmill Road Cemetery with his parents. A native of Foleshill, born 1st August 1892, he attended Red Lane Elementary and then went on to Bablake for four years from 28th August 1905 to 23rd July 1909, his attendance being awarded by the Governors of Bablake, the last two years being a resident. He

was the son of Henry, a turner, and Annie Selina Cantrill. In 1913 *'The Wheatleyan'* mentioned that at the London Matriculation Examination Cantrill and Loudon were in the 2nd division. After leaving school he became an analytical chemist, but changed this over time to an auto mechanic and chauffeur when he resided at 8 Stockton Place, Trenton, New Jersey, USA.

He was considered fit for duty on July 17th 1918 in Ottawa, Ontario, Canada. The *'Attestation Papers'* lists his brother Harry Cantrill RAF as next of kin. It was noted he had enlarged tonsils, was 5 feet 6 inches tall with 40 inch chest and a fair complexion, blue eyes and brown hair. Herbert died on board transport in Plymouth Harbour aged 26 on the 11th October 1918; originally buried at Plymouth he was later re-interred at Foleshill Cemetery and has a private memorial. This reveals his mother died before him on March the 10th 1912 aged 42 and he was preceded in death by his father Henry on Armistice Day 1927, aged 52. Harry survived the war and his name appears on the memorial as one of those who served.

The Private Memorial of Private Herbert Victor Cantrill

Hubert Arthur Morley, a cadet with No. 7 Squadron No. 7 Observers School of Aeronautics, RAF, died at Bath aged 18 on the 27th October 1918. A war hospital was situated nearby and in Bath (Locksbrook) Cemetery there are forty four graves directly related to casualties from the hospital. He was son of Arthur and Annie S. Morley, 67, Far Gosford Street, Coventry. Whilst his father was employed as a cycle works time keeper, Hubert was an engineers' apprentice. Enlisting in June 1918, he had completed five months with the RAF at the time of his death and is also commemorated in the War Memorial Park.

W. A. Roberts was listed in the Cadet Corps records as a Lance-Corporal and went on to become a Second Lieutenant in the RAF. His school record does not exist. The only W. A. Roberts to have died with the RAF was **William Alexander Roberts** who died on the 31st July 1919 making him the only post armistice casualty for Bablake. The circumstances of Lieutenant Roberts' death are not known although an influenza pandemic was occurring. He is buried in Shirebrook Cemetery in Mansfield, Derbyshire this cemetery contains ten WW1 graves. The name of W. Roberts appears on a stained glass window in St. John's church.

The War at Sea

Six Old Boys died at sea. Three of them were in the ranks of the Royal Navy, two died whilst on board merchant ships and Private Ambrose John Cole was the victim of a torpedo attack.

Battle of Jutland

The naval Battle of Jutland was to account for the loss of two Old Boys: Boy 1st Class Henry Gordon Farmer aged just 16 years, and 34 year old 1st Class Gunner Charles John Jones. Despite the loss of approximately 6,100 British sailors compared to 2,500 German sailors, the battle was indecisive and Earl Haig in his diary commented *"we have not won a great victory at sea, so we are a little disappointed"*: the critics were looking for a repeat of the Battle of Trafalgar.

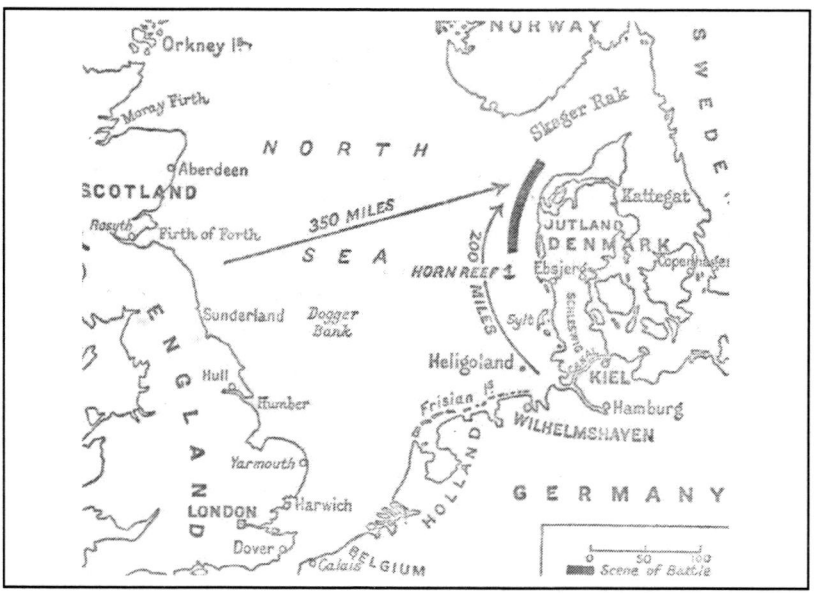

Scene of the Battle of Jutland

The Battle of Jutland was to be a major face-off between Sir John Jellicoe, Commander in Chief of the Grand Fleet, Admiral Sir David Beatty and German high seas commander Admiral Reinhard Scheer. In April 1916 Scheer's forces bombed the coastal towns of Lowestoft and Yarmouth. The grand fleet came out but missed them: Jellicoe set about making a trap to make sure the next time. Scheer too was planning a trap for the Grand Fleet in the same place between Jutland and Norway, and news of his departure on the 30th May from the German estuaries was detected by British interception of his radio, thus ensuring that the two plans would coincide. The battle cruisers' fleets came into action at about 3.30pm on the 31st May 1916 and the battle was to last some eighty minutes.

German shooting was indeed very good, their crews impeccably drilled; they had superior range- finding capability and better quality shells, which penetrated and then exploded. The Germans had the advantage as the British ships were silhouetted against the western sky making ideal targets. HMS Indefatigable was hit first, then suddenly blew up and sank. Shortly afterwards another salvo hit the HMS Queen Mary and she also sank a little after 4.20pm. Admiral Sir David Beatty said to the Captain of HMS Lion *"There seems to be something wrong with our bloody ships today"*.

Many of the Grand Fleet ships, though more numerous than the Germans, were obsolete and lacked new, virtually impenetrable, armoured plating. The vulnerability of British ships was exacerbated by the ease with which a shell could penetrate the magazine causing a massive explosion, as in the case of HMS Indefatigable and HMS Queen Mary. The German fleet which was created out of compulsive ambition by the Kaiser had newer, better armoured and armed ships.

Henry Gordon Farmer was born on the 10th August 1899 at Leamington, the son of George, a builder, and Mary Jane Farmer from Minster Road, Coventry. He entered the Navy eleven months before the Battle of Jutland and was previously employed as a coremaker. For seven months he was on the training ship HMS Victory and was then transferred to HMS Malaya, which was in the thick of the fighting, sustaining eight hits and requiring eight weeks of repairs. HMS Malaya was built by Armstrong Ship Builders and launched on 18th March 1915.

A memorial to their fallen comrades was erected in Lyness Royal Naval Cemetery by those that survived. Henry Gordon Farmer had served on HMS Malaya for four months prior to his death. One of Henry's responsibilities was that of a range finder to the gun crew and whilst carrying out this duty he was struck by a shell and died instantaneously. His body was buried at sea.

A Victoria Cross was awarded posthumously to a 16 year old, John Travers Cornwell, who had the same rank as Henry in the Battle of Jutland. John, who was not an Old Boy was aboard HMS Chester and part of his duty was to sight the 5.5 inch gun. Although severely wounded in the chest and under continuous fire, with the greatest fortitude he stood by his gun for more then fifteen minutes. He died in hospital on June 2nd 1916.

A Postcard of HMS Malaya in later life

Charles John Jones served on board HMS Queen Mary, built by Palmers and launched in 1912. Born the 23rd of June 1881, in Spencer Street, Charles resided at 44c. 1h, Gosford Street. He received his early education at St. Michael's Church School, and gained a scholarship tenable at Bablake which he attended for three and a half years. Charles was a sailor by profession: he had seen nineteen years of service, going straight into the Navy from Bablake at the age of 16. The *'Registers of Seamen's Services'* show he served on a variety of ships from 11th November 1900. He was passed educationally for Petty Officer on the 3rd March 1908 and then seamanship on the 6th November 1911 and promoted to rank of acting Gunner on the 14th March 1913 and which point his record ends.

At the outbreak of war he was on a torpedo boat but was transferred to the battle cruiser in November 1914. This was his second engagement as he had also taken part in the Battle of Dogger Bank, 24th January 1915, which saw a British tactical victory, though they failed to capitalise fully on the advantage of faster ships. In this encounter Warrant Officer Jones broke one of his fingers.

During the Battle of Jutland after receiving direct hits from the German ships Seydlitz and Derfflinger, HMS Queen Mary blew up with the loss of 1,266 crew with only a few survivors.

Two pictures of 1st Class Gunner C. J. Jones

Only a few months before his death he paid a visit to his mother who lived at 296 Swan Lane. Charles was a married man and just before the war was engaged in the training of naval cadets. His name appeared in the Admiralty list of officers who lost their lives during the sinking of the HMS Queen Mary.

Both Old Boys are remembered on the Portsmouth Naval Memorial, with 1st Class Gunner Jones having a plaque in the War Memorial Park.

The Merchant Ships

Sydney Charles Hitch was a Second Officer onboard SS Polymnia (London), a defensively-armed merchant ship. He died aged 38 on the 15th May 1917 with six of his colleagues after the ship was torpedoed without warning by an enemy submarine. SS Polymnia was attacked fifteen miles west from one of the most southerly points of England known as the 'Lizard'. Sydney was the son of Edward Hitch, and the husband of Sophia Amelia Hitch (nee Lubbock), of 84, Cotton Street, Poplar, London. He was born at Eastbourne and is remembered with honour on the Tower Hill Memorial. The First World War section of the Tower Hill Memorial commemorates almost 12, 000 Mercantile Marine casualties who have no grave but the sea.

Alfred Oswald Peart was an Ordinary Seaman on board SS Ravensworth. He attended Bablake twice, the first time from 25th August 1902 to the 23rd July 1908, the second time for a period of four months in 1910 from the 7th March to the 22nd July. He was previously educated at Little Heath School. Born 19th April 1892 at 7 Hertford Terrace he resided at 6 Melville Road with his parents William John, an engineer, and Elizabeth. After schooling he worked in several occupations, an electrical engineer, Ministry of Journalism and analytical chemist. A Royal Naval Volunteer Reserve (RNVR) he enlisted in July 1916 and drowned aged 25 with two comrades as a result of a collision on the 15th September 1917. SS Ravensworth is not recorded on the list of British Merchant ships lost at sea. Alfred became a marine casualty whilst on active service.

The bodies of Alfred's comrades, Leading Seaman David Hanlan and Engineer George Henry Trengove were recovered and buried together in Ballantrae Parish Churchyard, Ayrshire. Alfred's body was not recovered and he is commemorated on the Plymouth Naval Memorial.

Protecting the Convoys

The fifth Old Boy to die at sea was **Frank Kenneth Greening**, an Able Seaman on board HMS Strongbow who was killed in action protecting a convoy in the North Sea on the 17th October, 1917 aged 22. He was born in 1886 at 39, Cox Street, Coventry and his mother and father Samuel and Emily Greening still lived there at the end of the war. Frank was married to Rose Janet and they resided at 60, Weston Street, Coventry; he also had one brother and two sisters. Before joining the Navy he was employed by the Singer Cycle Co. Ltd as a cycle polisher and left the school in 1910. No stranger to naval action, Able Seaman Greening had been slightly wounded in action at the Dardanelles on board HMS Swiftsure. In one of his letters home to his parents, he included a sketch, which he had obtained from an unknown naval officer who witnessed the bombardment of the Dardanelles and saw HMS Ocean and HMS Irresistible sunk.

The sketch providing a vivid idea of the bombardment

The ship on the right is HMS Swiftsure, whilst the ship on the left is HMS Ocean, and in the centre some distance away is HMS Irresistible, both of which are depicted as sinking. The ship on the extreme left is HMS Prince George. In the background on both sides are the high hills of the Dardanelles which are being heavily shelled by the warships.

Able Seaman Frank Kenneth Greening served on board HMS Swiftsure almost continuously from the 12th January 1914 to the 10th May 1916. He had one more posting on HMS Pembroke before finally ending up on HMS Strongbow on the 10th November 1916, two months after her launch on the 30th September 1916. On the 15th October 1917, four ships, HMS Mary Rose, her sister ship HMS Strongbow (pictured) and two armed trawlers left Lerwick to escort an eastbound convoy. On the 16th at noon the two destroyers parted Company:

HMS Strongbow stayed with the eastbound convoy and HMS Mary Rose went to meet the approaching westbound convoy. Later that evening the two ships rejoined in a convoy of merchant ships bound for Shetland. The following morning at 6.00am, two German mine- laying cruisers, the Bremse and the Brummer, intercepted the convoy. In conditions of poor visibility they were mistaken for British cruisers. From 3,000 yards they opened fire on HMS Strongbow.

This had a devastating effect, killing many with well directed fire. The Germans had also jammed HMS Strongbow's signal so the other ships could not be warned about the immediate danger. Lieutenant Commander Brooke though injured would not allow anyone to leave the ship until all confidential papers had been destroyed; he then ordered that she should be sunk and anybody alive should save themselves. HMS Strongbow sank about 9.30am with the loss of forty seven officers and men.

The Germans then proceeded to sink four of the merchant ships. HMS Mary Rose, assuming an attack from a submarine, turned but then too late realised the superiority of the enemy. As HMS Mary Rose approached the enemy at high speed she was sunk by the enemy guns, with the loss of a complement of over eighty eight men. The attack on the convoy took the lives of over two hundred and fifty men, and only ten men from HMS Mary Rose and five from HMS Strongbow survived. Nine of the convoy ships perished, and the Bremse and Brummer returned to port safely.

'*The Times*' on October 22nd 1917 reported the engagement under the headline:
'*German Naval Raid, Convoy Attacked in North Sea, two Destroyers and nine Ships sunk*'.

The Secretary of the Admiralty makes the following announcement:-
"*Two very fast and heavily armed German raiders attacked a convoy in the North Sea about midway between the Shetland Isles and the Norwegian coast on October 17. Two British destroyers, his Majesty's ships Mary Rose (Lieutenant-Commander Charles L. Fox), and Strongbow (Lieutenant-Commander Edward Brooke), which formed the anti-submarine escort, at once engaged the enemy vessels and fought until sunk after a short and unequal engagement.*

Their gallant action held the German raiders sufficiently long to enable three of the merchant vessels to effect their escape. It is regretted, however, that five Norwegian, one Danish, and three Swedish vessels - all unarmed-were thereafter sunk by gunfire without examination or warning of any kind, and regardless of the lives of their crews and passengers. Lengthy comment upon the action of the Germans is unnecessary, but it adds another example to the long list of criminally inhuman deeds of the German Navy.

Anxious to make good their escape before British forces could intercept them, no effort was made to rescue the crews of the sunk British destroyers, and the Germans left the doomed merchant ships while still sinking, thus enabling British patrol craft, which arrived shortly afterwards, to rescue some thirty Norwegians and others, of whom details are not yet known. The German Navy by this act has once more further degraded itself by this disregard of the historic chivalry of the sea.

It is regretted that all eighty eight officers and men of HMS Mary Rose and forty seven officers and men of HMS Strongbow were lost. All the next of kin have been informed". Able Seaman Frank Kenneth Greening is commemorated on the Chatham memorial. His name appears on the school memorial but as one of those who served, '*The Wheatleyan*' reveals he was on HMS Strongbow.

Torpedoed

Private **Ambrose John Cole,** 310082, Warwickshire Yeomanry was the last Old Boy to die at sea on the 27th May 1918. Born the 25th November, 1899 at 8, Rothesay Terrace, Barras Lane, he resided at 152 Earlsdon Avenue, Coventry and was employed as an engineer.

Enlisting in September, 1914 he had served in Egypt and embarked on the 'Leasowe Castle' on the 24th May 1918 bound for Taranto, Italy with nearly 3,000 other troops who were being shipped to the Western Front. At 1.30am on the 27th May 1918 the 'Leasowe Castle' was torpedoed on the starboard side by UB-51 whilst in a convoy one hundred and four miles north-west of Alexandria. Working parties were sent to lower the life boats whilst those not involved assembled ready to disembark; men started to leave the stricken ship after forty five minutes with B Company of the Warwickshire Yeomanry leaving via the portside. Other ships in the convoy came to the aid of 'Leasowe Castle' mainly the 'Lily' which came alongside to speed up the disembarking process. At about 3.00am a bulkhead in the ship gave way and she sank rapidly with the loss of eight nine men.

Seven of the men were from the crew and nine, including Ambrose, were from the Warwickshire Yeomanry. The 'Lily' was prevented going down with the 'Leasowe Castle' as the quick- thinking crew cut the joining ropes with axes just prior to the sinking. 'Leasowe Castle' was previously torpedoed on April the 20th 1918 whilst serving as an ambulance transport ship off Gibraltar.

Ambrose was presumed drowned as no bodies were formally recovered. The survivors were taken to safety and eventually made it to Taranto on the 21st June 1918 where they were reformed as a Machine Gun Company (MGC). The nine men who drowned from the Warwickshire Yeomanry are commemorated on the Chatby Memorial.

The War In The Air

In 1911 the Air Battalion of the Royal Engineers was formed with the predominant function being that of a spotter and feeding information to the Army and Navy. A year later the Royal Flying Corps (RFC) was formed, the Corps did not have an independent command as the full potential use of aircraft had not been realized to date. At the start of the war aircraft were still mainly used for reconnaissance but after years of fighting, the potential was understood and with the increased threat at home from aerial attacks the Royal Air Force (RAF) was created on the 1st April 1918. The RAF were a completely independent force and combined the Royal Naval Air Service (RNAS) with the RFC.

Forty two of the Old Boys listed on the *'Roll of Honour'* were members of either the RFC, RNAS or RAF. Five Old Boys would die from these units, as already stated Second Lieutenants Herbert Nelson, William John Salmons and William Alexander Roberts died at home whilst Private Francis Cox and Second lieutenant Frederick Adams died as a result of enemy action.

Private **Francis Daulman Cox** (no relation to Francis Henry Cox) served with the 22nd Squadron, RFC and formerly with the 28th Battalion, London Regiment (Artists' Rifles). He died of his wounds on the 26th November 1916 aged 24. He was the eldest son of Walter James (post office clerk) and Mary Jane Cox, of 4 Coundon Street, Coventry. Francis joined the Artists' Rifles in October 1915 and went through a training school in the London district; later in France he was attached to the Flying Squadron as an observer and was severely wounded in an aerial action on November 17th, the penultimate day for the ending of the Battle of the Somme. He died of wounds in the Canadian General Hospital at Etaples on November 26th and is buried in Etaples Military Cemetery. He also has a plaque in the War Memorial Park

Private F. D. Cox's Headstone

Second Lieutenant **Frederick Adams,** 53rd Squadron was shot down over the German lines near Messines and died on May the 12th, 1917 aged 28. He was originally reported as missing and it was believed he was in the hands of the Germans but sadly this was not the case.

He was born on the 24th October 1888 in Coventry and resided in Allesley Old Road, Coventry, the son of W. H. and E. Adams of Coventry. Brother of Captain Arthur Joseph Adams killed on the 30th August 1918, Frederick was a trained mechanic prior to the war and found time during his service to write letters to *'The Wheatleyan'*: *"A Zeppelin visited us the other night about midnight at which hour all respectable aviators are in bed. The noise was terrific, as it managed to drop about fifteen bombs unpleasantly close before it took to its heels and ran back over the lines. I must tell you about Corporal Fitzgerald's exploit the other morning. He was out when they sighted a German machine. Of course they gave chase and having a faster machine quickly overtook the German. Fitz, waited for a favourable opportunity and then fired.*

Nothing happened, so they turned again and manoeuvred again for an opening. This time Fitz must have hit the pilot, for the machine dived towards the ground, but about fifty feet from the ground he seemed to recover, and then Fitz, lost sight of the machine. Nothing further was fought until yesterday when a Major commanding a section of the artillery behind our lines sent a message of congratulations to the aviators of the British machines on their success in bringing the German down. It appears that our troops watched the fight and saw the German drop. He recovered about fifty feet from the ground, only to fall just afterwards between the line. We immediately turned a machine gun into the wreckage, and there the tale ends – rather grim isn't ? Hope the censor passes this, as it is the first bit of news I have told you, but seeing that Fitz, is an Old Bablake Boy it is only right the people at home should know what the Coventry lads can do. From my previous letters you must think that all we do out here is to eat cakes and chocolates all day and then write home for more".

The 'Fitz' referred to by Second Lieutenant Adams was B. M. Fitzgerald MBE who was in the RFC and left Bablake in 1899. Frederick was commissioned from a flight sergeant on the 17th December 1916 for duty with the RFC as a Second Lieutenant. After being shot down, Second Lieutenant Adams was buried, probably close to the vicinity of his wreckage. In 1924 graves were relocated from the surrounding area and Frederick was reburied in Oosttaverne Wood cemetery, Heuvelland, Belgium.

Gallipoli

The *'Roll of Honour'* was to increase further when His Majesty's forces landed on the shores of the Gallipoli Peninsula on the 25th April 1915. For 260 days the combined forces battled the Ottoman Empire (now Turkey) in the Gallipoli campaign for control of the peninsula and a strategic waterway known as the Dardanelles. By controlling the Dardanelles, the Allies hoped to threaten the Ottoman capital, Constantinople (now Istanbul) and knock the Turks out of the war.

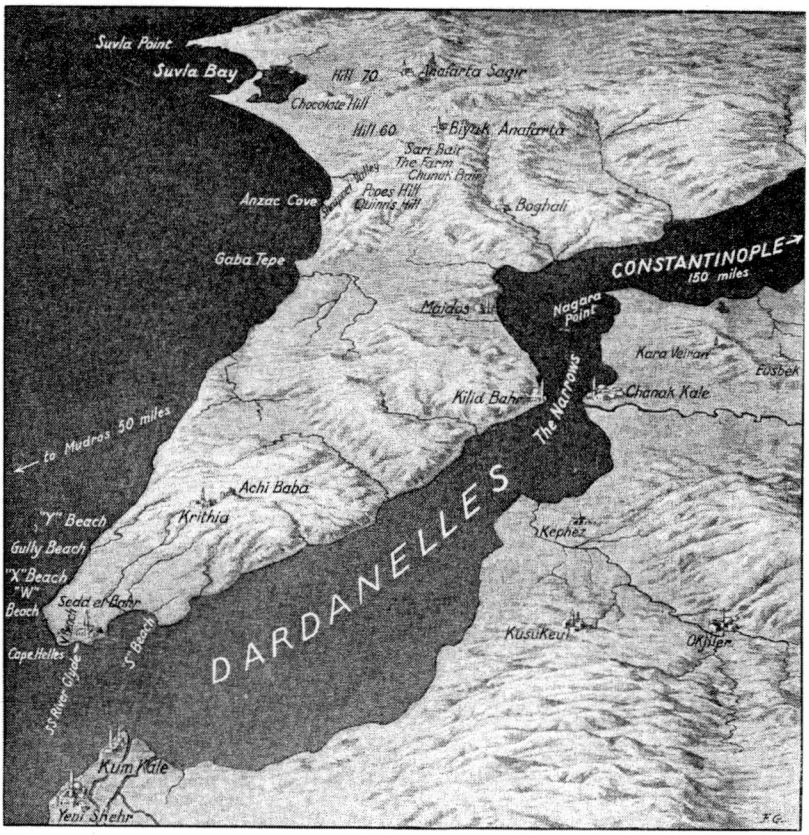

Map of the Dardanelles

This unsuccessful campaign was to prove rather costly and diverted much needed resources from the Western Front. When the order was received to withdraw, a number of ingenious methods were employed to give the illusion that the fighting forces were still there: guns were rigged to fire long after the owners had left; men ran along the trenches firing to give the impression of a bigger force and those going to the boats wore mufflers on their shoes. The withdrawal was planned with precision, so that every surviving man had been evacuated safely. The Gallipoli campaign was to account for the loss of four Old Boys, injuries to others and various award winners. *'The Coventry Graphic'* cited that of Old Boy Hugh Nelson, brother of Second Lieutenant Herbert Nelson (Refer to Died at Home).

"On the 11th May 1916 the Admiralty announced that Chief Petty Officer RNAS Hugh Nelson 272016 has "been mentioned in despatches by the Vice- Admiral commanding the eastern Mediterranean squadron for good services in action between the time of landing in the Gallipoli peninsular in April 1915 and the evacuation in December 1915-January 1916".

The first casualties of the campaign were Corporal Alfred Bailey, who was killed in action on the first day of the campaign, and Lieutenant Frederick Hugh Dodson whose exact date of death could not be verified but who was killed in action between the 25th and the 29th April. Corporal Bailey and Lieutenant Dodson were part of the Australian and New Zealand Armed Corps (Anzacs) who would have finished off their training in Egypt and sailed from Lemnos to the coast of Turkey ready for the landings.

Having disembarked onto small rowing boats the Anzacs were making their way to shore when flares illuminated the sky, quickly followed by the opening of machine gun and rifle fire from the Turkish positions. The Anzacs were shot in the boats or drowned as they attempted to get ashore. Those who managed to get ashore found they faced steep cliffs as through navigational errors they had not landed at the required point (a sandy beach) but a position one mile north. In this baptism of fire the Anzacs managed to make progress inland via the rugged cliffs but paid heavily.

Corporal **Alfred Bailey** was born in Coventry on the 18th June 1886, but he resided in Sydney having emigrated in 1909. This emigration could have been as a result of work with the Wesleyan Methodist Church and the Reverend J. Gawthorp as the *'Coventry Wesleyan Methodist Church Record'* included details of the missionary work required in Australia and New Zealand. The Reverend Gawthorp came to Coventry in 1890 and according to accounts *" At twelve years of age he was led into bad company, and ran wild with the wicked till the age of eighteen, when, like the wandering prodigal, he returned to his Father"*, an earnest evangelist he had the ability to recruit attendees at the young people's

class into the Christian fellowship and had done so in his previous positions.

Alfred enlisted on the 4th September 1914 with the 3rd Battalion, 1st Infantry Brigade. An engineer, he served his apprenticeship with Alfred Herbert Ltd at the Butts factory and previously resided at the Samson and Lion Hotel, Coventry. He was engaged to be married to a Miss Ida Bellchambers of Petersham, Australia and worked in a government workshop at Ranwick. He had previously visited Australia and the regime of Army life was not new to him as he served for four years with the 2nd Warwick Volunteers; this was viewed favourably on enlisting and he was made a corporal on enlisting, becoming an armourer. Alfred left Sydney on the 20th October 1914 on HMAT A14 Euripides. Whilst he was in Egypt a few of his friends received letters from him stating how anxious he was to get to the front.

His friend, also an Old Boy A. H. Langdon wrote to *'The Coventry Graphic'* explaining that a *"memorial service was held at Petersham Baptist Church on Sunday 6th June. The church was as full, with workmates, a Company of military and a large body of personal friends. The Minister was also from Coventry being Mr. Gawthorp, late of Queens Road Church"*. Also in attendance was Wallace Collett, an old school chum who left Bablake in 1910. He enlisted on the 3rd September 1916 aged 32 with the 53rd Battalion. Wallace had worked with Alfred at Alfred Herbert in Coventry and proceeded to France on the 5th December 1916. By the 15th February 1917 he reported as sick and was discharged on the 16th October 1917 suffering from bronchitis.

In Private Bailey's last will and testament he left his insurance money to his mother, a house in Earlsdon to W. Stratham, to his fiancée Mrs. Bellchambers all money except £50, to Wallace Collett £50 and finally to A. H. Langdon all his tools. In 1965 the Australian government launched a Gallipoli medal and Alfred's was applied for and granted to his fiancée in 1967. Private Bailey's body was not recovered, his possessions including photo and guide book were sent to Mrs. Bellchambers. His father, previously a landlord at the Samson and Lion hotel, had died a few weeks before he enlisted.

The name of F. Dodson appears on the memorial, and *'The Wheatleyan'* advises that a Lieutenant F. H. Dodson was killed with the New Zealand Expeditionary Force. **Frederick Hugh Dodson's** exact association with Bablake is not known as it appears he was born in Hukanui, Waikato, New Zealand. A single man he was employed at the New Zealand Loan and Mercantile Agency of Tauranga, New Zealand. Frederick Hugh's father was Albert Frederick and his mother Maude and they were named as his next of kin. He was one of the 2,721 New Zealanders who died in the campaign, roughly one-quarter of those who fought on Gallipoli, and

one of the 176 who are listed as being killed on the first day. Lieutenant Dodson, Auckland Regiment, 6th Hauraki Company is one of the 492 officers from the Anzacs who died in the Gallipoli campaign aged 23.

Both men are commemorated on the Lone Pine Memorial which records the names of the Anzacs who have no known grave and died in the area of Gaba Tepe. The original Lone Pine Ridge obtained its name after the Turkish army cut down almost all the pine trees, as roofs for their trenches, leaving only one pine tree standing. Owing to the horrific losses suffered by the Anzacs, the 25th of April is a national holiday in New Zealand and Australia, commemorated as Anzac day.

The remaining casualties in the Gallipoli campaign are remembered on the Helles Memorial to the missing. Gunner Samuel James Elliott was killed on the 17th May 1915 aged 21 and Pioneer Herbert Joseph Payne died aged 34 on the 8th August 1915.

Samuel James Elliott attended Bablake from the 27th August 1906 and left on the 23rd July 1909. Prior to this he was at St. Mark's Elementary School and he is pictured in the centre on the following page. Born on the 6th March 1894 at Worksop, he resided at 28 Highland Road, Earlsdon, working as a plumber and painter prior to the outbreak of war. He enlisted in November 1914 and at the point of his death was serving with the 14th Siege Battery, Royal Garrison Artillery (RGA). The siege batteries were almost immobile; as they involved the largest guns they were normally mounted on fixed concrete emplacements or on train tracks although the conditions at Gallipoli would have dictated this was probably not the case. He was one of three brothers, the sons of William, a millwright's engineer, and Emma Jane Elliott, who originated from Whittington Moor, Chesterfield.

The Elliott Brothers

All three brothers served: Private A. Elliott (left) went out with the Expeditionary Force to the Western Front and survived the war. He left Bablake in 1899 and served with the 2nd Company of the Coldstream Guards. Sergeant Ernest Clifford (right) also attended Bablake and lost his life with the King's Royal Rifle Corps. (Refer to 23rd April 1918) .

At 34 years old, **Herbert Joseph Payne**, a Pioneer with 72nd Field Company, Royal Engineers (RE), was killed in action on the 8th August 1915. Born 3rd August, 1882 at 72 West Orchard, he was 17 years old when he served in the South African War as a Trooper in the Imperial Yeomanry. Son of Alfred and Ellen Elizabeth Payne of Cox Street, Coventry, he was called up in August 1914 and was occupied as an examiner residing at 16 Gas Street. He also has a plaque in the War Memorial Park.

The four Old Boys who died at Gallipoli have no known graves. This is not only due to the conditions involved in the campaign at Gallipoli, which made it almost impossible to bury the dead safely, but also that the Allies could not return to the Peninsula until after the war and start the process of identification.

Mesopotamia

Turkey's entry into the war on the 29th October 1914 immediately prompted Britain to open a new front in the remote Ottoman province of Mesopotamia, now present-day Iraq. To protect British oil interests (a vital necessity to numerous campaigns), British and Indian troops were mobilized and dispatched to the Persian Gulf. Encountering minimal Turkish resistance the forces made good ground and by 28th September were one hundred and twenty miles south of the capital, Baghdad.

At the Battle of Ctesiphon on the 22nd to the 26th November 1915 under the command of General Townshend, events took a turn for the worse and the Turks withstood a large attack. Half of the British force numbering some 8,500 were killed or wounded. Survivors fled, retreating to Kut-el-Amara, without sufficient resources including medical and transport facilities. After the epic retreat Kut-el-Amara was finally reached on the 3rd December 1915.

Turkish reinforcements saw to it that the town was besieged for one hundred and forty seven days, during which time the men endured horrendous conditions, including an epidemic of sickness, before finally surrendering on the 29th April 1916. Attempts were made to rescue the besieged town including air drops but they all failed and the British suffered another defeat by the Turks. The Mesopotamia campaign continued, Kut-el-Amara was recaptured on the 24th February 1917 and Baghdad on the 11th March.

One Bablake Old Boy died in Mesopotamia, Second Lieutenant **Reginald Kenneth Drakeley** from the 9th Battalion, Royal Warwickshire Regiment. He was born on the 14th January 1894 at Birmingham and lived in Coventry, before moving to Wallasey, Cheshire. On leaving Bablake he was employed as a clerk in the Town Office but quickly followed his father's profession enrolling as a police officer. When he was admitted to Bablake in September 1907 his father was a Superintendent (living in the police station, Longford); he left Bablake in April 1910. Prior to this he attended Foxford Elementary School. Reginald was 6 foot 1 inch tall, weighed 11 stone 4 lbs and received his temporary commission on the 16th November 1914.

There were six attempts made to relieve those besieged in Kut–el-Amara. The final phase lasted from the 17th to the 22nd April, and this accounted for the life of Second Lieutenant Drakeley. At 7.15am on the 19th April 1916 in the region of Chalelah the 9th Battalion went forward to attack the enemy's front line. The flooded, marshy terrain made if difficult for the Battalion to advance; heavy rifle fire and terrific machine gun fire accounted for many casualties. During the attack two officers were killed, four were wounded , including Lieutenant Drakeley, who died of his wounds whilst in charge of a party of bombers. He is buried in Amara War Cemetery, one of over 20,000 in the British Army killed in the relief attempts. Of the other ranks sixteen were killed, sixty eight wounded, sixteen went missing in action and one died of wounds. The following men were then drafted into the Battalion, one officer and thirty eight other ranks from Basra, giving the Battalion an effective strength of six officers and 421 other ranks.

News of Lieutenant Drakeley's death was covered in *'The Birmingham Weekly Post'* , 6th May 1916 stating *"Lieutenant Drakeley, 13th Cyclist Division, formerly employed in the Town Clerk's Office, Coventry, and a son of Superintendent Drakeley, Warwickshire Police has died of wounds in Egypt. He enlisted early in the war"*.

Palestine

Lieutenant **Frederick James Poulton** died on the 2nd November 1917 in Palestine engaged in the Third Battle of Gaza, which began on the 27th October, ending with the capture of the ruined and deserted city on the 7th November 1917. Frederick's unit was the 9th Battalion of the Queen's (Royal West Surrey Regiment) but he was attached to the 1/8th Battalion, Hampshire Regiment. A Coventry resident, but born in Birmingham in 1894, he attended Albert Road Elementary School in Aston prior to Bablake. He spent six years at Bablake, May 1905 to April 1911, and gained a London Matriculation in January 1911. On leaving he engaged in private study with a view to entering the Civil Service, eventually

becoming an articled clerk to chartered accountants at Iliffe & Sons Ltd. His father was also an accountant in a printing works. Frederick received his temporary commission on the 17th June 1915.

Lieutenant Poulton is buried in Gaza cemetery. A member of the Queen's Road Church, he is commemorated on a stained glass memorial in the Church and on a tablet erected by the firm and employees to the memory of those from Iliffe & Sons Ltd who lost their lives during the Great War. This tablet contains thirty nine names.

Italy

Private **Henry Edwin Gunn** was born 12th August, 1895, at 56 King William Street; he resided at 46 Stockton Road, Coventry. A pupil at Wheatley Street Elementary School, he spent four years at Bablake from 2nd July 1907 to 23rd July 1911. He was awarded his four year term by the Governors, the last two years being spent as a resident. He was a clerk and an assistant in a chemical laboratory and enlisted in September, 1914 with the 1/7th Battalion Royal Warwickshire Regiment. He was one of the four sons of William F. (cycle hand) and Fanny L. Gunn, of Coventry. In April 1916 the patriotic family appeared in *'The Coventry Graphic'*. Private William Gunn (middle left) was with the 4th Worcesters and was invalided home from Suvla Bay; Horace Gunn (far left) served on HMS George V and was the only surviving brother who attended Bablake, leaving in 1912. He also served on HMS Erin; and Walter Gunn (far right) was attested under the Derby scheme and called to the colours. Henry is shown middle right, with the Royal Warwickshire insignia.

The Gunn Brothers

Private Gunn served in France from the 22nd March 1915 and the school memorial implies that Henry was awarded a Military Cross, this could not have been the case as this was not awarded to Privates. Neither the Commonwealth War Graves Commission or the Royal Warwickshire Regimental Museum show Private Gunn as the recipient of an award for gallantry and this would seem to be a genuine error. The Italians entered the war on the Allied side, declaring war on Austria, in May 1915. British forces were at the Italian front between November 1917 and November 1918, and rest camps and medical units were established at various locations in Northern Italy behind the front. Between April 1918 and February 1919 those who died from wounds or disease in the 9th , 24th and 39th Casualty Clearing Stations (CCS) were buried either at Montecchio Precalcino or at Dueville. Henry died on the 26th June 1918 and is buried in Montecchio Precalcino Communal cemetery Extension.

The Western Front

1914

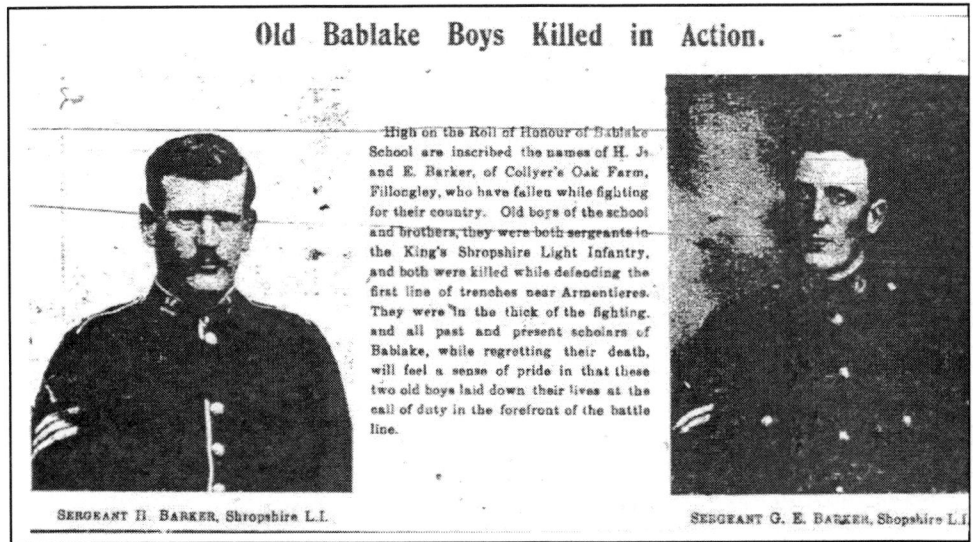

Old Bablake Boys Killed in Action.

High on the Roll of Honour of Bablake School are inscribed the names of H. J. and E. Barker, of Collyer's Oak Farm, Fillongley, who have fallen while fighting for their country. Old boys of the school and brothers, they were both sergeants in the King's Shropshire Light Infantry, and both were killed while defending the first line of trenches near Armentieres. They were in the thick of the fighting, and all past and present scholars of Bablake, while regretting their death, will feel a sense of pride in that these two old boys laid down their lives at the call of duty in the forefront of the battle line.

SERGEANT H. BARKER, Shropshire L.I.

SERGEANT G. E. BARKER, Shropshire L.I.

The Death of the Barker Brothers is Announced

The first two casualties on the chronological *'Roll of Honour'* are two brothers, Sergeant **George Edward Barker** and Sergeant **Henry J. Barker,** residents of Collyers Oak Farm, Fillongley. George, the eldest son, was born in Adelaide, South Australia in 1892 and shortly after his birth it is believed that his family emigrated as Henry was born in Coventry. Both brothers enlisted before the outbreak of war, Henry in Coventry, initially into the Royal Engineers but later transferred to the 1st Battalion King's Shropshire Light Infantry (KSLI) to be with his brother George, who had enlisted in Birmingham.

When war broke out, the brothers by this time were both Sergeants and stationed in Tipperary, Ireland as part of the 16th Infantry Brigade, 6th Division. Mobilisation orders were received at 6.00pm on the 4th August 1914 and on the 14th August the Division left Tipperary for Queenstown and by the 20th August were encamped in the neighbourhood of Cambridge for intensive training. All ranks were declared fighting fit on the 6th September and embarked at Southampton on the 8th, arriving in France on the 10th. The landing strength of the Battalion was 27 Officers, 1 Warrant Officer and 969 other ranks.

After ten days of manoeuvres taking in Mortcerf, Crecy, Jouarres, Rocourt, Buzancy, Mont Notre Dame and Courcelles the Battalion crossed the River Aisne on the 21st September and that night came into line in the left centre of the British front. Two companies of the 1st Battalion KSLI, C and D took over the trenches a quarter mile east of Vailly, A and B companies being in reserve. Having relieved the 1st Wiltshire Regiment the 1st Battalion KSLI were themselves relieved by the 3rd Coldstream Guards on the 1st October.

The Battalion moved less than a mile to the west of Vailly and took over trenches occupied by the Royal Scots Fusiliers and stayed there until the 12th October when they were relieved by the 287th Regiment of French Infantry. Over the coming days the 6th Division moved north and by the 16th were assembled south west of Cassel to take part in the First Battle of Ypres and the struggle for the Channel Ports. The 16th Brigade were placed in Divisional reserve whilst the main force advanced through Sailly on the 17th and by the 19th were three miles south of Armentières at Bois Grenier.

Heavy firing was heard all through the night; on the following morning the Germans attacked heavily along the whole of the front. In the evening the Battalion put their entrenching tools to good use digging a defensive position at Le Quesne Farm. The following day they took over the trenches of 2nd York and Lancashires and one Company of the Leicesters and were subjected to heavy shelling for the next two days.

At 4.15am on the 23rd October the Germans attacked in force, but were repulsed with heavy losses. The attacks continued until 5.00pm even though no ground was gained. By the end of the day over two hundred enemy dead were counted in front of the Battalion's trenches; it was during the defence of the trenches that George and Henry lost their lives. Exactly a day later the Germans renewed their attack and the Battalion held its ground, even though the distance between the two fighting forces in some places was less then fifty yards. The British headquarters were forced out of their position at 4.00am on the 25th October by heavy shelling, and by 2.00pm orders were received to withdraw.

Exactly a week later the Battalion returned to Bois Grenier, and owing to the steadiness and courage of all ranks, left an unbroken line. The total casualties for the five days were three officers killed, fifty two other ranks killed, seventy nine wounded and eleven missing. The brothers, who have no known grave, are remembered on the Ploegsteert Memorial and on the Fillongley war memorial along with thirty seven members from the Fillongley community.

Also remembered on the Ploegsteert Memorial is Private **John William Rossiter** I Company of the 2nd Battalion, Royal Warwickshire Regiment who was killed in action aged 27 on the 27th October 1914. John was the son of Charles James Rossiter and resided with him at 19, Stockton Road, Coventry. Born on the 28th August 1887, he was a native of Coventry and as a boy he attended Wheatley Street School prior to Bablake, which he attended for four years. He was employed as a turner until enlisting with the 4th Battalion, Royal Warwickshire Regiment. He served for three years in India and was at Malta for two years. After the outbreak of war, he left with his regiment the 2nd Battalion as he had been transferred several years earlier, they arrived in France soon after the fall of Antwerp.

For several days prior to his death the 2nd Battalion were involved in heavy fighting at Hazebrouck, France. On the 24th October orders were received to clear a wood and passing through it the Battalion came under heavy shell fire; a note is made in *'The Battalion war diary'* stating that *"the enemy retired obstinately leaving many killed and wounded in the wake"*. Later the same day a body of Germans were found occupying a house and further orders were received to take the farm. In doing so the Battalion received numerous casualties from machine gun and rifle fire. The enemy took some prisoners, captured ammunition and notably retained possession of their machine guns.

The following day the Battalion were placed in reserve and received a congratulatory message from Sir Henry Rawlinson stating *"the previous day they had saved the line"*. By the night of the 26th the Battalion were retired to Klein Zillebeke, having witnessed an English aeroplane shot down by its own gunners. Rising early at 5.00am on 27th October the Battalion advanced five to six hundred yards into a wood, where they came into contact with not only the remainder of the Brigade, but also had further encounters with the enemy and during this encounter Private Rossiter was killed. Probably owing to the severity of this action there are no further *'Battalion War Diary'* entries until the 11th November.

Following Private Rossiter's death his relatives must have received unofficial notification that he was buried in Hazebrouck Communal cemetery, which was a grave location known to be used at this time. Burials began in the Hazebrouck Communal Cemetery in October 1914 and continued until July 1918. At first, they were made among the civilian graves, but after the Armistice these earlier burials were moved into the main enclosure. The CWGC does not acknowledge that Private Rossiter is buried at Hazebrouck, and he is therefore commemorated on the Ploegsteert Memorial. However, of the 877 graves in Hazebrouck cemetery, seventeen remain unidentified. At the time of his death his brother, Alexander was serving with the 7th Battalion, Royal Warwickshire Regiment a pupil at Bablake his name also appears on the school memorial.

1915

Whilst the Gallipoli campaign was raging, 19 year old Private **William Wilkins,** 1st Battalion Royal Warwickshire Regiment was being buried at Wimereux Communal cemetery. An employee of the Humber works, William enlisted in August 1914. He had been at the front for two months when he was wounded in

both legs by shell fire, the resultant injuries requiring one of his legs to be amputated. He wrote a letter to his parents, Thomas and Rosina Williams of Cromwell Street, Coventry, saying he was progressing *"favourably"* but his condition must have deteriorated as he died of his wounds at Boulogne Hospital on the 4th May 1915.

'The Battalion war diary' on this day states the *"great relief felt by the Battalion after the last ten days"* that they had received orders to leave the area known as Shell Trap farm as they had been heavily shelled throughout its occupancy, having had numerous men killed and wounded every day.

The first Commissioned officer to pay the supreme sacrifice was **Herbert William Hyde,** Second Lieutenant Royal Sussex Regiment, son of Charles and Amelia Hyde from Rugby. Herbert was attached to the 2nd Battalion Royal Inniskilling Fusiliers. He appears in the army list of August 1914 as a Lieutenant in the special reserve Royal Sussex Regiment, being commissioned on the 13th September 1913. By April 1915, aged 25, he was attached to the Royal Inniskilling Fusiliers.

It was not until the Battle of Festubert, 15th to the 22nd May 1915, that the Inniskillings were to get an opportunity to prove their worth. During the winter they had suffered the cold and mud in Flanders but had seen very little enemy action, being posted to the 5th Infantry Brigade, 2nd Division. Three days prior to the start of the battle they had taken up positions in the 2nd Division's Front marching through Richebourg. The area was waterlogged and the trenches provided little protection against the enemy artillery. Before the attack began six men were killed and forty men were wounded.

Previous daylight raids and a further attack made on the night of the 15th had failed. For this attack along the 2nd Division front, the 2nd Battalion of the Royal Inniskillings were part of the attack on the left with the Worcesters. A and D Company led the assault on the far and near side respectively with B and C supporting. D Company's attack was successful: they captured the second line of German trenches and consolidated with C Company. The A Company attack was less successful: they captured the first line of the trenches but met with heavy losses, B Company came out of support and also met with heavy losses until falling back. The Worcesters had also failed in their attack.

D and C Company were ordered to fall back to the first line of trenches and they held this position until the evening of the 16th, when they again fell back to the original 2nd Division Front line. Herbert William Hyde died on the 17th May 1915 and his name is on the school memorial as W. H. Hyde. During the offensive a total of 19 officers (including Second Lieutenant Hyde) and 652 other ranks from the 2nd Battalion lost their lives. The Battalion were then withdrawn from the line and their gallantry rewarded by receiving numerous congratulations from Senior Officers.

Herbert has no known grave and is remembered on the Le Touret memorial, which contains the names of 13,000 missing who fell in the area enclosed on the north by the river Lys and a line drawn from Estaires to Fournes, and on the south near Grenay before 25th September 1915 (the eve of the Battle of Loos). In all, the Royal Sussex Regiment lost 6,800 members whose names are recorded in the Regimental Chapel of St. George in Chichester Cathedral; unfortunately Second Lieutenant Hyde is missing from the Roll, probably because of his attachment to the Royal Inniskillings. Similarly his name is not recorded in the Royal Inniskilling casualty list. This British offensive costs the lives of approximately 16,500 men, gaining 1,000 yards on a front of 2,000 yards.

Less then a month later a decision was taken to launch a further offensive at Givenchy, this action lasted for two days from the 15th to the 16th June. During the joint offensive two attacks were launched by the Canadians on a strong point known as 'Dorchester' with similar results the advancing troops being cut down by machine gun and rifle fire. The first attack was made on the evening of the 15th and the renewed attack in the afternoon of the 16th. In this action, the Roll increased further with the death of Private **John Samuel Harris**, 3rd Battalion Canadian Infantry (Central Ontario Regiment).

John was born on the 29th May 1884 at Attleborough, Nuneaton. He was the son of Enoch and Emily Harris of Kemscote, Lythalls Lane, Coventry and one of four brothers. Before emigrating to Canada he spent three years with the 7th Battalion Royal Warwickshire Regiment (Territorials) and was considered fit for the Canadian Expeditionary Force (CEF) on the 26th October 1914. At enlistment he was recorded as 5 foot 9 inches tall with a medium complexion, blue eyes and had a distinguishing mark on the back of his hand; he is one of 11,000 Canadians remembered on the Vimy Ridge Memorial who have no known grave.

Private **Hubert William Morris** was also killed in action in the vicinity of Givenchy on the 25th September 1915 aged 18 with the 2nd Battalion of the Oxfordshire and Buckinghamshire Light Infantry (OBLI).

This date is significant as the start of the Battle of Loos, an offensive incorporating the use of six divisions and the first use of gas by the British Army. The Givenchy attack was a diversionary one and to give this perception was launched thirty minutes prior to the main attack.

Initially gains were made, but on approaching the second line which had been heavily fortified with wire they received heavy machine gun fire and were counter attacked forcing a withdrawal to the original starting trench. By noon on the 25th September, Loos had been captured by the 15th and 47th Divisions , but the Battle of Loos was to last until the 19th October 1915 and account for over 50,000 casualties.

Hubert was a native of Wolston and the son of John Charles (a miller) and Miriam Morris. His name is recorded on the memorial as W. H. Morris. *'The Coventry Graphic'* on July 2nd 1915 revealed that the inhabitants of Brandon and Wolston were proud of the fact that a large proportion of the men eligible for military service had left the two villages to join the colours; this particular article showed forty seven men, one of them being a Private H. Morris from the Oxfordshire and Buckinghamshire Light Infantry. William attended Bablake from 1908 to 1911, one of over nine hundred and fifty men killed in this diversionary attack he is buried in Guards' Cemetery, Windy Corner, Cuinchy.

His relatives, who reside in Stoney Stanton, Leicestershire, are in possession of the following notification from the War Office:

Army Form B. 104—82.

No. _____
(If replying, please quote above No.)

_____ Infantry Record Office,

_____ WARWICK _____ Station,

_____ OCT 6 1915 _____, 191 .

Sir,

It is my painful duty to inform you that a report has this day been received from the War Office notifying the death of

(No.) *11096*   (Rank) *Private*

(Name) *Wm H. Morris*   (Regiment) OXF. & BUCKS. LT. INFY.

_____ which occurred at _____

_____ *Givenchy* _____ on the *25th* day

of *September 1915* _____, and I am to express to you the sympathy and regret of the Army Council at your loss. The cause of death was

Killed in Action

If any articles of private property left by the deceased are found, they will be forwarded to this Office, but some time will probably elapse before their receipt, and when received they cannot be disposed of until authority is received from the War Office.

Application regarding the disposal of any such personal effects, or of any amount that may eventually be found to be due to the late soldier's estate, should be addressed to "The Secretary, War Office, London, S.W.," and marked outside "Effects."

I am,
Sir,
Your obedient Servant,

_____

Officer in charge of Records.

Notification Received by the family of Hubert Morris

The name of Hubert Morris is recorded on the Wolston War Memorial with the names of twenty six other men from the village.

Sapper **Harry Hassall Underwood** is one of fifty four casualties who have a special memorial at Menin Road South Military Cemetery. With constantly changing battle lines the cemeteries and graveyards were not sacrosanct and subjected to

shelling as per other areas of the battlefield. Sapper Underwood was originally buried in Menin Road North Cemetery; his grave was probably destroyed by shell fire and could not be found after the Armistice when these graves and other in isolated positions were consolidated into Menin Road South Cemetery.

Sapper Underwood was a member of Wall Street Congregational Church, employed as an apprentice at Alfred Herbert, and an enthusiastic cricketer playing for the West Orchard Club. He was an only son, and resided at 100 Newcombe Road, Earlsdon. He enlisted in Coventry and died on the 26th September 1915 aged 18 whilst serving with the 89th Field Company, Royal Engineers. His name is recorded correctly in *'The Wheatleyan'* as H. Underwood but shown as A. Underwood on the memorial.

The last casualty of 1915 and the first married man was Bombardier **Charles John Hopkins,** of the 1st North Midland Brigade, RFA, who died aged 36 on the 13th October 1915. This was a day for the renewal of a British attack and came shortly before the end of the Battle of Loos on the 16th October. Charles's parents occupied the Elms in Coundon then a lodging house and he was employed as a school teacher. He was married to Lizzie May and resided in Boston, Lincolnshire. Bombardier Hopkins would have been deployed in the use of medium calibre guns and howitzers near the front line. He has no known grave and is commemorated on the Loos Memorial to the missing. This memorial records the names of over

20,000 Officers and men who have no known grave and stands in Dud Corner cemetery, so called because of the number of enemy duds found after the Armistice.

1916

Four days into 1916 saw the death of **Herbert Charles Collingbourne,** a Gunner with the 1st Warwick Battery, Royal Horse Artillery (RHA), who had responsibility for the light mobile guns. Gunner Collingbourne was in the Coventry section of the Warwickshire RHA, during their fourteen months of action in France they had been immune from casualties, but this excellent and fortunate record has had to be sacrificed as the result of a bombardment when several Coventry men were injured by the bursting of a high explosive shell. The battery was the first territorial regiment to go to France arriving there on November 1st 1914, they claimed they had been more in action than any other battery and have been complemented on their splendid work by General French. The incident occurred when the man sought safety in an old cellar protected by sandbags, one of the enemy shells forced its way through the structure and according to local papers *"played havoc amongst the men".*

An account of the disastrous bombardment was given in a letter from Gunner Croydon who in writing home says :-" *We all went down a cellar for safety because they were shelling us. And as soon as we got down there one of the 5.9 shells came in and burst. The result was bricks and bits of shrapnel were flying all over the place. About six of us got hurt, Fletcher, Short, Collingbourne, Barklett and myself. I believe Chattaway was hit but I don't know, (Spot) Phillips was not there at all so was not hurt thank God. I was the only one able to stand so got out and went for help. I believe I am on my way for England but don't know. I must look funny. I was hit in the face and you can only see one eye and enough of my mouth to but a fag in. The nurses are very good to me and the Doctor is a Leamington man (Dr. Gibbons Ward Medical Officer of health for Leamington is one of the best). I am on a barge on the canal on the way to the coast. Chattaway it is believed is seriously hurt".*

The Chattaway referred to was Herbert Walter, the son of Architect of the City who had attended King Henry VIII, later reports advised he was seriously injured, but a successful operation has been performed and he had been visited in hospital in France by his father. Other reports suggested Gunner Richard Hunt Croydon also a former King Henry VIII pupil and son of Mr. Richard Croydon has been brought back to Colchester Hospital. The other men who were injured and well known locally were Collingbourne, Short, Traherne (probably Herbert Leslie a former King Henry's pupil from Chapelfields) and Reginald Fletcher. This was the only other Old Boy known to be amongst those injured, he was pictured with his brothers in the 'Enlisting Section' and left the school in 1911.

Herbert also known as 'Bert' was treated at the hospital centre in St. Omer. The extent of his wounds ultimately led to his death and he was buried in Longuenesse (St. Omer) Cemetery. The General headquarters of the British Expeditionary Force (BEF) were based at St. Omer until March 1916. Herbert was one of five children. He was born in Colchester Street, Coventry and resided at King Richard Street. In 1906, Herbert was awarded a prize of an annual in the yearly prize giving and the Programme where Herbert's prize was declared is shown on the following page. The signatures around the edge are Herbert's and his fellow classmates, the signature at the top being that of the Head F. W. Humberstone. Herbert also expressed an interest in photography and on one occasion photographed Bablake at Midnight from Nauls Mill Park.

A territorial Herbert chose to enlist in Leamington in 1914, swapping his uniform from that of a telegraphist and sorter at the Post Office to that of the RHA. His brother, George also served with the RHA as a Sergeant he did not attend Bablake and survived the war. Herbert had been home on a short leave in August 1915. After the war to commemorate the loss of a son and brother his family bought a plaque in the War Memorial Park and his name is one of sixteen men recorded on the Post Office Memorial.

Nine months after the death of John Samuel Harris, Givenchy was to claim another Old Boy: Lance-Sergeant **Henry Smith Craven**, The Buffs (East Kent Regiment) died on the 6th March 1916 and along with Charles John Hopkins is commemorated on the Loos Memorial. He also has a plaque in the War Memorial Park.

Born 22nd February 1892, Henry was the only son in a family of five, with sisters Dorothy, Emmie, Florence and Mabel and lived with them at 27, Spencer Street. He enlisted in October 1914 in Canterbury, six years after leaving Bablake which he had attended from 1904 to 1908. Prior to this he was educated at St. Peter's School. In Bablake he had proved himself a splendid tackler in football for the first XI and excelled at batting in cricket.

He secured a boy clerkship in the Civil Service occupying 16th position in the entrance exam out of 1,001 entrants; in July 1912 he came 9th out of 1,500 in the Excise and Customs Examination. A man of ambition he pursued his desire to be at the opening of the Panama Canal and got there working as a purser on the 'Orduna'. The opening was delayed until August 15th, 1914. One of Henry's roles was to announce in four languages that war had broken out and the remainder of the return journey was spent avoiding submarines.

Shortly before his death he had been wounded and returned to England for convalescence near Ipswich. Using his experience of working part-time for a Scottish newspaper he wrote the following poem, which appeared in the February 1916 edition of '*The Wheatleyan*':

Soliloquy of a Disabled Soldier

No more except in dreams,
Or in those haunting visions of the past,
Which soon dissolve in air, yet while they last
Bear all the imprint of reality,
Hear we the roar and thunder of the guns,
Or grimly wait at break of day the Huns'
Blind onrush towards Eternity.

No more shall we at night
By cloud-veiled moonbeams' misty light
Bury in earth the silent dead, or bear
The wounded comrades, groaning back to where
There's healing and security.

No more the Maxims' bane, nor yet again
In damning witness of unfettered hate
The shattered home, and ruins desolate
Of peaceful shrines and altars consecrate!

All these are over now.
Their price in flesh and blood alone is paid;
The pleasures of the heart and mind are made
More glorious in their fateful loss; and here
Mid sylvan glades where English red deer run,
And beeches redden in the Autumn sun
The soul renews its purity.

And as entranced I lie
On bracken couch to gaze on high
Where flimsy cloudlets float, me seems
The fairy magic of youth's dreams
Awakes anew to ecstasy.

In gardens fair
'Mid perfumes rare
Where linnets gaily sing,
Where laughter gay
Soothes care away
And pain has lost its sting.

Regretting nought, I think with awe and pride
Of you who follow, you who still must fight,
Knowing the toil, yet glorying in your might
And will to conquer, for Britain and the Right.

He then returned to France, having become engaged to Miss Carrie Morgan, (daughter of Frank Morgan, a Bablake Master), who later was to be headmistress of Moseley Avenue junior school for many years. On the 6th March 1916, he was killed aged 24.

Sergeant **John Weston Burton** of 1/7th Battalion, Royal Warwickshire Regiment died on the 26th June 1916 aged 24. He was the son of Thomas and Louisa Jane Burton, of 6, Starley Road, Coventry. Enlisting in September 1914, a tailor by trade, he was the youngest of three children. The 26th June was a fine day; smoke candles were lit all along the Battalion's front and at 10.15am the enemy responding to previous shelling put down a heavy barrage on the trenches occupied by the Battalion, which caused considerable damage.

This resulted in the deaths of two men, with twelve wounded; four were subsequently able to return to duty. Sergeant Burton, born the 18th July 1892 at St. Mark's, Coventry, was one of the two casualties from the 1/7th Battalion killed on this day and is buried in Hébuterne Military Cemetery.

The following two men, Sergeant William Toms and Lance Sergeant Herbert Ward were killed after the start of the Battle of the Somme, the areas in which they were killed were not part of the Battle and they have been taken out of chronological order for this reason.

Sergeant **William Toms** was killed on the 3rd July aged 24. Sergeant Toms was married to Mrs. M. A. Toms and resided with his wife at 190, Spon Street, Coventry. Born in Coventry on 14th February 1892 he was employed in the city as an elementary school teacher, before enlisting in September 1914 at Oxford. This probably influenced his decision and he joined the 2/4th Battalion Oxfordshire and Buckinghamshire Light Infantry. The first part of his education was spent at St. Michael's Elementary School; he then spent four years at Bablake, starting on 28th August 1905 and leaving 23rd July 1909, then went on to Culham Training College.

His stay at Bablake was paid for by the Coventry education committee. In 1909 he gained two certificates, Part I & II of the preliminary certificate (Distinction in history and science) and 2nd Class in the Matriculation Exam from London University. He is buried at Laventie Military Cemetery, La Gorgue. After the armistice a number of graves were removed from other burial grounds and re-interred in this cemetery. Billets were placed at Laventie as it was approximately two miles from the front line, this area was however subject to shelling as it came within range of the German field guns. William has a plaque in the War Memorial Park and is also commemorated on a plaque in the Council House to those who fell from the Education Department.

Lance-Sergeant **Herbert Ward**, 2/7th Battalion, Royal Warwickshire Regiment, was the next casualty who died on 19th July 1916 aged 35. He was married to Alice Ward (formerly of Cheltenham), and lived with her at St. Georges Road, Coventry. Herbert enlisted in November 1914 and swapped the position of Engine & Pumping Station Workman at the sewage pumping station, Coventry Corporation for the regiment. He was also a member of the Well Street Congregational church and a volunteer player for Humber C.C. for many years.

Lance- Sergeant Ward is remembered with honour at Laventie Military Cemetery, La Gorgue. The graves in this cemetery are mainly associated with the 61st South Midland Division at the attack on Fromelles on the 19th July 1916. This attack was aimed at preventing the enemy moving troops away from this area to support those involve in the Battle of the Somme. The early morning was misty and two companies each of the 2/6th and 2/7th Battalions who had been resting at Riee Bailleul reached Laventie at 7.45am and were successfully sent up to the front without loss. At 11.00am, zero hour the disposition for the 2/7th Battalion was three companies B, C and D lining front parapet from Fauquissart to Trivelet Road, one Company A in reserve.

The objective for the 61st South Midland Division and the Australian 5th division was the village of Fromelles and a ridge which overlooked the battlefield, the attack was centred around a position known as Sugar Loaf. At 11.00am the British Artillery bombarded the German positions, however this failed to suppress the enemy and when the infantry attacked they were mown down by well directed machine gun fire and artillery.

The losses reported were high for the 2/7th Battalion, for the officers; 1 killed, 9 wounded, 2 missing believed killed and 1 missing. Other ranks reported 200 men wounded and 170 men missing. The 61st Division lost 79 officers and over 1,400 men and the Australians 178 officers and over 5,300 men. Prior to the attack there was some debate whether the operation was required and in hindsight there is no evidence to suggest the attack prevented troops moving to the vicinity of the Somme.

The grave of his parents in Coventry Cemetery reveals his father Walter died on the 11th January 1938 aged 76 and his mother died two days later on the 13th January 1938 aged 78. The main inscription reads *"In death they were not divided"* with a smaller inscription stating *"also of Sgt H. Ward killed in action 19th July 1916 aged 35"*. Herbert is also commemorated on the Sewage Disposal Memorial in the Council House.

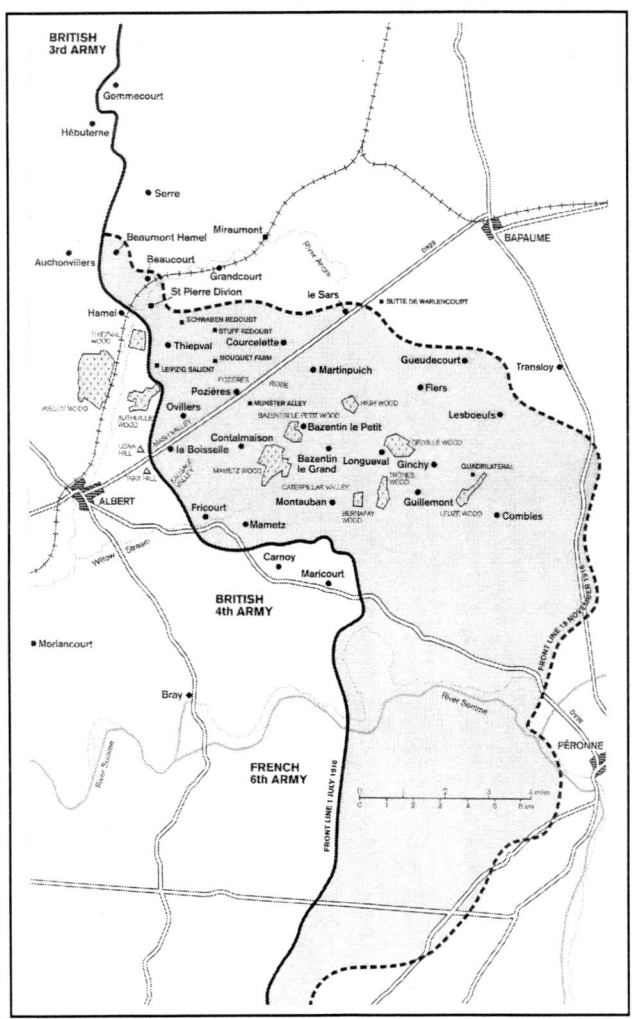

Map of the Somme

The Battle of the Somme started on the 1st July 1916, thirteen divisions launched an offensive on a line from North of Gommecourt to Maricourt. Prior to the start of the battle, an intense artillery bombardment pounded the German lines for seven days with the intention of eliminating any likely resistance. When zero hour came on the 1st July at 7.30am, the men went over the top and worked at a steady pace towards the enemy positions. In spite of the shelling many of the German positions were unscathed and were able to open fire with machine guns on the advancing masses which were met with this unexpectedly fierce resistance. Ground that was gained initially was lost over the coming days. In the first few days of the Somme the British Army lost over 52,000 troops.

The first Old Boy to fall at the Battle of the Somme was Captain **Harold Meredyth Adcock,** D Company, 10th Battalion, Lancashire Fusiliers who was previously Master of Modern Languages at Bablake. He commenced his employment in September 1913 and ended in September 1914 when he enlisted. Prior to this he worked for one year as a schoolmaster at Real Gymnasium, Frankfurt-an-der-Oder, Prussia. Born on the 23rd August 1890 at Horsham, Sussex he resided in Meriden Street whilst working at Bablake. He was the son of Charles and Alice Margaret of Charleville Mansions, West Kensington, London.

Captain Adcock spent his early years in Australia, but was educated in England – at Ellesmere College, Shropshire and Christ's College, Cambridge. At Ellesmere College he was the Captain of Hall, a colour sergeant in the OTC and obtained the school colours for cricket, hockey and football. He then spent six months in Hanover, and entered Christ's College in 1909. He read for the Medieval and Modern Languages tripos, in which he obtained his B.A honours in 1912. He was a member of the OTC, played hockey, coxed the 1st Lent and 2nd May boats in 1910, and edited the college magazine. He was a college scholar and prizeman.

In Michaelmas term 1910 he was awarded an exhibition of £20 for medieval and modern languages and this was repeated a year later being awarded a Medieval and Modern Languages scholarship of £30. As a cox his weight was recorded in the *'College Magazine'*. In Michaelmas term 1910 he weighed 8st 13lbs, Lent term 1910 8st 11lbs and finally Lent term 1911 where his weight increased to 9st 4lbs.

A member of the Debating Society in October 21st 1911 he proposed *'That this house believes the time to be ripe for a general reduction in armaments'*: the motion being lost thirteen votes to nineteen. A week later *'That this house considers the present system of dramatic censorship to be pernicious and useless and would welcome its abolition'*, again motion lost by five votes to eighteen. Several months later in Lent Term, on Saturday January 20th 1912 he opposed *'That in the opinion of this house the halfpenny press is a standing disgrace to the nation'*. The outcome was not recorded.

In the Easter 1912 *'College magazine'* he wrote an article about an annual visit to Cambridge and a Working Boys' Home. He was also referred to in the same magazine as he was a forward in the second division of the league *"one could not wish for a better defence, but the forwards were very weak; they would combine well at times but seemed incapable of scoring, showing the splendid keenness of the team. Although they met with defeat time and time again they never gave up the task as hopeless till the match was over"*.

He then spent a year in Prussia and on his return started at Bablake. One of his first interests there was the formation of the Cadet Corps; and he was at the summer camp with the members when war was declared. In September he received a commission to the Lancashire Fusiliers through the Cambridge OTC and was stationed with them until he went to the front in July 1915. He served with the 10th Battalion in the trenches until December 1915, when he was invalided home with a slight attack of enteric (inflammation of the intestines).

During this period, he wrote letters that appeared in *'The Wheatleyan'*; and whenever he came back for a day or two, from camp or from the trenches, he showed that he still retained the keenest interest in the Corps. On his last visit though only just recovering from an illness, he managed to give the Non Commissioned Officers (NCO), some useful lectures on fire-orders, drawing on experiences he had brought back from France.

Extracts from two of his letters are below:

"At present September 20th 1915 we are in reserve holding some redoubts behind the firing line in a wood. The weather is very fine and it is as good a life as man could wish for. Six or seven hours' work on the defences by day, draining or trench digging or working with sandbags – and the night to rest in. We are indeed living under the greenwood tree. And with this weather I ask for nothing better. I might also add "Here shall he see no enemy but winter and rough weather". For so far I have seen exactly three Germans and these I saw

with field glasses some 600 or 800 yards away. We hear them, and by night a fair number of stray bullets come whistling through the wood. But all you see if you look over the parapet is a long winding line of sandbags heaped up anyhow, some white and some black in wise confusion. We shell one another spasmodically and we bomb one another spasmodically, and very rarely at night we hear a rustling and clicking in the wire and then something black scuttles off in the darkness". Two months later on November the 11th the following appeared: *"All the country round this part of the line has been heavily shelled for months now and is a howling wilderness. Not a sign of life. Everything wet and muddy"*.

He rejoined his Battalion in February 1916, and returned to France early in April, when he obtained his captaincy aged 25. On the 5th July his Company was under orders to occupy a portion of the second line of the German trenches, when leading his men and close to the trench, he was struck by a bomb and killed instantly. The Company took and held the trench. After a year in France, he was buried in Sheeter Wood near Pozières and as his exact grave location was not known he is commemorated on the Thiepval Memorial and locally on the stained glass window in St. John's church. The *'Battalion Records'* indicate Captain Adcock was killed at Contalmaison during action in the vicinity of Shelter Alley, Quadrangle Trench and Pearl Alley in the Ancre Area.

Tributes were paid to Captain Adcock both from his employers and his educators. His obituary at Christ Church states " *There was a quiet strength of determination in Adcock's character which made him a marked factor for good throughout his college life"* and *'The Wheatleyan'* stated *"It is given to few to make in the space of a short year so marked an impression on the life of the school as H. M. Adcock made here during 1913-1914. He will be chiefly remembered by the devotion by which he threw himself into the organisation of the Cadet Corps…. He was never content with any standards short of the highest; whatever fell to him to undertake he pursued without respite, until it was completely and efficiently carried out. He was a man, in short, for whom a more than ordinarily distinguished career could have been prophesied unless indeed extreme modesty is a hindrance to such a career"*.

W. C. V. Thomas replaced Captain Adcock from 1914 to 1915 until he also joined the forces, becoming a Lieutenant in the 12th Welch regiment. He was wounded in France but made a good recovery and survived the war.

Four days later Bablake was to lose another member of staff, **Harold Masters Brown MC,** Second Lieutenant with the 5th Battalion Royal Berkshire Regiment, died of wounds on the 9th July 1916 aged 27. Harold was born at Slinfold, West Sussex on the 31st July 1888 and the third son of William and Keziah Harriett Brown. Initially Harold was educated at Horsham Grammar School, from 1909 to

1910 he attended a part time course in Chemistry at King's College, London. In 1913 he was listed with King's College as an external student meaning that he never matriculated in one of the University of London colleges and that most of his study was undertaken privately, he gained a 3rd Class Honours BSc in Chemistry.

His father William was Head Master of Slinfold Church of England and Harold followed him into the teaching profession as Science Master at the King's School, Canterbury. As war broke out he accepted a vacancy at Bablake School but never took up his position, enlisting in the Coldstream Guards on the 11th September 1914 as a Private. He was at the front for some time and became a Corporal prior to being commissioned as a Second Lieutenant to the Royal Berkshire Regiment on the 10th March 1915. Whilst a Corporal he was wounded three times.

The 5th Battalion did not take part on the initial day of fighting on the Somme. On the 2nd July 1916 at 3.00am, the Battalion were near the village of Ovillers la Boisselle, B and C companies were occupying the front system of trenches with A and D supporting in Rycroft Street. Battalion headquarters was situated in Vincent Street, with the 37th Infantry Brigade holding the trenches on the left and the 19th Division on the right. The trenches reflecting the outcome of events 24 hours earlier were found to be in a very filthy state, with many dead and wounded lying about. In the evening orders were issued that at dawn the following day the intention was to capture the village of Ovillers la Boisselle.

The war diary starts again at 4.00pm on the 3rd of July with the Battalion at Ovillers la Boisselle, no explanation of the events which occurred in the evening of the 2nd and the morning of the 3rd July are stated. The Battalion which now consisted of about seventy men, and the Commanding Officer were ordered to go to the Albert defences for the night. Here the men made bivouac shelters, and the officers and NCO's who had been left at the transport lines rejoined, and cookers were brought up. In the evening Second Lieutenants Breach and May, and about sixty men who had been dug in, in 'No Man's Land', rejoined under the cover of darkness, which brought the number up to approximately one hundred and thirty.

The 4th of July was extremely wet; the survivors moved into some vacant houses in Albert and spent this and the following day testing and refitting. The impact of the events for operations against Ovillers were not fully known and the following was recorded in the *'War diary'*: *"Officers Killed 2, Other Ranks Killed 2, Died of Wounds 2, Wounded 215, missing 111.*

The medical officer and the stretcher bearers remained behind in the Aid Posts in Standish Street; when the Battalion was withdrawn from the trenches; they performed excellent work in bringing in many wounded".

In the operations on the 2nd July 1916, Second Lieutenant Brown was wounded and awarded the Military Cross. The citation states *"for conspicuous gallantry in action on several occasions, notably when he carried out a dangerous reconnaissance of the enemy's trenches and afterwards led his Company to the attack with great dash. He was wounded in five places"*. He died of his wounds on the 9th July at the Duchess of Westminster's Hospital, Touquet and is buried at Etaples Military cemetery. His epitaph reads *"Thy will be done"*.

His Colonel wrote: *"He was a most popular and gallant officer, and led his Company across to the enemy's line splendidly,"* and his Captain: *"He was a magnificent officer and made his platoon the most efficient in the Battalion; he was a great favourite with all the men and officers"*. One of his brother officers also wrote: *"He had earned quite a reputation by having trained the platoon that won the competition for general efficiency and smartness, open to the whole Brigade"*. His two elder brothers also served and at this point were serving as Captains in the RAMC.

On the 20th August 1916 at Wanquetin, France the General Officer Commanding (GOC), 12th Division presented decorations given to Officers and men for operations on the 2nd and 3rd of July. Second Lieutenant Brown was awarded the Military Cross (MC).

Another member of staff, **John Claude Murray** Second Lieutenant, 2nd Battalion, South Wales Borderers, went missing on the 1st July the first day of the Battle of the Somme, his official date of death is the 9th July 1916.

He was a member of the staff from 1908 until 1913. He was commissioned as a Second Lieutenant (temporary) on Christmas Day 1914 and a Lieutenant (Temporary) on the 1st April 1916. He joined the 2nd Battalion just two months before his death, he has no known grave and is commemorated on the Thiepval memorial.

From the 1st July to the 9th July 5 officers died with the 2nd Battalion and 128 other ranks.

Also on the Thiepval Memorial is Corporal **George Cyril Biggs** 1/7th Battalion, Royal Warwickshire Regiment, who died on the 14th July 1916 aged 21. Born in Chilvers Coton, Nuneaton to George Robert and Ada Mary Biggs, of 52, High Street, Nuneaton he was the only son from a family of four. He was admitted to Bablake on the 2nd September 1907 and left 22nd July 1910. Prior to this his education was at Chilvers Coton Elementary School. On leaving Bablake he was a clerk in a quarry works and probably worked for his father, who was employed as a quarry manager.

On the 13th July, a fine and warm day, the Battalion were at Bouzincourt. At 1.30pm the Battalion moved by motor lorries to just outside Bouzincourt and from there they moved in fighting order to Albert, where they lay down in a field until midnight. Orders were received that the Battalion would attack north east of la Boisselle at 7.30am.

The next day the Battalion moved into position in trenches and were heavily shelled going into la Boisselle. Zero hour was 7.30am, and after artillery preparation, A and B companies proceeded to assault and reached their objective. Many casualties resulted, chiefly from machine guns, four officers were killed, one of them Lieutenant Bullock, a former King Henry VIII pupil. The Battalion held the trench for seven hours but had to evacuate it on account of the enemy's extremely heavy enfilade fire, both shell and machine guns. Lieutenant Colonel Knox, who led the attack and who had shown the greatest bravery throughout, was wounded. Major Hanson then took command of the Battalion. The casualties were estimated at 150, of whom 68 were reported killed.

Three more Old Boys with the Royal Warwickshire Regiment, 48th South Midland Division would become casualties on the 24th to the 25th July 1916 at Pozières. On the 24th July 1916, Second Lieutenant Matthew Frank Matts was killed in action with the 1/5th Battalion, with the 1/7th Battalion Company Sergeant-Major William Henry Croft Wood and Private Howard Round dying of their wounds on the 25th.

Matthew Frank Matts was born on the 16th June 1891 in Paynes Lane. He resided at 7 Grantham Street and was one of three sons. Employed as a builder's clerk prior to his enlistment in August 1914 he probably worked for his father Arthur, who was a builder's manager. He was pictured previously with other Old Boys whilst a Lance- Corporal.

William Henry Croft Wood (recorded as Croft Wood) was born the 28th February 1886 at St. Giles, Kensington, London, the son of George and Annie Wood with whom he resided at 19 Stanley Road, Earlsdon. A cashier, he enlisted August 1914.

Howard Round at 20 years old was the youngest of the three men. Born on the 4th April 1896 at Dudley he resided at Whoberley. He attended Bablake from May 1907 to the 25th July 1911, previously attending Earlsdon Elementary School. After

leaving Bablake he was initially a clerk at an auctioneer's office but went on to become a draughtsman with Messrs. Harper, Son and Bean at Dudley; his father Isaac was a millwright at Alfred Herbert Ltd. Howard enlisted slightly later than his comrades on the 3rd September, 1914 in Coventry and went to France in March 1915. A letter made available to his parents from Sergeant A. H. Jarnard reads *"Howard Round was an admitted hero by all who used to witness his work. He was a stretcher bearer, and did his work nobly. He, too, did some glorious work in the early days, and when he was killed he was actually going to bring in a wounded man…I have seen a lot of him since being out here, and I can tell you he was a cool customer and a real comrade"*. Howard was also a member of Well Street Congregational Church.

On the 19th July 1916 the 2/5th had reached Bouzincourt at 6.00am whilst the 1/7th were relieved by the 1/4th Royal Berkshire and proceeded to bivouac in the same location. The 20th and 21st saw the men taking the opportunity to have a bath and the couple of days were devoted to cleaning and inspection with curios performed in the evening.

On the 22nd July the 2/5th moved up to Ovilliers and Crucifix from the billets at Bouzincourt to join the 144th Infantry Brigade. The 1/7th were attached to this brigade as reserve leaving Bouzincourt at 8.00pm. A and D companies of the 1/7th remained to the east of Albert, while B and C companies went forward at 11.00pm and occupied support trenches immediately east of la Boisselle, as garrison for the trenches when the 144th Brigade went forward to attack.

The 23rd of July was a fine and warm day. The 2/5th Battalion were engaged in efforts to meet up with the Anzacs; despite attempts using stokes mortars and bombs they were unsuccessful owing to an enemy strongpoint. Meanwhile D Company of the 1/7th moved up to la Boisselle. Both A and D companies 1/7th were employed as a carrying party all day. B and C Company remained in the support trenches, repairing them and doing a certain amount of carrying. Orders were received from the Brigade to send out patrols to get in touch with the Anzacs in Pozières, and find out who was occupying the main German trench just west of Pozières as some signalling had been observed from that trench. At night the whole of C Company went to Pozières with orders to bomb up the German trench. On arriving at Pozières they found that the Anzacs were occupying part of the trench which had a bomb stop in it. After discussion with the Commanding Officer of the Anzacs' Battalion, it was agreed that the Anzacs should bomb the trench at dawn and C Company was subsequently withdrawn.

The following day at 7.30am and 4.30pm further attacks were made by the 2/5th Battalion; again these were unsuccessful even though they were aided by artillery and stokes mortars. Subsequent aerial photographs and intelligence from prisoners revealed that the position known as X.3.B.64 was strongly fortified and held by three machine guns with 300 men available to hold the position.

The 1/7th Battalion spent all morning carrying bombs and stokes mortars ammunition. That afternoon they received orders to relieve the 5th Battalion in the front line at 5.00pm. A and B took over the front line with C and D in support. Orders were received late in the evening that one of the support companies was to attack across open ground a position that had been identified as a German strong point. For the 2/5th the day ended with 1 Officer (Second Lieutenant Matts) killed along with four other ranks, twenty two wounded and two missing.

With the 2/5th now in brigade reserve, the action on this day resided with the 1/7th Battalion. At 2.00am on the 25th owing to a bombing attack on the left the Germans put up a very heavy barrage on our trenches which prevented the Company from coming up in time to make the attack before daylight. So the scheme had to be abandoned. Second Lieutenant Loveitt, a Coventry resident and former Henry the VIII pupil, was killed by rifle fire whilst reconnoitring the ground in front preparatory to the attack.

"At about 9.00am on this day after a short bombardment of the strong post by the stokes mortars, it was endeavoured to bomb the trench but owing to the Germans' heavy bombing etc the 1/7th were unable to get past their barricade. About 1.00pm another attack was organised. Two stokes guns were ordered to fire on the point for five minutes; bombing parties were to approach as near as possible under cover of the stokes gunfire and were then to rush the trench. Unfortunately for some reason (it is thought owing to the gun sinking in the soft ground) the stokes bombs all fell short and killed about seven of our men and wounded about 10. Naturally this disorganised the bombing parties and all the men were reportedly "very shaken". At about 8.00pm we had orders from the brigade to attack the strongpoint and take it at all costs. Casualties for this day amounted to approximately 18 men killed and 27 wounded and 2 missing. Pozières was eventually taken by the South Midland Division and the Anzacs later in the day".

Lieutenant Matts is buried in Pozières British Cemetery, Ovillers la Boisselle. A resident of Stoke, Coventry his name is inscribed on a stone tablet in the Porch of St. Michael's church along with twenty six other men who fell from the community in the Great War.

Company Sergeant- Major Wood is buried at Heilly Station cemetery, Mericourt l'Abbe. This cemetery is unique in that the burials were carried out under extreme pressure, and many of the graves are so close together that they could not be individually identified. Company Sergeant-Major Wood also rests with Private Frederick Murdoch, 20th Battalion Royal Fusiliers who died aged 25 on the 21st July 1916 and Lance-Corporal Dennis Taylor, 1/4th Oxfordshire and Buckinghamshire Light Infantry, who died on the 20th July 1916. Owing to the space limitations on the headstone the insignia of the relevant regiments are carved on a cloister wall on the north side of the cemetery. Locally his name is recorded in St. Barabara's Church and in the Earlsdon Working Mens club as one of the five members who died, in both cases he is commemorated as 'Croft Wood'.

Private Howard Round has no known grave and is commemorated on the Thiepval memorial

With the Battle of the Somme continuing Private **Kenneth Barry**, 23rd Battalion, Royal Fusiliers was killed in action at Deville Wood, on the 27th July 1916 aged 20. He was the son of Oliver Barry (photographer of Process Block books) and Amy Barry of 83 Grafton Street, Coventry.

He attended St. Peter's Elementary school and went on to Bablake on the 2nd September 1907. After four years he left on the 28th July 1911, his final two years being paid for by the Governors of Bablake. Kenneth continued his education at Manchester University as a student of textiles, he also previously worked as a clerk in a textile works. Kenneth enlisted in February 1916 in Manchester. Following the successful raids of the 14th July the right side of the new British Line was threatened by Deville Wood and uncaptured parts of Longueval village, for attacks to continue these areas needed to be captured. The task originally fell to the South African Brigade starting on the 15th July. After initial gains the Germans counter attacked forcing a withdrawal. Fighting for the wood continued until the 3rd September 1916. A renewed attack was made by the 2nd Division on the 27th July in which Private Barry lost his life. He is commemorated on the Thiepval Memorial and in the War Memorial Park; an appeal was made in 'The Coventry Herald' by his family for any information.

Exactly a month later Gunner **Alfred George Middleton,** D Battery, 240th South Midland Brigade, RFA, was killed in action at Aveluy, France on the 27th August 1916 aged 23. He was the third son of Edward (a gas works engine wright) and Rebecca Middleton, of 78, Richmond Street, Stoke, Coventry. A native of Collycroft, Bedworth he was born in 1893 and resided at 572 Foleshill Road. An engineer by profession he enlisted in October 1914 and had been in France about 18 months. He was home on leave at Easter 1915 with his younger brother, Rupert who was a Corporal in the same battery; they both returned looking extremely well.

Gunner Middleton prior to enlistment was employed at the Triumph works, was 23 years of age and single. Major Fowler, in writing to the deceased's parents, mentions that *"Alfred was one of the best gunners in the battery and a popular favourite with the officers and men"*. The Chaplain, Reverend Cyril A. Brown, writes *"There is not a man in the battery who does not feel his loss"*.

The story passed down through generations of the family is that he was killed as a result of a dud going off prematurely. At Bablake he *"gave promise of a very bright future"*. He is buried at Aveluy Communal Cemetery, commemorated in the War Memorial Park and on the memorial to the sixty seven employees of the Triumph and Gloria Works who gave their lives for liberty in the Great War. This memorial stands in London Road Cemetery.

Three more Old Boys were to die in the month of October: on the 7th Rifleman Pails and Lance-Corporal Price, and on the 23rd, Second Lieutenant Cox. All are remembered on the Thiepval Memorial. The 7th October saw the start of the Battle of the Transloy Ridges, the start being delayed due to atrocious weather conditions. The attack involved six divisions with only one success, the capture of Le Sars by the 23rd Division. German machine guns caused the greatest problem for the attack and the enemy remained vigorous in their defence, continuous rain at night prevented further advances and removal of casualties. The battle lasted until the 20th October.

Rifleman **Hugh Conrad Pails,** 1/12th Battalion, London Regiment (The Rangers), formerly of the Queen's Westminster Rifles, was killed in action, aged 19. He was born the 16th of April 1897, at 7, Starley Road and resided there with his parents Hugh William (a warehouseman) and Clara Emma Pails. A pupil at St. John's Elementary School, he attended Bablake from 6th September 1909 to 1st August 1912 on receipt of a grant from the Governors. Hugh was a designer in a textile factory after leaving and enlisted in April 1916. He is also commemorated in the War Memorial Park.

Lance-Corporal **Leonard Joseph Walker Price**, 9th Battalion, Royal Fusiliers died age 21. The only son of Joseph (watchmaker) and Alice Price, he was born on 16th August, 1895, at 9, Stanley Terrace, Allesley Old Road and resided at 58, Craven Street aka the Craven Arms. Leonard attended Bablake for almost three years from January 1907 to October 1909, receiving his previous education at Spon Street Elementary School.

He joined the Public Schools Corps attached to the Royal Fusiliers in January 1916, being drafted to France in July. Before the war he was a clerk in a motor works and for a number of years was a member of St. John's Church choir and his name is recorded on a stained glass panel. An officer of his regiment in writing to his parents says *"He was killed in action on the 7th October whilst attacking with his Company"* and adds *"He was an NCO of great promise and his death is a big loss to his regiment"*.

Second Lieutenant **Francis Henry Cox**, 1st Battalion, Royal Warwickshire Regiment, died on the 23rd October 1916 aged 19, enlisting when he was 18 in April 1915. Born the 13th July, 1897 in Trafalgar Street, he resided at 56 St. Michael's Road. He attended Wheatley Street Elementary School, and then entered Bablake on the 5th April 1910 leaving on the 31st March 1915. He spent his last two years as a resident, courtesy of the Governors of Bablake. On leaving he immediately enlisted. He very quickly passed the Entrance Examination into the Military College at Sandhurst, receiving his commission into the Royal Warwickshire Regiment on the 14th September 1915. His father Henry was a detective in the police force and he had two siblings (Enid and Clarice); his mother's name was Florence.

The events of the 22nd to the 24th of October are recorded in the *'Battalion War Diary';" The 22nd of October was a cold fine day, and the 1st Battalion spent it preparing for the attack the following day. At 4.00pm General Lampton visited all the troops and wished them good luck. At 6.45pm the companies marched off in support of the 2nd Royal Dublin Fusiliers and took up their positions, A, B and C in Shamrock trench and D Company in Fluff trench. Companies were in position by 12.00pm.*

A 14 point plan was issued for the 23rd. At zero hour the 1st Battalion Royal Warwickshire were to move forward and occupy the trenches left by the 2nd Royal Dublin Fusiliers, then advance at zero plus 10 and pass through the brown line and at zero plus 30 follow the barrage to the green line. Point 14 was to send back guides as soon as objective was gained.

At 10.30am a message was received to say zero hour had moved forward to 2.30pm by which point the 2nd Royal Dublin Fusiliers were already in a sunken road in preparation for zero hour. At 2.20pm two German planes were observed overhead and eight minutes later the Germans shelled the sunken road as a result of communication with the planes. Two minutes later the attack was launched and the barrage fire opened; initial reports from the returning wounded implied the attack was going well.

The first of several messages that were to come in that day, arrived at 3.50pm, stating prisoners were coming in from Gun Pits. Less then an hour later another returning wounded stated " his Company were about 400 yards north east of Strong Points at Hazy Trench, but no one was on his right".

The next message was received at 5.05pm (even though it was recorded as timed at 3.30pm), the front line of strong points has been captured but machine gun fire on all sides is holding up the advance. Heavy casualties so reinforcements with bombs required. This position was too weak to withstand a German counter- attack.

The next message was received at 5.30pm via a runner from A Company, timed 4.30pm. A mixed party of 50 Royal Warwickshire Regiment and Royal Dublin Fusiliers are close to Hazy and digging in. The German machine guns were about 300 yards ahead of the position, with approximately 20 Germans. Troops were observed on the right but not on the left.

At 6.45pm a wounded Lieutenant from A Company confirmed that Gun Pits had been cleared and also they were holding the ridge on the other side of Pits. He was still, however, unsure about those on the left. At 6.50pm a message (timed at 3.45pm) arrived with a runner from C Company: they were in the south end of Gun Pits with 25 men and being fired at from left rear. Germans were also in the north end of Gun Pits and in shell holes behind. The Officer commanding D Company specified he wanted to clean up Gun Pits but had suffered heavy casualties along with the Royal Dublin Fusiliers.

Another message came in at 7.30pm (this was 1 hour 45 minutes old and from the officer commanding D Company) stating his position that he occupied the German strong point, but he had only 14 men.

On to the 24th, a report was sent back at 4.30pm that the day was quiet and a feeble counter- attack had been stopped with rifle fire. The valley was now clear of the enemy. Relief took place at 2.00am by the 20th Royal Fusiliers, 33rd Division and in the two days of fighting 2 officers had died of wounds, with a further 6 officers wounded, 150 other ranks killed, wounded or missing". Second Lieutenant Cox was originally posted as missing but it was confirmed later that he had lost his life on October the 23rd.

Private **Noel Raymond Averns**, 7th Battalion, Royal Fusiliers (City of London Regiment), had possibly more reason to enlist as he was born on 8th December, 1896 in Brussels. After coming to the UK, he attended Earlsdon Elementary School and then went on to Spon Street Elementary. At Bablake he entered Form 3G on the 6th September 1909 and left on the 30th July 1914 when he was in the Upper 6th, having passed the London Matriculation. His first year at Bablake was granted by the Board of Governors, the remaining four by the Education Committee of Coventry where he was in residence from 1910 to 1912. Noel was one of three sons. Rene Ernest, the oldest son, was also born in Belgium, whilst the youngest, Erie, was born in Swanage. The three were sons of Ernest Lloyd, who was employed in cycle manufacture, and Mary Louisa who was a school mistress. The family resided at 38 Shaftesbury Road, Earlsdon, Coventry.

Like his mother Noel was employed in education as a teacher in a public elementary school, and he enlisted in December 1915. Noel died of wounds aged 19, 11 months after enlisting in France on the 19th November 1916. The Battle of The Ancre lasted from the 13th November to the 18th November and this final engagement in the Battle of The Somme could have resulted in Private Averns being mortally wounded. He is buried in St. Sever Cemetery Extension, Rouen.

During the war, camps and hospitals were stationed on the southern outskirts of Rouen. They included eight general, five stationary, one British Red Cross and one Labour Hospital, and No. 2 Convalescent Depot. The majority of the dead from these hospitals were buried in the city cemetery of St. Sever. Demand was such that in September 1916, it was found necessary to begin an extension. Private Noel Averns is remembered in St. Barbara's Church in Earlsdon and has a plaque in the War Memorial Park. In St. Barbara's Church his name is commemorated not only on the brass plaque at the rear of the church but also on a lectern dedicated to the Averns brothers. The lectern was originally in Palmerston Road but moved with the church to Rochester Road; the plaque reads *"Rene Ernest died 18th July 1919 and Noel R. Averns killed in the Great War November 19th 1916 from their loving parents"*.

Lectern dedicated to the Avern Brothers

The circumstances of Rene's death are unknown; his name is not commemorated in the *'City of Coventry: Roll of the Fallen'* or by the CWGC. No evidence could be found to prove he attended Bablake or his death was war related, the name of R. L. Averns appears on the list of those who served.

Starting on the 1st July 1916 and finishing on the 18th November, the Battle of the Somme lasted for four and half months, thirteen Old Boys lost their lives in this battle. The gain made at the end of this period was a strip approximately twenty miles wide and six miles deep.

1917

Three months into 1917 saw the death of Private **Wilfred Hibbert Sidwell,** 17th Battalion, Royal Fusiliers, who died on the 25th March 1917 and like Private Cox is buried in Etaples Military Cemetery. He was mortally wounded three days before his 19th birthday and fifteen months after enlisting. A native and resident of Coventry, he lived at 'Branksome', 9 King Richard Street, Coventry. He attended Bablake for four years via a grant from the Governors, entering in Form 3B on 2nd September 1907 and leaving in the 6th Form on the 28th July 1911 the latter two years being spent as a boarder. Prior to this he attended St.

Peter's Elementary. He worked with his father, Isaac Septimus, as a clerk in the weekly wage department at a cycle works before joining the clerical staff in the Public Health Department, Coventry Corporation.

The Sidwell Brothers

Wilfred was one of four sons who all served in the forces and all of whom attended Bablake. The remaining brothers were Petty Officer F. A. Sidwell (left), Private Edgar Sidwell (middle right) and Trooper Cecil Sidwell (middle left). In August 1916, *'The Coventry Graphic'* recorded that Wilfred (right) had been wounded. However, this was not the wound that led to his death. Wilfred's name is recorded on the Public Health Department Memorial in the council house. His brother, Cecil also died during the war with the Warwickshire Yeomanry on the 30th January 1918. (Refer to died at home.)

Three Old Boys lost their lives during the month of April 1917: Gunner Frederick Caldicott, Bombardier Harold Rollason and Corporal Frederick Harris. The two Fredericks were members of Queen's Road Church and both names are recorded on the stained glass panel in the church. The 9th of April 1917 saw the first day of the Battle of Arras; the British forces were attacking a defensive fortress known as the 'Hindenburg Line' to which the Germans had retreated and consolidated. Zero hour was 5.30am. This battle would last thirty six days until the 15th May and was a diversionary attack for the French assault on the Aisne. Like the Battle of the Somme an initial bombardment had proceeded, which began on the 4th April, and more then 2,700,000 shells were fired over a front of twenty four miles.

Gunner **Frederick Walter Caldicott,** 15th Warwick Brigade, Royal Horse Artillery was killed in action on the first day of the Battle of Arras aged 25. Frederick was named after his father, who was a commercial traveller. His mother was Hannah Caldicott; his parents lived at 3, Warwick Avenue, Earlsdon, Coventry. Frederick was born in Foleshill on the 7th February 1892, and resided at 280, Foleshill Road; he was a printer.

Frederick is buried in Beaurains Road Cemetery. Beaurains was captured by British forces on the 18th March 1917 and the Germans at this time were still in nearby Tilloy-les-Mofflaines, having strategically withdrawn from Beaurains. The major British assault on the 9th April 1917 was named the First Battle of Scarpe. The attack was directly east of Arras, the 12th Division were attacking north of the Arras-Cambrai road and elements of the 3rd Division south of this road with Tilloy-les-Mofflaines as one of its primary objectives. By the end of the first day the advance had managed about two miles.

Bombardier **Harold Eugene Rollason,** 1st Warwick Battery,15th Brigade, Royal Horse Artillery was killed in action on the 11th April, 1917 aged 24 and is buried in Tilloy British Cemetery, Tilloy-les-Mofflaines. This was taken by British troops on the 9th April 1917, two days prior to Harold's death. Harold was the only son of James Eugene Herbert and Nellie Annie Rollason, of Norfolk House, Grantham Street, Coventry, who also had one daughter, Gladys. He was in the first territorial battery to go to France (October 1914) and had taken part in major battles including Loos, Ypres and the Somme. Originally a sailor, Harold changed trades

and he worked in his father's tailoring business as a tailor's cutter. Harold received his education at St Peter's Elementary and then Bablake which he attended from 27th August 1906 to 23rd July 1909.

During the period from the 1st August 1907 to the 23rd July 1909 he was a boarder at the school, as specified by the grant received by the Governors.

Corporal **Frederick Arthur Harris,** like so many Old Boys, has no known grave and is commemorated on the Thiepval Memorial as he died in the Somme sector. After the Germans fell back to the Hindenburg line there were no significant battles in this area until the German advance of March 1918. Frederick enlisted in November 1914 in Oxford and joined the Oxfordshire and Buckinghamshire Light Infantry. He died near St. Quentin serving with the 2/4th Battalion on the 28th April 1917 aged 20. Like his father Thomas Henry he was a draughtsman with an

engineering firm. His mother was Emma Harris. He was born at 17 Grove Street, Coventry on the 4th October, 1896 and also resided there.

Frederick was admitted to Bablake on the 6th September 1909 in Form 3B initially, receiving a two year grant, and left on the 30th July 1913 when he was in the Lower 6th receiving a further two- year grant from the Governors. On leaving he received a Minor Scholarship of £1 a year for three years tenable at a Technical Institute or School of Art. Prior to Bablake he attended Wheatley Street Elementary School.

Second Lieutenant (Acting Captain) **Percy Hood Hollick,** 3rd Battalion, Royal Warwickshire Regiment, was attached to the 15th Battalion at the time of his death. He was killed in action on the 9th May 1917 at Fresnoy Wood, near Arras. He was promoted from temporary Second Lieutenant to Lieutenant on the 3rd March 1916 when he was attached to the 2nd Battalion moving from them to the 3rd Battalion on the 22nd May 1916. He gained a further promotion in December 1916 to Acting Captain, A Company, having started his military career as Private 1267 with the Honourable Artillery Company (HAC).

Born the 29th January, 1891 at Allesley, in the 1901 census he is listed as a boarder with a family in Kenilworth. By July 1912 he was an articled pupil to Mr. R. A. Rotherham Solicitor having passed the Final Solicitors' Examination. Though residing in Tile Hill his parents, Alfred and Fanny Hollick had lived at 'Brooklands', Balsall Common. Percy enlisted on the outbreak of war.

Early on the morning of the 6th May 1917, parties of the enemy were observed wiring; they were quickly dispersed by means of a Lewis gun and snipers. 3.00am saw the commencement of a heavy and continuous bombardment of Fresnoy Wood together with the adjoining trench running south. The enemy also registered with guns of different calibres and had aeroplanes flying directly overhead. The line north of trench junction including the bombing stop at that point and the strong point established, was handed over to the 1st East Surreys, 95th Infantry Brigade. The platoon of B Company and one platoon of D Company withdrew to B Company's trench, whilst C Company furnished a working party on the trench.

Next morning a patrol visited the enemy wire and reported work at different points: the wire which had been cut up by shell fire was still 15 to 20 feet thick. The guards were vigilant and fired on the patrol. The 2nd King's Own Scottish Borders (KOSB) relieved the Battalion. In wet weather C Company and two platoons of B Company remained to work until 2.30am on D Company's trench and A Company remained to work until 2.30am completing their trench.

On the 8th May the Battalion were in a new position. At 8.30am telephone orders were received for the Battalion to be taken back to the region of Orchard Dugout. By 11.10am the Battalion was in close support trenches near headquarters. At 12.30pm verbal orders were received that the Battalion would attack and take the village of Fresnoy and the wood to the south west. Two hours later the commanding officer made his dispositions and explained them to the Company commanders.

A and D were to lead the attack, A Company on the left with C supporting, and D Company on the right with B supporting. The left boundary was formed by the Arleux – Fresnoy Southern Road and the right boundary the south eastern edge of wood. The objective was Fresnoy village and the wood and a 'dig in' line; C Company were to do the mopping up. At about 10.00pm zero hour was fixed at 2.00am on the 9th May. At 11.00pm companies moved forward, A Company leading from near Battalion headquarters to the assembly area.

At zero hour on a very dark night the barrage and attack commenced. C and B companies had moved up close to the companies they were supporting and all companies got away from the assembly area clear of enemy barrage. The pace of the British barrage (100 yards every 5 minutes) proved very slow and with the enemy barrage shortening the troops were "pinched" between the two sets of barrages. Casualties were very heavy but the companies on the right succeeded in almost reaching their objective. One party commenced digging in at Fresnoy Wood, and another entered the trench running south east. A and C companies on the left succeeded in getting into Fresnoy, and a few more penetrated Fresnoy Park. Captain Hollick, Officer Commanding A Company, was killed in the wire close to the left boundary road almost in the village; he was aged 26. Close encounters were made with the enemy who were defending with machine guns.

Unable to establish touch on either side, Captain Rutter, Officer Commanding D Company, was the only Company commander left, together with three other officers. Finding the Battalion entirely in the air on either flank, and very weak in numbers, he made the decision to withdraw all the details he could muster to the jumping off trenches. These included some details of other units, plus Lewis guns, all of which in spite of a very heavy proportion of casualties amongst the Lewis gunners, had been brought back. Captain Rutter then manned and held the original assembly area. During the whole of the day shelling was heavy and continuous. The Battalion was relieved by 16th Battalion, Royal Warwickshire Regiment and withdrew to reserve trenches.

During this operation the casualties suffered were six officers killed, one of whom was Captain Hollick, with a further six officers wounded, seven other ranks were killed, one hundred and thirty seven wounded and fifty missing. Captain Hollick's body was never formally recovered and he is remembered with honour on the Arras Memorial. He was mentioned in despatches by Sir Douglas Haig on the 9th April 1917 and the following paragraph appeared in *'The Coventry Graphic'* with the headline *'Posthumous Honour'*: *"Among those mentioned in Sir Douglas Haig's despatch for distinguished service appears the name of Captain P. H. Hollick, Royal Warwickshire Regiment a Coventry solicitor who was killed in action"*.

Gunner **Harry Clarke** was with the Royal Garrison Artillery when he was killed in action at Vlamertinghe, Belgium on the 3rd June 1917. He was formerly service number 8915 with 156th Oxford Heavy Battery, RGA. He was born on the 4th April 1896 at Birmingham and resided at 68 Adelaide Street. He enlisted in October 1915 and prior to this worked as a clerk.

Harry's education started at Frederick Bird Elementary. He was admitted to Bablake on the 6th September 1909 to Form 3G, with a grant for two years from the Governors. He left on the 28th July 1911 when he was in form 4A at the end of the tenable period. Aged 21 he was buried in Vlamertinghe Military Cemetery. This cemetery is remarkable for the care with which men were buried side by side if they died at about the same time. In Gunner Clarke's case his grave is next to Sergeant Joseph Thompson, The Loyal North Lancashire Regiment and Private William Varndell, Hampshire regiment, who died on the same day.

Four days after Harry's death saw the start of the Battle of Messines, the bombardment had begun on the 21st May and involved over 2,300 guns and 300 heavy mortars. The bombardment ceased at 2.50am on the 7th June and twenty minutes later over six hundred tons of explosives were detonated in twenty one mines under the German positions. Meticulous planning had gone into this attack and all initial objectives were taken within three hours. Counter attacks were made but these were fought off successfully and diminished over time.

The next major battle after the taking off Messines Ridge was the Third Battle of Ypres or Passchendaele; the overall aim was the destruction of the German submarine bases on the Belgian coast. The unrestricted sinking of unarmed boats by the U-boats had bought the USA into the war but the Germans needed to be deprived of their submarine sanctuary, this action would enable the American contribution to be effective. The German base at Bruges was less then thirty miles away from the allied front line and Haig's other concern was to dislodge the Germans from a ridge that ran from Westroosbeke to Broodseinde. This battle was to last from the 31st July until the 10th November and would become synonymous with heavy rains and mud; this combination turned the battlefield into a swamp until eventually ending with the capture of Passchendaele village. The bombardment prior to the battle started on the 18th July. Over 4,250,000 shells were fired in ten days giving the Germans adequate warning of an imminent attack and also destroying the drainage systems necessary for the mobility of the tanks and infantry.

During this time, operations still continued away from the battle of Passchendaele and by the 10th November and going into the Cambrai offensive the number of the fallen would increase by ten.

The next two casualties, Henry Courts and Frank Yardley, were members of staff at the Education Department in Coventry and are commemorated on the Memorial in the Council House. Having started on the 31st July, the Battle of Pilckem ended on the 2nd August owing to the ceaseless rain although over 6,000 prisoners had been taken.

Henry (or Harry) Amos Courts, a pioneer with A Special Company, Royal Engineers, was killed in action in Belgium on the 4th August 1917 aged 28. The husband of Sarah Lilian Courts, they resided at 65 Park Road, Bedworth. Born in 1889 at Longford, he was employed in Coventry as a school teacher in an elementary school and enlisted in London. He came from a family of seven children, with the head of the house being Amos, a coal miner. He is buried in Mendinghem British Cemetery, near the village of Proven, Belgium. This area had seven casualty clearing stations.

Just three days later would see the death of Second Lieutenant **Frank Yardley** of the 246th Company, Machine Gun Corps (Infantry), who was killed in action on the 7th August 1917 aged 29. He was one of three sons of Walter and Laura Yardley, of 77 New George Street, Coventry.

The sons were pictured in *'The Coventry Graphic'*, David was a Petty Officer on HMS Ajax (right), their eldest son Frank (middle), and the youngest son, Sidney were transferred to the MGC, but at the time the picture was taken the brothers were in the Royal Warwickshire Regiment.

Frank was a school teacher in an elementary school, born in 1888 in Brewery Street and resided at 83, Somerset Road, Coventry. He enlisted in September 1914, commissioned on the 25th March 1917 and is pictured left in the Machine Gun Corps. In similar circumstances to that of Private John William Rossiter. *'The Roll of the Fallen'* lists him as being buried in Oosttaverne Wood Cemetery, Wytschaete, Belgium but his grave could not be formally identified and he is commemorated on the Menin Gate Memorial. This cemetery contains 1,119 first world war graves 783 of which are unidentified.

The next Battle for those at Passchendaele was the Battle of Langemarck, which lasted from the 16th to the 18th August. During these dates one Old Boy would be fatally wounded and the village of Langemarck was effectively reduced to rubble.

James William Guise was a Second Lieutenant with 5th Battalion, Oxfordshire and Buckinghamshire Light Infantry. He seemed destined for a career in the military: he was born on the 15th March, 1899, at Cowley Barracks, Oxford. His father was Captain James Guise and his uncle Sergeant John Guise; both men were also in the Oxfordshire and Buckinghamshire Light Infantry.

Captain James Guise (Senior) had a distinguished service history: he originally left the Army in 1909 as a Colour Sergeant Service Number 2765, 1st Battalion having served 22 years and 9 months. During this time he fought in South Africa and in 1900, was awarded the Queen's South African Medal with two clasps. On the 23rd September 1909, he was discharged to pension; at this point he was being paid 2s 11d per day. He rejoined the Regiment at the start of the war and was a Regimental Sergeant- Major at the depot until February 1915, when he received a commission as Territorial Captain, 7th Battalion. He was discharged again in November 1919 and died in Coventry on the 26th July 1927 aged 63 years.

James William Guise enlisted into the ranks of the 4th (Reserve) Battalion, Royal Warwickshire Regiment on the 5th of August 1914. He served in France with the 2nd Battalion of the Royal Warwickshire Regiment as a Company Sergeant- Major and then a Regimental Sergeant- Major. He then returned to the 4th Battalion Royal Warwickshire Regiment in England and applied for a commission in January 1917.

After passing through No.9 Cadet School, he was gazetted as Second Lieutenant into the 5th (Service) Battalion, Oxfordshire and Buckinghamshire Light Infantry and joined the Battalion in Flanders on 16th March 1917. The 1917-1918 *'Regimental Chronicles'* for the 17th August 1917 state *"Second Lieutenant J. T Rose and Guise were wounded by a 77mm shell on the way to the trenches, and the relief were gas shelled at Zillebeke Lake"*.

These wounds led to James' death, and he died on the 19th August 1917 at Ypres; Second Lieutenant J. T. Rose survived. James is buried in Brandhoek New Military cemetery, No. 3 Vlamertinghe, Belgium. Field ambulances and Casualty Clearing Stations were posted there for the on- going offensive. James William Guise, son of James and Norah and brother of Ellen of 51 Paynes Lane, Coventry, would have received some treatment at one of the stations prior to his death. During research these were the only father and son found who were both engaged in active service simultaneously.

The family gravestone in London Road Cemetery reads *"In Loving Memory of James Guise who died June 26 1927 aged 63 years also of Norah Guise his wife who died Feb 19 1933 aged 63 years and of James Guise son of the above 2nd Lieut. OBLI who died of wounds received in France August 19 1917 Aged 18 years. R.I.P"*.

William Arthur Imber was the third Second Lieutenant to die in the space of less than three weeks.   He served with the 7th Battalion, Royal Warwickshire Regiment and lost his life on the 27th August 1917 aged 23.

Born 6th July 1894 at Coventry, he was the son of William (a police superintendent) and Hannah Imber, of 'Astbury', 43 Spencer Avenue, Earlsdon, Coventry. An attendee at Spon Street Elementary School he started at Bablake in Form 1 on the 27th August 1906, exactly 11 years before his death. He left Bablake after four years in July 1910 in the 6th Form, the final two years being awarded by the Governors. On leaving he was employed as a clerk to a Medical Officer of Health and then a banker's clerk at Barclays Bank. He joined the Army in December 1914 and was for a time attached to the University and Public School Corps. He was commissioned on the 16th June 1915.

Just over a year later, on the 26th June 1916 at 10.15am whilst serving with the 1/7th Battalion Royal Warwickshire Regiment Second Lieutenant Imber was slightly wounded. The enemy had put a barrage on the Battalion trenches causing considerable damage. 2 other ranks were killed, 12 were wounded. On the 27th August 1917, Second Lieutenant Imber was killed in action near St. Julien, Belgium and is remembered with honour on the Tyne Cot Memorial. He also has a plaque in the War Memorial Park.

The *'Battalion war diaries'* show that the 1/7th Battalion started an attack at 2.00pm. D Company captured Springfield and handed it over to the 8th Battalion Worcester Regiment who relieved them. The details of A Company and a portion of B Company were relieved from the line on the 27th by the 8th Battalion Royal Warwickshire Regiment and went by train to Poperinghe. Unusually Second Lieutenant Imber is not named in the diary and the casualty numbers are not recorded.

Vincent Arthur Bloxham enlisted in August 1914 and became Gunner, 840327, D Battery 240th Brigade, Royal Field Artillery (South Midland Howitzers). A pupil at Earlsdon Elementary he went on to Bablake and attended for three years from the 2nd September 1907 to the 21st July 1910.

Vincent was born and raised in Earlsdon, Coventry moving from Moor Street where he was born in 1896 to 38, Earlsdon Street and then finally; 8 Stanway Road. He was the son of George and Alice Bloxham. Like his father he was employed as clerk and store assistant at a cycle works. He enlisted in August 1914 and died of wounds in Boulogne on the 18th September 1917 aged 21. He is buried in Wimereux Communal Cemetery. Also buried here is Bablake Old Boy Private William Wilkins and Lieutenant Colonel John McCrae, author of the poem "In Flanders Fields". Gunner Bloxham also has a plaque in the War Memorial Park.

One of those pictured is V. A. Bloxham

Private 34032 **Henry Buckland,** 1st Battalion, Duke of Cornwall's Light Infantry, (formerly 20179 Royal Warwickshire Regiment), was killed in action on the 2nd October 1917. Born 16th July, 1875 at 35, Norfolk Street, at 42 years he was one of the oldest Old Boys to die in the Great War. He was the son of William Buckland and lived with him at 23, Chester Street, Coventry. Together with other members of his family he was employed as a gold watch case maker.

Private Buckland is buried in Meteren Military Cemetery, France this cemetery contains 768 burials and was made in 1919 by the French authorities who brought in graves from the local battlefields and neighbouring cemeteries. He also has a plaque in the War Memorial Park and is commemorated on a stained glass panel in St. John's church.

Arthur Whinfrey was an engineer's apprentice prior to enlisting in July 1916, before becoming Gunner 107303 with the 256th Siege Battery, Royal Garrison Artillery. He was born on the 2nd April, 1896, at Berkswell and also resided there prior to his death. His parents Frank and Annie Whinfrey lived nearby in Bradnock Marsh, Hampton-in-Arden. Gunner Whinfrey was killed in action at Broodseinde on the 4th October 1917 and is buried in Buffs Road Cemetery, St. Jean-les-Ypres, Belgium. This cemetery was created and used by fighting units (particularly the Royal Sussex and the Royal Artillery) between July 1917 and March 1918 and was the name given to a small lane just to the north of the hamlet of Wieltje.

The 4th of October was the date for the Battle of Broodseinde; this attack along a front of 8 miles with 12 divisions gained the ridge from Gheluvelt to Broodseinde. This battle had followed on from the Battle of Polygon wood which had lasted from the 26th September to the 3rd October and had taken the remaining uncaptured part of Polygon Wood.

Second Lieutenant **Walter Ernest Grew** was with the 16th Battalion, Royal Warwickshire Regiment, having previously been a highly respected NCO in the Cadet Corps. He entered Bablake on the 5th September 1910 from St. John's Elementary School and spent five years there, leaving in the Lower 6th on the 29th July 1915. He boarded at the school for his final two years via a grant from the Governors.

On leaving school he was employed as a bank clerk until joining the army in November 1916. At this time his father was an editor for a motorcycle journal having previously been a manager at a motorcycle works. He was gazetted as a temporary Lieutenant on the 26th April 1917, but less than one year after enlisting he was killed in action near Ypres, on the 7th October 1917. Born on the 15th July 1898 and living on Holyhead Road, he was aged only 19 when his life was lost trying to capture an objective south of the Reutelbeek.

111

On the 5th October the 16th Battalion moved into support headquarters, having two companies digging in trenches immediately North of the Ypres – Menin Road. At 12.10am a message was received by Battalion headquarters from D Company saying that they were digging in but had suffered several casualties; the other companies confirmed they were in position. After 5.00pm that evening preparations were being made for an attack with an objective south of the Reutelbeek.

On the night of the 7th and 8th October the 16th Battalion were to capture the Polderhoek Chateau and spur and then relieve the 1st Norfolk regiment. A Company 1st Bedford regiment moved forward at dusk to 100 yards in front of their Battalion headquarters. A Company, 16th Battalion then moved into these vacated trenches.

The signs were ominous for the forthcoming attack; at 1.05am on the 7th October SOS signals were received from the Battalion's right and ten minutes later a dressing station was blown in, killing nearly all the aid post staff and RAMC bearers. At 6.30pm the relief of the 1st Norfolks was meant to commence but owing to an enemy barrage the leading companies did not move off till 9.00pm. By 2.25am on the 8th October the relief had been completed. However, Second Lieutenant W. E. Grew had been killed along with thirty nine other ranks during the relief. His body was not formally recovered and he is commemorated on the Tyne Cot Memorial and in St. John's church.

Captain **Alfred Ernest Mander** B.A fell in action at Passchendaele. Born 15th September 1879 at Spon End, he resided in Spon House, Spon End. He was the third son of Alderman Mander and Mrs. H. Mander, and his brother Second Lieutenant P. G. Mander, 4th West Riding Regiment, also attended Bablake, leaving in 1896. The actual date that Alfred left Bablake is unknown; however, it would have been slightly earlier than his brother.

On leaving Bablake, he furthered his education at Trinity College, Dublin and became a schoolmaster. He enlisted on September the 14th, 1914 and was commissioned as a Second Lieutenant to the Duke of Wellington Regiment on the 10th April 1915, formerly being a Sergeant in the 2nd South Midland Brigade, Royal Field Artillery. He proceeded to France in December 1915.

'*The Coventry Graphic*' of July 21st 1916 contains details that he had been wounded probably at the start of the Battle of the Somme, and was now lying in the Duchess of Westminster Hospital at Le Troquet, Paris. He made a sufficient recovery and was able to rejoin his Battalion. At the time of his death in the Battle of Poelcapelle on the 9th October 1917, aged 38, he was the Captain of A Company, 4th Battalion, Duke of Wellington's (West Riding Regiment). The affinity with this regiment is not clear but it obviously appealed to Alfred and his brother. Captain Mander has no known grave and is remembered on the Tyne Cot Memorial and in the War Memorial Park. His brother survived the war and is on the school memorial as P. G. Mander.

Lieutenant **Sidney George Wolfe** of the 7/18th Battalion, Lancashire Fusiliers is also commemorated on the Tyne Cot Memorial. Sidney resided at 45, Berkeley Road, Earlsdon, Coventry with his wife and one child. He was a well known footballer in Coventry and district, having played for Coventry F.C and regularly for the Midland Counties as a forward. After staying at Saltley College for scholastic training he became an assistant master at a school in Rugby. Sidney joined the forces in September 1914 being one of the 400 who volunteered to make up foreign service with the 1/7th Battalion, Royal Warwickshire Regiment. He was attached to the cycle company of the division and went out to France in early 1915.

After only a few days in France he was badly wounded, he came home and was ill for some time before going back to the front on May 1st 1917. Lieutenant Wolfe obtained his commission in 1916 being gazetted to the Lancashire Fusiliers.

Two pictures of Lieutenant S. G. Wolfe

The only son of George and Julie Wolfe, he was born on the 14th February, 1890 at Rugby and was killed in action at Passchendaele on the 22nd October, 1917. *'The Coventry Herald'* printed extracts from a letter written by a comrade and received by his wife which stated " *He was leading a company into action and was unfortunately killed during the advance. He had scarcely advanced more then 75 yards when an enemy shell fell close and he was killed instantaneously and his servant was badly wounded"*. The letter continued *"He will be a great loss to the Battalion and he will be missed by all who knew him. As a soldier I cannot speak too highly of him and as a man I had the greatest affection for him. He was always cheery whether in the line or out, a great sportsman and always thoughtful for his men"*. A resident of Earlsdon his name appears on St. Barbara's memorial.

The next battle was the Battle of Cambrai which lasted from the 20th November to the 30th December 1917, two Old Boys would lose their lives in between these dates. Over 4,700 Royal Dublin Fusiliers died in the Great War, however, there is only one casualty from Bablake associated with this regiment. Second Lieutenant **Bernard Michael Ward** was killed in Cambrai with the 11th Battalion. As November 1917 ended, the Regiment had some success in a diversionary assault for the Cambrai offensive which hid the true place and scale of the attack.

The environment in the area around Cambrai was conducive to the use of tanks, and over 350 were used in the offensive. In addition to this the element of surprise was employed as the preliminary bombardment used previously to breakdown the enemy's defenses but also warned them of an imminent attack was to be left to the tanks, with the infantry following close by. Within ten hours the German front had been penetrated to a depth of five miles, however the momentum would be lost due to insufficient reserves and the Germans would counter attack so by the 30th November a large part of the ground gained would be lost.

Bernard was one of five children born to John (bicycle rim maker) and Mary Ward of Ballinrobe, County Mayo, Ireland. Born in Coventry on the 20th August 1898, he was the only one of their children not born in Ireland. Attending Wheatley Street Elementary School he entered Form 3B at Bablake on the 5th September 1910 and left five years later on the 24th July 1915 after completion of the Upper 6th . Mainly attending on a daily basis, he spent his final year as a boarder at the school and during this time he was a highly respected NCO in the Cadet Corps.

In 1913 he gained a junior school certificate from Birmingham and in July 1915 was awarded a minor exhibition having his fees paid for three years at a technical institute or school of art. Prior to his enlistment Bernard was employed as a registrar's clerk at a motor works up to August 1916, a year later on the 1st August 1917 his name appeared as a temporary Second Lieutenant, Royal Dublin Fusiliers in 'The London Gazette'. Bernard died on the 20th November 1917 aged 19, and is buried in Croisilles British Cemetery, near Arras and has a plaque in the War Memorial Park.

The last casualty of 1917 was Captain **Frank Septimus Neville**, 6th Battalion Northamptonshire Regiment. He was killed in action on the 24th November 1917 aged 26. He was born in Dunchurch the son of Mr. T. J. Neville and Mrs L. Neville, of 1 Bilton Road, Rugby.

Westvleteren, Belgium was outside the front held by British forces during the First World War. However, in July 1917, in readiness for the forthcoming offensive, groups of casualty clearing stations were placed at three positions which were named ironically by the troops Mendinghem, Dozinghem and Bandaghem.

The 4th , 47th and 61st were posted at Dozinghem and the military cemetery was used by them until early in 1918. Captain Neville is buried in Dozinghem cemetery, probably having received treatment at one of the casualty clearing stations. His exact link to Bablake could not be established. His name appears on the memorial and in *'Roll Of Honour'* as one of those killed (Captain F. Neville, Northants Regiment.)

1918

With the British having sustained heavy losses at the Battle of Cambrai, Passchendaele and earlier in 1917 at Arras and Messines, the German Command decide to opt for an intensive attack. In addition to this Russia's withdrawal from the war had freed up experienced men that could move to the Western Front. The imminent arrival of the American forces was also an important factor and the date chosen was the 21st March 1918. By gathering intelligence the forthcoming attack was known about and early on the morning the Germans started a brief but intense bombardment with the aim of cutting communications and return artillery fire, effectively preventing any form of counter attack or defence.

Along the forty mile front the weather was also ideal for the attacking forces as they were concealed by mist, in some sectors troops were outnumbered 4:1. By the end of May the advance had bought the Germans guns in range of Paris, however the speed and ferocity of the advance could not be maintained. The logistic issues of feeding and arming the troops was taking an effect. On the 15th July an attack was made that threatened Rheims and this was successfully fought off by the Americans on the 18th, at this point the Allies remained on a continuous attack.

Company Sergeant Major **Alfred James Suddens**, 2/4th Battalion, Oxfordshire and Buckinghamshire Light Infantry died after the German Offensive began on 21st March 1918. Born in 1890, he resided in Coventry as a school teacher in Coventry and enlisted in Oxford. He was the son of Thomas, (a preacher), and Clara, brother to Harold.

He died whilst a prisoner of war in German hands, 21st March 1918 and is buried in Premont British Cemetery. This cemetery was not established until October 1918 and some years later 165 graves were added to it: 155

from Bohain Station Military Cemetery, six from Seboncourt Communal Cemetery, and four from a site near Honnechy. CSM Suddens would have originally been buried in one of these cemeteries. Alfred and his brother Harold are commemorated on the Education Department memorial in the Council House. Harold, who survived the war and also served with the Oxfordshire and Buckinghamshire Light Infantry achieving the rank of Corporal is commemorated on the school memorial as H. T. Suddens. In the first few days of the offensive over 90,000 prisoners had been taken and more then 1,000 guns.

Second Lieutenant **Frederick Charles Vincent,** DCM 7th Battalion, King's Royal Rifle Corps, also died on 21st March 1918 aged 25. He was the son of William Charles and Emily Laura Vincent, of Walsgrave-on-Sowe, Coventry.

Originally reported as missing, he was awarded his DCM in early 1916 whilst Sergeant R/2038 with the King's Royal Rifles and entered France on the 21st July 1915. He received his commission in November 1916 and his was the third DCM to the school, but during research the details of his citation could not be found. Frederick is commemorated on the Walsgrave memorial. The memorial was erected in 1922; the villagers raised the £300 required as a tribute to fifteen members of their community who lost their lives. Frederick has no known grave and is remembered with honour on the Pozières Memorial. This memorial commemorates over 14,000 men who fell in the Somme region from the 21st March to the 7th August.

On the 23rd March two more Old Boys were to lose their lives. Lance Corporal **Walter S. Bailey,** 1/7th Battalion, Argyll and Sutherland Highlanders was killed in action. He was born and enlisted in Coventry, but resided in Chiswick, London. He is remembered on the Arras Memorial and more locally on a brass plaque in the Methodist Central Hall. Walter was the brother of Annie and Marian, his father also Walter was a tailor. (Note: no relation to A. Bailey). This memorial to the missing covers 35,000 men who died in the Arras sector up to the 7th August 1918.

Private **Sydney Mornington Pickerill,** 2/7th Battalion Royal Warwickshire Regiment, was originally posted as missing and then subsequently as killed at St. Quentin aged 22. He was the son of Isaac (manager of a meat retail business) and Rose Pickerill, of 'Oak Mount', Windmill Lane, Berkswell. Born the 8th April, 1895, at Sutton Coldfield, he resided at 69, Shakespeare Street and worked for his father as a butcher's assistant. He studied at Bablake for 18 months from the 15th January 1908 to the 23rd July 1909. His admission records show his attendance was very irregular through illness and he entered and left whilst in Form 1; he previously attended

Radford Elementary school. An only son, he enlisted in October 1914, in Coventry.

Having been at the front for two years his parents received notification in May 1918 that he had been wounded and an appeal was made by his parents via *'The Coventry Herald'* in January 1919, for any details of their son who was still posted amongst those missing.

On the 21st March, the Battalion were billeted at Germaine and ordered to man battle stations. They then marched to act as a counter attack Battalion at Attilly Huts. En route they suffered from heavy artillery and gas shelling with twenty two wounded. In heavy mist the Battalion were dispersed in various trenches. At 5.00pm they moved to dugouts to avoid the shelling and six hours later were requested to act as a counter attack Battalion south of Holnon Wood. It was explained this was not possible due to the various locations of the troops.

On the 22nd March the mist was again heavy and at 9.00am verbal orders were received to move into the area of Holnon Wood. Four hours later orders were received to withdraw and fight a rearguard action. Shells were falling all around the Royal Warwickshire Regiment. The sight of masses of the enemy advancing, the superiority of enemy aero planes, the lack of artillery support, the useless trenches all sought to unsteady the troops but they were still the last to leave the line. The Battalion marched to Matigny and then to Offy, to cross the Somme and occupy trenches at a bridgehead. One hundred and twenty other ranks were picked up and joined the Battalion.

On the 23rd March the Battalion moved into assembly position in reserve and dug in. At 8.30am reports were received that the enemy were breaking through on the right; troops began withdrawing but they were assembled and sent forward by the Commanding Officers. By 11.00am the enemy were gaining, their artillery and trench mortar fire becoming heavier and the retirement of the troops was becoming more obvious. Three hours later the left flank was opened by withdrawing King's Royal Rifles but quickly filled; the enemy artillery lengthened its range and kept the line under well- directed fire.

At 5.45pm as part of the rearguard action orders were received to destroy a footbridge and prolong the King's Royal Rifles line; troops not supporting the line were moved to Cazigny. During the night there was considerable enemy artillery and trench mortar activity on the front. By midnight 14 officers and 248 other ranks had been killed. Private Pickerill's official date of death is the 23rd March 1918 and he is commemorated on the Pozières Memorial and in the War Memorial Park.

Before the end of March one more Old Boy would lose his life: Private **William Alexander Loudon, 40470, 7/8th** Battalion, King's Own Scottish Borderers formerly 4159 in the Royal Scots, who died on the 28th March 1918. He was posted as missing and then presumed killed.

Born 8th February, 1896 at Holyhead House, Holyhead Road, Coventry he resided further afield at Portobello in Edinburgh, where he enlisted in February 1916. The son of a physician he spent eight years at Bablake from the 25th September 1905 to 30th July 1913, entering in Form 1 and leaving in the 6th Form.

He boarded at the school from 1910 to 1912 under the conditions of his award by the Governors and before Bablake attended an unknown private school. At the end of April 1913, in a critique of players in the second football team, Loudon was described as *"most useful back or half back – the sort of player one can rely on when in difficulties- he does not waste energy- all that is put in is profitably expended"*.

In 1913 it was noted that at the London Matriculation Examination, Loudon and Herbert Victor Cantrill were classified as being in the second division. On leaving school he became an assistant in a chemical laboratory at a cycle works, though he was awarded a minor scholarship of up to a £1 annually tenable at a technical institute or school of art. He has no known grave and is remembered on the Arras Memorial.

Also posted as missing and then presumed killed in France on the 2nd April 1918 was Private 45196 **Thomas Herbert Allchurch** with the 1/6th Battalion (Territorial), Northumberland Fusiliers formerly 9816 Army Cyclist Corps. A resident of Coventry, he was born on the 6th August, 1889 at Worcester but enlisted in October 1914, in London. The son of Emma and George he was employed as an accountant's clerk and was a member of Queen's Road Church, where he is commemorated on a stained glass memorial and ultimately the Pozières Memorial. Thomas's Battalion started March 1918 with 21 officers and 664 other ranks, and during the latter stages of this month were involved in a ten day battle with the enemy and this ended with 326 casualties; 16 officers, and 310 other ranks.

The *'Battalion war diary'* dated 3rd May 1918 states *"The war diary of the 6th Northumberland Fusiliers will be forwarded as soon as possible. The following has been received from the Officer Commanding that Battalion:' Owing to the exceptional nature of the heavy casualties suffered by this Battalion lately which include the Commanding Officer, adjutant and intelligence officer, great difficultly is being experienced in obtaining authentic data for the continuous operations in which this unit has taken part during the period covered by the war diary in question. Major G. Leathart, at present at Le Touquet, is the only surviving officer who can supply certain necessary facts and he will not be returning to the Battalion, until the end of the present week. I fear that it will not be possible to submit the war diary for April at the stipulated time. It will be forwarded at the earliest possible moment"*.

Private **Edgar Herbert Buckingham,** of the 2/7th Battalion, Royal Warwickshire Regiment, was the next casualty. Born on the 27th May 1898 in Coventry he resided there at the time of his enlistment. An attendee of Bablake for five years from 28th September 1908 to 4th July 1913 entering in Form 1 and leaving in Form 5B, prior to this he was educated at Spon Street Elementary.

Edgar went on to become a confectioner, working for his father who was a baker and a shopkeeper. The 1901 census shows the family to have five servants, however three of these were occupied as bread makers. Herbert enlisted in May 1916 in Cheltenham, probably when he reached his 18th birthday.

On the 13th April 1918 the 2/7th Battalion were in the Calonne Region. At 5.00am the British artillery opened a heavy bombardment on the enemy's line. By 1.35pm the enemy had worked his way up and by 2.50pm the enemy's machine guns had increased activity. The situation was good for the British troops as they were back in their old line and houses reoccupied, even though the enemy kept firing on the barrage lines and on Battalion headquarters. The Battalion were due to be relieved by the 2/6th Battalion Royal Warwickshire Regiment. However, the relief proceeded very slowly, owing to an especially black night which resulted in the platoons getting lost in the darkness. On the 14th April the Battalion arrived at Hamet Billet; the men had breakfast and rested. The Battalion strength was sixteen officers and 536 other ranks. Killed in the period from the 11th April 1918 to 14th April 1918 were four officers and twenty eight other ranks. One hundred and forty six were reported as wounded, with sixty one missing.

One of the twenty eight other ranks was Private Buckingham, who was killed in action on the 14th April 1918, less then two years later after enlisting. The name of E. H. Buckingham is inscribed in a brass plaque in St. Barbara's Church, Earlsdon, in the War Memorial Park, the Ploegsteert Memorial and finally a plaque in the Methodist Central Hall.

The next day Private **William Charles Beacham**, 2nd Battalion, Royal Berkshire Regiment (formerly 39954 Royal Warwickshire Regiment), died aged 18. He was the son of William (carpenter and joiner) and Emma Beacham, of Raglan House, Allesley Old Road, Coventry. He also had two older sisters Edith and Mabel. Born in Allesley in 1900 he also resided there, a carpenter by trade. William enlisted in 1917, by the 20th April 1918 the Battalion had relieved the 54th Australian Battalion in the line on the night of 20/21st April 1918 and were employed as a counter attack Battalion, north of Villers-Bretonneux.

The Battalion undertook a counter offensive on the 25th April at 6.30am on Villers-Bretonneux. The village was cleared and mopped up; thirty five machine guns and three hundred prisoners were captured. The Battalion were still in Villers-Bretonneux on the 26th and 27th; and by the 28th had come out of the line. With no relief taking place they proceeded to billets in Glisy; by the 30th the billets had changed to Boutilliere. The counter attack costs the lives of fifty five men from other ranks, one hundred and sixty six wounded, nineteen gassed and ten men were missing.

One of the fifty five, Private Beacham is buried in Adelaide Cemetery, Villers-Bretonneux. After the Armistice a large number of graves were brought into the Cemetery from small graveyards and isolated positions on the north, west and south of Villers-Bretonneux and they were, without exception, those of men who died in the months from March to September 1918.

The last casualty in April 1918, on the 28th, was Sergeant **Ernest Clifford Elliott**. His brother Samuel James, also an Old Boy, had already been killed almost three years earlier. Sergeant Elliott was with the 20th Battalion, King's Royal Rifle Corps (KRRC), a British Empire League Pioneer Battalion. It provided military labour for improving trenches and wiring, and improving roads and railways. The 20th KRRC crossed to France in March 1916 and was part of the 3rd Division until the end of the war. On the 12th April 1918 the 20th Battalion, KRRC moved to Gonnehem, and after a couple of days' wiring and digging, south west of La Bassee canal moved on to Chocques, where it continued its pioneer work for the remainder of the month, mainly digging trenches and putting up wire.

Aged 23, Ernest lost his life in this work and is buried, in Chocques Military Cemetery, having served for over 3 years. From April to September 1918, during the German advance on this front, the burials were carried out by field ambulances, divisions and fighting units. Most of the burials from this period are of casualties who died at the clearing station from wounds received at the Bethune front. Ernest was educated at St. Mark's Elementary and then Bablake for three years from 27th August 1906 to 23rd July 1909.

The Royal Warwickshire Regiment were to suffer a further loss in June with the death of Sergeant **Joseph Howe MM**, 14th Battalion, who died on the 29th June 1918, aged 20. Joseph was the son of William, a gardener, and Elizabeth Howe, of 170 Gulson Road, Coventry. Joseph was born on the 18th January, 1898, in Harnall Lane West. He was the youngest of six children, three boys and three girls. The dates he attended Bablake are not known, but in the April 1913 edition of 'The Wheatleyan', a critique of the Football Second Team players described Joseph as "*a steady half back , needs a little more dash, worries*

well – will improve". Prior to his enlistment he was a clerk in the Guardian's office, Little Park Street, Coventry.

In October 1917 the death of his oldest brother Willie (who had not attended Bablake but was also a gardener,) was announced. Willie, aged 30, was a driver with A Battery, 317th Brigade, Royal Field Artillery and formerly employed at the Rudge-Whitworth Works, enlisting soon after the outbreak of war in the South Midland Howitzers, subsequently transferring to the RFA. He is buried in Duhallow Cemetery, this cemetery took casualties from the Advanced Dressing Station, a medical post one mile north of Ypres. Willie is pictured left on the following page with Joseph on the right.

The following month, his parents, grieving from the death of the eldest son, would have received notification that, Joseph, then aged 19, was in a convalescent camp suffering from a gunshot wound to the face. In this action he could have won his Military Medal which was awarded for bravery in the field. Joseph recovered sufficiently and was sent back to his Battalion.

On the 28th June 1918 the 14th Battalion had managed to take all the objectives and the *'war diaries'* note *"a great number of Boche dead are lying about and many prisoners"*. At night a wiring party was sent forward to wire a new front 1,000 yards long in a defensive arrangement known as a *'double apron'*. The 29th was a quiet day and at dusk the wiring continued, resulting in three fatalities: Privates F.A. Brown and F. L. Clarkson and Sergeant Joseph Howe; six privates were also wounded during the operation. The three soldiers' bodies were recovered and they are buried side by side in Tannay British Cemetery, Thiennes, occupying Grave 3 to 5, Plot 3, Row F.

His death was announced in *'The Wheatleyan'*: *"Sergeant J. Howe has died a gallant death in action. The notice of his decoration was only issued last term and it comes as a very bitter grief to learn that such a valuable soldier has passed away. His bravery and noble character was emphasized in the high words of commendation with which his commanding officer accompanied the announcement of his loss"*.

July 1918 saw the death of Lance-Corporal **Victor Leslie Clarke**, 2/7th Battalion, Royal Warwickshire Regiment attached to the 182nd Trench Mortar Battery. He was one of three serving sons of John (a gardener) and Mary Jane Clarke, of 66, Villa Terrace, Radford, Coventry. On the following page Victor is pictured on the right, and the two remaining brothers who didn't attend Bablake were Henry (middle) and Ernie Clarke (left). Henry lost a leg in the Battle of the Somme and Ernie survived the war.

All three names of the Clarke brothers appear on the Engleton Road Memorial in Radford near St. Nicholas Church; a cross next to Victor's name signifies he died during the war. It is believed that German prisoners of war, who were based in the nearby Villa Road assisted in the construction of the memorial which was originally on the opposite side of the road. There is also a plaque to Victor in the War Memorial Park paid for by his mother.

Born 7th April 1894, Victor went to Radford Elementary and then on to Bablake, entering Form 3 in 1908 and leaving in Form 4B in 1910, going on to be an office boy at an unknown works and then an assembler. On the day of his death, Victor's Battalion were in reserve with a strength of 19 officers and 522 other ranks, resting at La Miquellerie. From the 25th June to the 1st July they spent six days in the line on the Right Sub-Sector Robecq Section. Despite excellent weather during this tour they had suffered 1 killed and 10 wounded.

Having enlisted at the age of 20, Victor died of wounds on the 3rd July 1918 aged 24 and is buried in Aire Communal Cemetery. At this time the 54th Casualty Clearing Station was in Aire and Victor probably received treatment there for his wounds.

The Clarke Brothers

On the 4th July, Corporal **Herbert William Hawthorne,** 15th Battalion, Royal Warwickshire Regiment (formerly H/310505 Warwickshire Yeomanry) was killed. He is buried in Aire Communal Cemetery. The 15th Battalion were involved in an attack at the end of June and by the 4th of July withdrew to Spresiano Camp in reserve. Herbert was born in the City in 1885. He was the husband of Lily Hawthorne, of 26, St. Michael's Road, Coventry. A tobacconist, he enlisted in October, 1914 in Warwick.

By the end of July there was one further casualty, Private **Raymond Frederick John Averns,** Queen's Own (Royal West Kent Regiment) 6th Battalion, formerly Royal Fusiliers. Born the 9th of June, 1896, at Coventry, he initially attended Radford Elementary and then was admitted to Bablake on the 14th September 1906 and left in the Upper 6th on the 30th July 1913. From 1910 to 1912 he was a boarder, and had been awarded a Minor Exhibition.

Furthering his education he went on to become an undergraduate at Selwyn College, Cambridge. The *'College Admission Book'* and the issues of the annual College publication, *'The Calendar'*, show that he matriculated at Selwyn College in October 1914 and seemed to be exempt from the initial examinations. He then gained a Third class in the 'Previous examination' in December 1914; this was probably part of the general exams to try to bring all students up to the same standard.

His first year room was B15, which is in the Tower staircase and hence the gateway to the College. His second year seemed to be far more successful in academic terms and he gained a First Class for Medieval and Modern Languages and in fact was a Junior Soph, (awarded to one of the highest scoring students). He was also awarded an Exhibition of £20. He joined up in June 1916 with the Public Schools Battalion, Royal Fusiliers at the end of the Summer term as he is in the list of students for that year who were in the services, then at some point he was transferred to the Royal West Kent Regiment.

The son of Raymond Herbert and Laura Dean Averns, he died on 30th July, 1918 in France aged 22 whilst a prisoner of war. His obituary appeared in both *'The Calendar'* and *'The Wheatleyan'* and he is buried in Conde-Sur-L'Escaut Communal Cemetery. This contains the graves of 90 servicemen of the First World War, all of whom died in German hands between June 1917 and October 1918. A resident of 12, Lydgate Road, Radford his name appears on the Engleton Road Memorial and on the stained glass memorial in St. John's church.

Private **John Spencer**, Machine Gun Corps (formerly Royal Warwickshire Regiment) was killed in action on the 2nd August 1918 aged 38. Research for J. Spencer initially proved rather difficult: the CWGC lists 129 whilst the *'City of Coventry Roll of the Fallen'* records 4 occurrences. Eventually entries of donations made to the War Memorial Fund provided a means of identification; Mrs. Isabella Spencer, widow of John made a donation of 10 shillings. John was born on the 16th October 1880 at Stockingford, Nuneaton and also resided in Stockingford at 44, Church Road. He was the son of Henry and Mary and is buried in La Clytte Military Cemetery in Belgium.

The Somme was to continue claiming victims from Bablake. On the 8th August 1918 Second Lieutenant **Aubrey Frederick Hall,** 92nd Field Company, Royal Engineers, was killed in action aged 22. He died in a position previously fought over in 1916. Born the 12th June 1896 at Parkside, he resided at 20 Britannia Street with his parents William, a tailor and Emma Jane Hall (nee Dewis).

Enlisting in April 1915 he gave up his occupation as an architect's pupil and joined the Royal Engineers. A pupil of Wheatley Street Elementary, he furthered his education at Bablake for a period of four years from 31st August 1908 to 1st August 1912. He attended on a daily basis for the first two years and then boarded at the school, this being the regulations set by his four year grant from the Governors. In 1912 he was awarded a Bablake minor scholarship and in 1913 the school magazine announced Aubrey had passed Royal Institute of British Architects (RIBA) Preliminary Examination.

Having fallen in the Somme, Second Lieutenant Hall is buried in Franvillers Communal Cemetery extension, which was used from April to August 1918 by units and field ambulances engaged in the defence of Amiens.

The next casualty was Private **Sidney Frank Ward**, 94119 King's Liverpool Regiment 1st Battalion formerly 38092, Royal Warwickshire Regiment. He was born on the 5th December 1885 at Stoneleigh Cottage, The Butts, and was killed in action in France on the 25th August 1918 aged 32. He was the son of George Ward of 74 St. Patricks Road and the husband of Gertrude Ward of 11 White Street, Coventry. In 1915 he changed his occupation from bookseller and stationer to a Private. Frank is commemorated on the Vis-En-Artois memorial, which bears the names of over 9,000 men who fell in the period from 8th August 1918 to the Armistice in the advance to victory between the Somme and Loos, and who have no known grave.

Captain **Arthur Joseph Adams,** 1st Battalion Royal Warwickshire Regiment, served for four years, enlisting in August 1914 as a Private in the Public Schools Battalion. He was killed in action, 30th August 1918. He was commissioned as a Second Lieutenant in October 1914 with the 3rd Battalion this appearing in the Gazette on the 14th May 1915. After 12 months training he went to France where he joined the 2nd Battalion. He went into action in the Battle of the Somme on July 2nd 1916 and was severely wounded in the leg. He was sent to France again in April 1918 and joined the 1st Battalion.

Born 22nd January 1885 he was the son of Mr. William and Eliza Adams of 28, Allesley Old Road, Coventry. He was one of seven children, four boys and three girls. One of his brothers was Second Lieutenant Frederick Adams, who also attended Bablake and was shot down on the 12th May 1917. His father William Adams was a watch manufacturer and employed the eldest family members as watch polishers.

Arthur was educated at Bablake School and afterwards became a solicitor. In July 1912 *'The Wheatleyan'* reported he had *"passed his Final Solicitors' Examination of the Law Society at the recent Trinity sittings and George William Moore has obtained a first class at the Intermediate Solicitors Examination. Both are articled to Mr. Chas. J. Band (Messrs Band Hatton and Co)"*. He later moved to London and practised at 25 Bedford Row and Coventry. G. W. Moore went on to become a Second Lieutenant with the 13th Battalion, Royal Warwickshire Regiment having left the school in 1910.

On the 27th August 1918, the villages of Vis-En-Artois and Haucourt were taken by the Canadian Corps and attacks on the enemy continued in this vicinity in the following days. On the 29th orders for a forthcoming attack by the 1st Battalion were issued by the Brigade and the Commanding Officer had a conference with the Company commanders. Zero hour was not notified at this point and the Battalion were heavily shelled by the enemy.

The following day, the Battalion moved south east of Remy Wood and Village. The companies dribbled forward but the movement was observed and a heavy machine gun and artillery barrage was put down. B and C companies were much disorganised and suffered severe casualties. Captain A. J. Adams was killed in this engagement. The allied artillery were then asked to shell the opposite ridge and the hostile fire was considerably reduced.

Owing to reduced strength A and C companies amalgamated, B and D also. These were then known as Composite 1 and 2 companies; they moved up to support the Duke of Wellington's, who together with 2nd Seaforth Highlanders, made an attack at 8.45pm on a third objective from the previous day. The objective was still not reached on the 31st August as the men, on their way to the second objective, had to cross a stream and swamp, wading waist deep in mud. Owing to this delay the artillery barrage got too far ahead and with the shortage of men this prevented the third objective being taken. Captain Adams aged 32 is buried in Vis-En-Artois, Haucourt British cemetery near Arras. He left a widow and two children. The cemetery was begun immediately after the taking of Vis-En-Artois and Haucourt.

In similar circumstances to Private Sydney Frank Ward, Private **Albert Knight,** was transferred from the Royal Warwickshire Regiment to the King's Liverpool Regiment 1st Battalion. Born and residing in Bedworth, he actually enlisted in Coventry. He died of wounds a month later than his colleague on the 29th September 1918 and was buried in Grevillers British Cemetery. The village was lost in the German advance of March 1918, but recaptured on the 24th August by the New Zealand Division. In September, the 34th , 49th and 56th Casualty Clearing Stations came to the village and the cemetery and burials recommenced.

Private **Frank William Wells,** service number G/17145, was with the 13th Battalion, Royal Sussex Regiment. The G stood for 'general service' and replaced the GS sequence in November 1914. The 13th Battalion was one of three Battalions, the others being the 11th and 12th, raised by Colonel Claude Lowther of Herstmonceux in response to Lord Kitchener's call to arms. Their mascot was a Sussex sheep- hence the nickname 'Lowther's Lambs'. They were recruited mainly from the downland villages and coastal towns of East Sussex. They trained at Cooden Camp at Bexhill and at Witley Camp near Godalming. They went over to France as the

116th (Southdown) brigade of the 39th Division in March 1916 and suffered heavy casualties at Aubers Ridge on 30th June 1916. The three Battalions fought at the third Battle of Ypres later in 1917 but the 11th and 13th in particular sustained very heavy losses in the struggle to stem the German offensive south of the Somme in March 1918. Both Battalions were practically wiped out and what remained of the 13th was finally destroyed at Ypres, in the German attack at Kemmel on 9th April 1918.

Frank Wells was captured in the spring of 1918, and *'The Coventry Graphic'* of July 19th 1918 cited it had been confirmed that he was a prisoner of war and had been missing officially since April 26th. He enlisted in September 1916 leaving the engineers office of the London & North Western and Midland Railways at Nuneaton.

Frank was born on the 7th September 1898 at Coventry and resided at 64 Arden Street. He was the son of Frank W. Wells, a railway barman, and Alice Wells, and brother of Arthur, who was two years younger. From Earlsdon Elementary he went to Bablake for two years from 8th September 1910 in Form 2 to the 30th July 1913 leaving in form 4B, the grant being received from the Coventry Education Committee. Before joining the colours, he was employed as a clerk and eventually died of his wounds in France, whilst a prisoner of war aged 21 on the 3rd October 1918. Along with other allied prisoners and German soldiers he is buried in Glageon Communal Cemetery Extension, the village being occupied by the Germans for practically the whole of the War. He is also commemorated in St. Barbara's Church, Earlsdon and the War Memorial Park.

Private **Joseph Edward Roots** enlisted as number 2044 in the Warwickshire Yeomanry in August 1914. He served over four years and at the time of his death on the 6th October 1918 he had transferred to the 100th Battalion, Machine Gun Corps (Infantry). He was with C Squadron when the Yeomanry left Coventry for the front. A pupil at South Street Elementary, his stay at Bablake was short-only 10 months, from the 6th September 1909 to 20th July 1910, never leaving Form 3C. Born the 18th July 1896 he was the eldest son of Mr. and Mrs. George Roots of 55 Highland Road, Earlsdon. At the outbreak of war he was employed by the Rover Company as an electrician and resided at 18 Croft Road.

In the same month as his parents, Mr. and Mrs. George Roots of 55 Highland Road, Earlsdon, received notification of his death they were also informed that their second son, Private George Roots 2/4th Hants Regiment had been wounded in France aged 19 and spent time in hospital at the Crieff. George had received very early military training as a member of the 2nd Cadet Battalion, Royal Warwickshire Regiment. George joined the colours in December 1917, three years after his brother, and by August 1918, was on active service in France. He was employed by the Coventry Chain Company. George did not attend Bablake but survived the war, whilst Joseph has no known grave and is remembered on the Vis-En-Artois Memorial.

Second Lieutenant **Frank Nevey**, 6th Battalion, Duke of Wellington's (West Riding Regiment), was one of the oldest Old Boys to die during the Great War when 36 years old. He was educated at Bablake between 1893 and 1897. He was the only son of Mr. George Richard and Annie Nevey, who were retired and living in Eltham, London. George was well known locally as for many years he was a schoolmaster at Keresley, and then at the end of his career a teacher at the Technical Institute.

Following his time at Bablake, Frank was educated at King's College, London, achieving B.A Honours 2nd Class in English in 1909 and then in 1916 an M.A with Honours in English. From 1915-1916 he was a member of the Faculty of Arts. He then became a master in L.C.C. Central School and the husband of Gertrude Lizzie Nevey residing at 29, Therapia Road, Honor Oak, London.

Shortly after the outbreak of war he enlisted as a Private in the Duke of Wellington's West Riding Regiment. According to the regulations then in vogue, he was too old to train for a commission in the University of London OTC. He obtained his commission in August 1917, and shortly afterwards was sent to France. He died on the battlefield after receiving a mortal wound from a machine gun while acting as Captain, and leading his men in an attack at Nieuvilly, about two miles from Le Cateau, on October 12th, 1918. One of his fellow officers who was wounded in the same battle said *"He was a man we could trust"*, expressing that he was much liked both by his fellow officers and the men under his command. The Chaplain also saw him fall and wrote a kind letter to his widow of the esteem in which he was held.

Second Lieutenant Nevey is buried in Selridge British Cemetery, Montay, which contains 60 graves, dating from the 10th October to the 1st November. These casualties were received in the Pursuit to the Selle. *'The Wheatleyan'* published his obituary stating *"He bore an irreproachable character throughout. In the after years he fitted himself for a high place in the scholastic profession of the future, which he no doubt would have filled"*. At King's College London his name appears on the *'Honour Roll'*, which takes the form of a board of photographs with biographical information pinned underneath.

"Frank Nevey MA 2nd Lt of the Duke of Wellington's West Riding Regiment; killed in action near Le Cateau 1918 Oct 12".

Private **Harold George Bonham** spent time with several different regiments. He was originally with the 20th Battalion London Regiment and then transferred to the 883rd Area Employment Company. At the time of his death he was attached to the Troops Office, Labour Corps. He died at Le Havre aged 27 on 20th October 1918, having received treatment at one of the general or stationary hospitals, and is buried in Ste. Marie Cemetery, Le Havre and commemorated on a plaque in the War Memorial Park

He was born, enlisted and resided in Coventry, with his parents Alfred (watchmaker foreman) and Fannie Bonham living at 'Bangor', Friars Road, Coventry. He spent five years at Bablake awarded by the Coventry Education Committee (August 1904 to April 1909) and prior to this attended St. John's Street Elementary. On leaving he became a clerk in the Gas Office until he enlisted in March 1916.

Private **Leslie Thomas Jones** of the 1/8th Battalion, Royal Warwickshire Regiment was killed in action at Landrecies, France aged 19, exactly one week before the Armistice on the 4th November 1918. Landrecies was the scene of rear-guard fighting on the 25th August 1914, after the Battle of Mons, and from that date it remained in German hands until it was captured by the 25th Division on 4th November 1918. At 6.15am the 1/8th Battalion attacked and after a very severe fight secured the objective which was the line of the River Sambre at Landrecies, establishing a bridgehead there. The Battalion then received orders at 3.40pm to concentrate in another area and they moved in accordance with these orders.

Born on the 29th December, 1898 in Queen Victoria Road, Coventry. Leslie resided at 'Avonmore', 33 Earlsdon Avenue South, Coventry with his parents Charles Arthur and Frances H. E. Jones. An electrical engineer, he enlisted in June 1918 in Warwick and had served only five months. He is buried in Landrecies British Cemetery. His name appears on the memorial in St. Barbara's Church in Earlsdon and in the War Memorial Park.

The last casualty on the Western Front was Private **Reginald Thomas Beaufoy,** 1st Battalion, Norfolk Regiment and like Private Jones he was killed in action, in the Sambre Area on the 8th November 1918 aged 20, having served five months. He lived with his parents Mr. and Mrs. Thomas Beaufoy, of 'St. Keyne', Queen Mary's Road, Coventry, but was actually born in Lockhurst Lane on the 18th September 1898.

At 5.30am on November 5th the Norfolk Battalion led an attack with the 1st Bedford at Jolimetz in immediate support. The weather, which had been splendid, had now broken and the advance was made in a downpour. At first no opposition was met and by 7.30am, when the first objective had been gained well within the forest, the Bedford Battalion passed through to continue the attack. The 1st Norfolk re-formed at the crossroads at Le Godelot, ready to give assistance, which, however, was not required.

On the 6th the Battalion went on to La Haute Rue, near the eastern edge of the forest, for a further attack. At 5.30pm it was ready for an attack across the Sambre, which flows north-eastwards along the eastern edge of the forest. A bridge in front had been reported safe, but by 7.30pm it was found to have been blown up by the retreating enemy, as well as a footbridge.

Late that night a working party was detached to help in the reconstruction of the bridge at the lock. By 6.00am on the 7th work had to be abandoned owing to the hostile machine gun fire. At 7.30am the attack was launched across the river, with the railway running north to Maubeuge as its objective. The passage was made by a pontoon bridge constructed during the night by the Royal Engineers. The railway was reached and made good by the Cheshire Battalion and a platoon of B Company of the Norfolk Battalion.

About 4.30pm the Devonshire Battalion of the 95th Brigade passed through the Norfolk and Cheshire Battalions to continue the attack. Fontaine on the right, was taken but the Devonshire men were held up at St. Remi-Mal-bati on the left. At 5.30am on the 8th the Devonshire Battalion were attacking near Avesnes-Maubeuge road, and at 9.30am the 1st Norfolk were withdrawn to the railway, whence, on the 9th and 10th , they went back to rest and reorganise at Jolimetz on the west of the Mormal Forest.

Private Beaufoy lost his life in the fighting on the 8th and is buried in the south corner of Bachant Communal Cemetery, this cemetery contains only four burials from WW1. He also has a plaque in the War Memorial Park.

The Unverified

Of the ninety six names on the school memorial, three of these could not be fully verified. This issue is compounded by the fact that as Bablake was a boarding school those concerned could in theory come from anywhere. In addition the Old Boys served with Australian and Canadian Battalions, a search of these databases revealed no possible matches and concentrated the search on the British regiments.

The unverified are D. Barber, G. N. Barber, and A. Wilkinson.

The *'Roll of Honour'* for Bablake indicates this was David Barber, who left the school in 1900, and this would mean he was in his late 20's, early 30's during the war. There is one David Barber listed with the CWGC, a Private in the Army Service Corps, 33rd Motor Ambulance Company, who died aged 34 on the 26th February 1917, son of Mr. and Mrs. Frederick Barber, of Berwick Pond, Rainham, Essex, and husband of Lillie Barber, of 96, High Street, Uxbridge, Middlesex. He is remembered on the Basra memorial.

The CWGC for G. N. Barber shows only one, Private George Norman Barber with the 1/4th Duke of Wellingtons (West Riding Regiment), who died aged 19 on the 12th March 1917 and is buried at Etaples Military Cemetery. Various Old Boys had joined the West Riding Regiment, so this was not unusual. A search for G. Barber on the CWGC web site reveals thirty four but none show any close associations with Bablake.

Whilst the name A. Wilkinson is written on the School Memorial, a B. Wilkinson appears in the *'Roll of the Fallen'* with the words *"Educated at Bablake, Killed in Action"*. The list of those who served suggests a B. Wilkinson was in the Warwickshire Yeomanry but this could not be found, and there are 19 B. Wilkinson's listed with the CWGC and one hundred and three for A. Wilkinson. One possible factor for the difference in initial is that his name was shortened from something like Albert to Bert.

Not appearing on the War Memorial, but included in the *'1919 Bablake Roll of Honour'*, published in *'The Wheatleyan'* as being killed in action, are A. E. Harris and W. Kirby.

There were two A. E. Harris who attended Bablake, the first being medal winner Sub Commander A. E. Harris who left the school in 1910 and is explored in the *'Medals Won'* section, the *'Admission Records'* for the second A. E. Harris show he left the school in 1913 and *'The Wheatleyan'* mentions he was in the Oxfordshire and

Buckinghamshire Light Infantry. There is one casualty registered with the CWGC who matches these details: Private Alfred Edward Harris, 2nd Battalion, Oxfordshire and Buckinghamshire Light Infantry, died on the 5th February 1918 aged 21. The son of Mrs. Millicent J. Harris of 201, Iffley Road, Oxford, he is buried in Rocquigny-Equancourt Road British Cemetery.

The name W. Kirby is in the *'City of Coventry: Roll of the Fallen'* and simply states *"educated at Bablake, Killed in Action"*. There are forty one names listed by the CWGC. The most likely seems to be Lance Corporal William Percival Kirby, 1/8th Territorial Battalion, Royal Warwickshire Regiment. He was born in Rugby, making it feasible for him to attend the school, although he enlisted in Aston, Birmingham and resided in Witton, Birmingham. William was killed in action on the first day of the Somme aged 20. He was the son of William and Clara Kirby of 53 Wyley Road, Witton, Birmingham and is remembered on the Thiepval Memorial.

Cross- checking the list of those who served against the databases revealed the addition Able Seaman Frank Kenneth Greening. There is not enough evidence to substantiate adding more names to the Roll. Erroneously two names appeared in *'The Wheatleyan'* as being killed: N. White probably Norman and P. Oldham. By the time the 1919 list was compiled they had moved onto the list of those that served.

Back from the Dead

The name J. A. White appears on the school memorial and the *'Roll of Honour'* reveals he was in the Royal Field Artillery and left the school in 1912. In *'The Coventry Graphic'* of the 31ˢᵗ January 1919, a story about Sergeant J. A. White appeared.

At this time he was on the headquarters staff of the 211ᵗʰ Brigade, RFA having been awarded the Meritorious Service Medal (MSM). The article states *"He joined the 3/4ᵗʰ South Midland Howitzer Brigade in May 1915, and had been in France nearly three years. White was previously employed as an assistant inspector in the weights and measures department, Coventry Corporation and was educated at Bablake School. His parents resided at 58 Colchester Street, Coventry"*.

Sergeant White was awarded the MSM for *"constant devotion to duty and untiring energy as Brigade Clerk, particularly during the period 23ʳᵈ February 1918 to the 22ⁿᵈ September 1918, under the most trying conditions"*.

'The Coventry Corporation Roll of Honour' was compiled in 1927 and this has J. A. White in the list of those who served. There is no mention of J. A. White's death in the local papers so it seems he lived through the war and his name is recorded as a genuine error. The *'City of Coventry: Roll of the Fallen'* in contrast names J. A. White with the inscription *"Educated at Bablake Killed in action"*.

Not appearing on the War Memorial, but included in the *'1919 Bablake Roll of Honour'*, published in *'The Wheatleyan'* as being killed in action, was H. Daulman. The name does not appear on any of the databases or at any other point in *'The Wheatleyan'*. It is also noted that a P. Daulman also appears but again no details are provided.

The fate of Lance Corporal H. Daulman, Warwickshire Yeomanry, was mentioned in *'The Coventry Graphic'* dated April 6ᵗʰ 1917 under the headline *'Not Dead, But a Prisoner of War'*. It was reported that he was a prisoner in the hands of the Turks, having been reported as dead three times, drowned once and twice killed in action. A further article on the 3ʳᵈ January 1919 ran a piece entitled *'Back from the Dead'*. This was concerning Trooper H. Daulman, son of the oldest tenant farmer on the Arbury Estate of Sir Francis Newdegate. Daulman went out with the Warwickshire

Yeomanry and was on the ill- fated ' Wayfarer' when she was torpedoed just off the west coast of England.

He was subsequently reported killed in the East by a fall from his horse and the family actually received a photograph of a grave, believed to be that of the young Daulman. They went into mourning but at a later stage the glad tidings came through that he was a prisoner in the hands of the Turks. Trooper Daulman returned to his parents' home at Chilvers Coton at the end of 1918 and *'The Coventry Graphic'* quotes from the family *"it turned out to the happiest Christmas the family had ever spent"*.

Medals Won

During the Great War, the Old Boys won a variety of gallantry medals and awards. The following were won multiple awards Corporal W. L. Shortridge DCM MM, Major A. Gould DSO MC and Sub Conductor A. E. Harris MM also received the MSM.

Distinguished Conduct Medal

The Distinguished Conduct Medal (DCM) was first instituted in 1854 as an award to recognise *"distinguished, gallant and good conduct"* in the field for Warrant Officers, NCO's and lower ranks. Nearly 25,000 DCMs were issued during the War, four to the Old Boys: Frederick Charles Vincent DCM who fell, Corporal W. L. Shortridge DCM MM, Gunner Roderick Coombes DCM and C. W. Baker DCM.

Corporal W. L. Shortridge DCM, MM left Bablake in 1906 and originally enlisted as a Sapper. He was promoted to a Corporal in the 16th Signal Company, Royal Engineers and was awarded his DCM *"for conspicuous gallantry on the 26th September 1915, near Hulluck, when he laid a telephone wire to the gun trench under heavy fire, and remained on the end of it for half an hour in the open in rear of the gun trench until ordered to withdraw. He showed great coolness, bravery and devotion to duty."*

Gunner Roderick Coombes, Telephony Section, 4th South Midland Howitzer Brigade, RFA, was awarded the DCM. Roderick was just 18 when he bravely stayed with an officer under heavy shellfire at La Gare observation station near Ploegsteert Wood on the 26th June 1915. Roderick left Bablake in 1912 after three years at the age of 14 to join Mr. Davis of Mount Farm, Meriden as a pupil. Before enlisting with the Howitzer Brigade at the age of 17 he worked as a dairyman for Robert Minton of Kensington Road, Earlsdon as he lived nearby at 22 Cromwell Street. His father was Mr. Walter Coombes a foreman at the works of Alfred Herbert Ltd. Thinking his father might object to his enlistment he wrote an explanatory letter with the words *"Your son will at least be honourable and be a man"*. The family resided at 'Ashdene', 24 St. Patrick's Road,

Coventry.

The news of his gallantry was announced in *'The Coventry Graphic'* and *'The Coventry Herald'* in January 1916. Describing the event that led to his award, Gunner Coombes stated *"We came out of action on Saturday the 26th of June, 1915 and we had a lively time that morning. The observation station we were in was a ruined house at some crossroads. A little further up the road was a German barricade. We had twelve rounds to use up so the officers said we would have a smack at it. We started off and gave them a few iron rations, one shell dropping under a tree at the back of the barricade and bought down either a sniper or an officer observing. That seemed to upset them and they got quite nasty over it and started to reply. The first and second shells nearly did for us-they were using fair-size high explosive shell-one of them bursting in front of the house. I must say a word of praise of Lieutenant Hayes, who was with me at the time of observing the fire. He never moved and gave the orders as cool as you like. He is 'some' officer"*. The next shell came through the room at the back of us, making a great hole, but luckily it never harmed either of us"*. Lieutenant Hayes was awarded the Distinguished Service Order (DSO), for continually firing despite being heavily shelled.

Gunner Coombes also wrote several letters home describing his life and work with the Howitzers; the following appeared in *'The Coventry Herald'* in January 1916:-
"I have had some exciting times lately and I am beginning to think I am lucky or must have as many lives as a cat. We went up to the trenches for three days on Saturday morning to the forward observation station. This was a fresh order, as we never slept as near before, so we made our home in the cellar of a ruined house. First of all we did our best to make ourselves as comfortable as possible. We scrounged a table and two chairs and also a spring mattress bed which the officers of a relieved regiment had left, put some straw in bags to serve the place of mattresses and to put the finishing touches on we got a vase full of beautiful roses from nearby which could be had by scrambling over the trench barricade and keeping very low. Then as the grass is so long you cannot be seen. Well, we then cooked our supper after having a busy day. We turned in about ten o'clock, thinking to have a bonny night's sleep, as it was the first bed I laid on since leaving England.

We did not get much sleep as they kept turning a maxim on the house, and the lead don't half splash up against the walls I can tell you. We kept testing the line and all went well till about 6.15am when we rang the battery again and found it all correct. I dozed off again, when suddenly-Bump! Bang! Boom!. The Germans had blown up two of their mines under one of our trenches. I had never heard such a din, you could not hear your own voice let alone talk to anyone on the 'phone'.

Well to get on with the tale; we grabbed for our garments. I got my mate's boots and he got mine, but after wishing one another best wishes etc., profusely, we changed around as quickly as possible. We had only got our trousers on when they started shelling the house which we were in. We bolted down the communication trench, when we were stopped, as it was no use going on further, for they were shelling a house about twenty yards further on which the trench ran through. So we snipped the wire and lay in the trench with some infantry supports about three deep trying to get through to the battery. I never saw anything like it and don't want to again. It was hell. Talk about rapid fire. I should think every German had a maxim gun. They absolutely swept the trenches. Trench mortars, rifle grenades, hand grenades, jam tin bombs, maxims, rifles- this backed up with shell fire; you can imagine what it was like. As we could not get through to the battery we knew there was a break somewhere so we made a dash for it, getting through safely. I found the break near the dressing station. We then got in communication again, but by this time the situation was once again normal and all was quiet except for the usual sniping and occasional shell coming over. Of course this was only a minor affair. Lord knows what it would be like if they were going to make an all-round attack. But keep smiling. I expect we shall be giving some of them return tickets shortly. I believe we dropped a shell into a party of them cooking this morning".

The Bablake war memorial records the name C. W. Baker DCM; his name is not recorded in *'The Wheatleyan'* or at any point in the school records. During research a Company Sergeant Major William Baker was found, he was awarded a DCM with the Royal Warwickshire Regiment on the 13th February 1917. *'The London Gazette'* stating *"for conspicuous gallantry in action, he assumed command and led his company with great courage and determination and performed consistent good work throughout".*

Military Cross

The Military Cross (MC) was first instituted on the 28th December 1914 as an award for gallantry or meritorious service for officers with the rank of Captain and below. In August 1916 it became possible to award a bar or bars to the MC for repeated acts of gallantry. All awards were announced in the London Gazette, usually with a citation, although awards made as part of the King's Birthday or New Year's honours were made for meritorious service and do not usually have a citation. 37,081 MC's were awarded in the war, 2,992 men were awarded a bar to the MC (that is they won it again); 176 a second bar and four men a third bar. The Old Boys were awarded thirteen MC's. Second Lieutenant Harold Masters Brown was awarded his posthumously. Four of the remainder were with the Royal Warwickshire Regiment. Captain Luther James Kelsey left the school in 1910 and served with the 8th Battalion before transferring to the South Staffordshire regiment. He was gazetted as a temporary Lieutenant on the 27th April 1917, an Acting Captain of A Company on the 8th June 1917 and temporary Captain on the 20th September 1917. His name appears in the *'Army List of Officers'*, January to

March 1918 edition as having been awarded an MC, as this was not specified In the October 1917 edition his award must have been won in the latter stages of 1917.

E. J. Blakemore served with the 7th Battalion and H. E. Storer who left Bablake in 1905 was with the 12th Battalion and finally Sergeant L. Allen (pictured). He was one of the four serving sons of Mr. J. Allen a well known member of the Coventry Board of Guardians.

Major Arthur Ernest Gould DSO, MC was awarded his MC whilst a Captain with the Royal Engineers and added his Distinguished Service Order early in 1918. The DSO was a high award for meritorious or distinguished service rather than an act of gallantry and was instituted in 1886 when it was realised that no adequate award for distinguished service was available to junior officers apart from the Victoria Cross (VC). In many cases during 1914-1918 it is not easy to discriminate between these two reasons for granting an award and appears that a DSO was awarded when perhaps a full recommendation for a VC could not be justified or corroborated.

From July 1918 to July 1919, Major Gould DSO, MC had appeared in 'The London Gazette' three times. His first mention in July 1918 was when he was a Lieutenant and retained his acting rank of Major with the Royal Engineers. In October 1918 he had resigned his commission in the Territorial Force, but retained his temporary commission in the Royal Engineers and finally in July 1919 he had relinquished the acting rank of Major on ceasing to be employed by the Ministry of Munitions on the 27th March 1919.

'The Wheatleyan' carried the announcements of former master K. E. Wootton, 10th London Regiment (pictured left) MC award in 1917, Captain Frank Leslie Morgan who had served with the Royal Warwickshire Regiment and North Lancashire Regiment and finally Lieutenant Jack Parsons, a Warwickshire County and England Cricketer, who attended the school until 1905 and served with the Warwickshire Imperial Yeomanry.

The Bablake war memorial reveals that a further three MC's were awarded. Private W. Coleman (pictured) left the school in 1908 and served with the Warwickshire Yeomanry and resided in either Brandon or Wolston, F. Mills left the school in 1903 and served with the Royal Engineers and finally D. Gee whose date of leaving and regiment are not known.

Military Medal

The Military Medal was instituted by Royal Warrant on the 25th March 1916 to be awarded for *"acts of gallantry and devotion to duty performed by non-commissioned officers and men of our army in the field"*. During the War, 115,000 MMs were awarded, with 5,800 first bars and 180 second bars. There was one award of the MM and three bars.

Eight MM's were awarded to the Old Boys, two of these were awarded to the fallen: Sergeant Joseph Howe and Second Lieutenant William John Salmons. A further two were awarded to Corporal Shortridge who also won the DCM and one of the 5,800 awards of MM with Bar was awarded to Bombardier Stanley Hulme. He enlisted in October 1914 at the age of 17 and had been in France since March 1915, his parents resided at 58, Kingsway. His first award covered in *'The Coventry Graphic'* of the 3rd December 1915 stated *"he carried a wounded comrade to safety whilst under heavy shell and machine gun fire"* and for MM with Bar *'The Wheatleyan'* announced with *"much pride that we hear of the investiture of Bombardier S. Hulme ("*

late assistant of Mr. F. Morgan in the manual work department) with the double honour of the Military Medal and Bar for bravery under fire". He attended Bablake school from 1909 and left the school in 1913, he was however employed at the School as an assistant to the Head of manual training before enlisting with the 4th South Midland Brigade RFA.

Sub Conductor Albert Eagleston. Harris won his MM for action in between the 18th to the 20th of August 1917 whilst at St. Idesbalde. His citation states *"The ammunition railhead was being heavily shelled, Sub Conductor A. E Harris was instrumental in getting Decauville trucks loaded with heavy ammunition pulled out of the shelled area into safety. Though shells were dropping close to the line he personally accompanied the engine and assisted in coupling up the loaded trucks. His behaviour and coolness undoubtedly inspired the men and was instrumental in averting what would probably have resulted in serious loss of life and ammunition. Sub Conductor Harris was awarded the immediate award of the MM by the Fourth Army Commander"*. He was additionally awarded the MSM on the 17th June 1918 for valuable services rendered with the forces in France. His medals are pictured on the following page and one of only four of this combination awarded to the Royal Army Ordnance Corps. The picture shows Sub-Conductor Harris in 1915 whilst a Sergeant at this time he was living in Church Lane, Allesley but by the time he was cited in the awards he had moved to Stoke, Coventry. He attended Bablake from 1908 to 1910 and on leaving became an apprentice to an engineering firm.

Left to Right: Military Medal (MM), 1914-15 Star, British War Medal (BWM), Victory Medal and the Meritorious Service Medal (MSM)

Further awards of the MM were made. Silas Poxon (pictured) of the Royal Engineers resided in Wolston and won his award whilst a Corporal, *'The Coventry Herald'* informed its readers on the 29th June 1917 that he had been promoted to Sergeant and on a recent visit home the residents were proud of his distinction. Other MM winners were A. A. Pickering, also of the Royal Engineers who left the school in 1896, and finally C. R. Banning, who left the school in 1916 and joined the Royal Lancashire Regiment.

Meritorious Service Medal

Four Meritorious Service Medals (MSM) were won by the Old Boys, one of these to a member of staff. This award was originally for long service or acts of particular merit from 1916. It was also for gallantry or meritorious service when not in the face of the enemy. As previously discussed, two were awarded to the Old Boys one to Sergeant J. A. White the other to Sub Conductor A. E. Harris, the final award was to Corporal J. Reynolds, Royal Engineers. He had enlisted at the outbreak of war, being present in the Battle of Ypres, Neuve Chapelle, Loos and the Somme. He was formerly a well-known figure in local cricket circles, who left the school in 1904 and was formerly with the Motor Cycle Corps. The award of a MSM to a member of staff was made to F. Core who served with the Machine Gun Corps, his award was not covered in *'The Wheatleyan'* and his citation could not be found.

Mentioned in Despatches

The lowest form of recognition was being *'Mentioned in Despatches'*. This was awarded for acts which were judged of sufficient merit to be officially mentioned in the despatches sent by the officer commanding a theatre of operation, back to the War Office in London. Individuals were mentioned in *'The London Gazette'*. In despatches Captain James Humberstone, Captain Percy Hood Hollick, Lieutenant M. B. Fitzgerald and Second Lieutenant R. E. Moore were mentioned for distinguished service. Second Lieutenant Moore had been wounded on four occasions whilst serving with the 4th South Midland Howitzer Brigade (RFA) and left the school in 1903. Chief Petty Officer Hugh Nelson was mentioned in despatches by the Vice-Admiral commanding the Eastern Mediterranean squadron for good services in action between the time of landing in the Gallipoli peninsula in April 1915 and the evacuation in December 1915 to January 1916 and on one further occasion.

Order of the British Empire (Military)

Major A. Palmer was awarded the OBE (Military). This award was created in December 1918, to reward distinguished service in action by officers and senior NCOs for 'The Most Excellent Order of the British Empire'. OBE denotes an Officer in The Most Excellent Order of the British Empire as opposed to the CBE which denotes a Commander in The Most Excellent Order of the British Empire. Major Palmer's exact citation in *'The London Gazette'* could not be found but would have been similar to: *"The King has been graciously pleased to confer the Medal of the Military Division of the Most Excellent Order of the British Empire for services in connection with the war"*.

Member of the British Empire

Member of the British Empire (MBE) was awarded to Lieutenant M. B. Fitzgerald MBE who served with the RAF and left the school in 1899. The MBE is the lowest rank within the Most Excellent Order of the British Empire. Lieutenant Fitzgerald MBE received this award prior to the 16th March 1919, at this point he was cited as one of those deserving of a special mention in Earl Haig's despatch. Lieutenant Fitzgerald was previously mentioned as one of his encounters whilst flying was observed by Second Lieutenant Frederick Adams.

Campaign Medals and Memorial Plaque

The Old Boys who served were entitled to several campaign medals; those that had to leave their native shore from 1914 to 1920 whilst on active service were entitled to the British War Medal (BWM). This was awarded even if the individual didn't enter a theatre of war. The Victory Medal was awarded to all those who entered a theatre of war, so it follows that the recipients of this medal also received the BWM. Over 6,600,000 BWM's were issued and over 5,700,000 Victory medals.

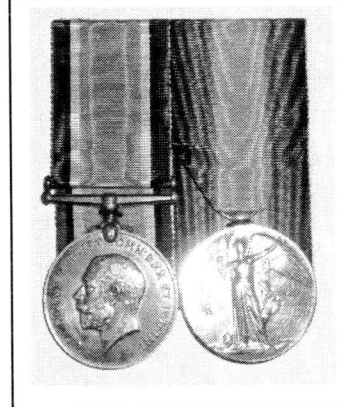

The 1914 Star (popularly known as the Mons Star) was awarded to those who served with the establishment of their unit in France and Belgium between August 5th 1914, and midnight of November 22/23rd, 1914. 365,622 stars were issued during this period. A star similar to the 1914 star known as the 1914-1915 star was awarded to those who served in a theatre of war before December 31st 1915 but did not qualify for the 1914 star. Approximately 2,100,000 stars were issued.

The pair of medals pictured were awarded to 42853 Acting/Sergeant Francis Albert Buckler 2/4th Royal Berkshire Regiment who was born on the 21st May 1891 and a baker by trade. He initially served in Ireland and then France where he served from the 24th April 1918 to the 8th March 1919.

The next of kin of the Fallen would have also received a 120mm round bronze Memorial plaque. This was awarded to the next-of-kin of those who lost their lives whilst on active service during the war. The inscription around the edge reads "He died for freedom and Honour". Over 1 million plaques were issued.

Even though the name has been wrongly recorded, the Memorial Plaque of Private Hubert William Morris who was killed in action on the 25th September 1915 aged 18 with the 2nd Battalion of the Oxfordshire and Buckinghamshire Light Infantry appears below.

The death plaque of Private Hubert William Morris

Post-War

News of the signing of the armistice on the 11ᵗʰ November 1918 did not appear in *'The Wheatleyan'* until July 1919 as the deadline had been missed for the December Issue. The school notes show the school received the news of the signing of peace with quiet enthusiasm and *"The first intimation was the sound of the church bells on the memorable Saturday afternoon. A match was in progress on the school pitch. Save for the hasty raising of the school flag upon the tower, and for the discordant clanging of hand bells by some hilarious person the match proceeded"*.

The former headmaster of Bablake J. I. Bates was Mayor of Coventry at the end of the war and he wrote the following letter to the local papers on the 9ᵗʰ November 1918, which appeared as follows:

How City will Celebrate Conclusion of Armistice

Sir, I shall be obliged if you insert this letter in your issue tonight so that the inhabitants may be acquainted with the arrangements which are being made officially for announcing to the public, when that news is received, that the armistice terms have been agreed by Germany.

So soon as official notification has been received, flags will be hoisted on St. Mary's Hall and the Council House and the church bells will be rung. The Town Crier will also proclaim the news throughout the city. If the news is received while the factories in the city are in work, the sirens or hooters of the factories will be sounded at a given hour, and it is expected that for the remainder of that day and the day following, a general holiday will be observed in all the industries in the city.

Arrangements will also be made for granting a holiday to all the school children. I trust that this announcement will avoid any misunderstanding, and that the citizens will restrain themselves until the official notification is given.

> *Yours truly*
> *J. I. Bates, Mayor*

The End of the War Is Announced

In July 1919 a 'Godiva Pageant' was held in Coventry, with various Bablake boys and masters taking part. Mr. F. W. Humberstone writing in *'The Coventry Graphic'* stated " *If a historical pageant is a moving picture illustrative of local history, the Bablake boys have an undoubted right to be represented on it"*.

The centre pages of the Programme showed an illustration of Mary and Jesus around the words from the Mayor *"We rejoice that peace has been declared but our rejoicing is mingled with sorrow: the whole City knows that many sad hearts are amongst us. Those who have returned know the price that has been paid. Those who remained at home and waited, think of those who will never return again. Therefore the Citizens of Coventry pray that The Most High, in his Infinite and compassionate memory, will, in His Own good time, heal the wounded hearts and comfort the sorrowing. May our brave dead Rest in Peace, In the name of the whole City"*.

J. I. Bates, Mayor

The Bablake Boys and Masters in the Pageant

On the extreme left is Mr. A. Carter, in the centre Mr. J. Bates, in the forefront the Headmaster Rev. Dr. Frankland and on the extreme right Mr. F. W. Humberstone. The boys pictured are those who represented Bablake in the event.

The potato patch, having done so much valuable service, was returned to its former duties as a football pitch and the demobilisation of members of staff meant the services of the female teachers would be lost. By the middle of 1919 with the exception of Mr. F. Pearson all members of staff who had been serving in His Majesty's forces had returned to school. Many of these would have a long association with the school.

Mr. Gerald Atkinson, who had been a Second Lieutenant with the Royal Engineers, started at the school in 1914 and left in 1958. Mr. Frank Core, the Gymnastics instructor, started in 1912 and remained for 30 years. The initial period for him was difficult as he was suffering the long- term effects of being gassed whilst serving with the Machine Gun Corps. Lieutenant Kenny E. Wootton MC, formerly of the 10th London Regiment who returned to the school as an art master, stayed at the school until 1948, completing 34 years of service.

Other masters also returned: Mr. J. J. Bates, who had started in 1900, remained until 1933; Captain F. L. Morgan stayed until 1926, having 35 years' service; Lieutenant A. Wilson, 11th Gordon Highlanders, who started in 1912, left in 1943.

C. H. Lawrence, formerly of the Royal Field Artillery, only stayed for a further year, having commenced employment in 1911. He had no physical scars from the war but didn't see eye to eye with the new head on his return.

Mr. F. Pearson, who was seriously wounded, having a cranial plate fitted and serious injuries to his left arm, was able to return to the school in September 1919. The demobilisation of the masters presented problems for the headmaster Dr. Frankland: to protect the school, temporary contracts had been given to a number of teachers and these had to be 'paid off' so those returning from the front could occupy their previous roles. The Old Boys also returned to their previous roles and the 'Certificate of Demobilisation' for Acting Sergeant F. A. Buckler is shown below, he returned to an occupation of a baker.

Serial No. / R. Berks R/ 2707.

Army Form Z. 21.

CERTIFICATE of* ~~Discharge~~ / Transfer to Reserve / ~~Disembodiment~~ Class Z / ~~Demobilization~~ on Demobilization.

Regtl. No. 42853 Rank a/Sergt.

Names in full Buckler. Francis Albert. (Surname first)

Unit and Regiment or Corps from which *~~Discharged~~ Transferred to Reserve Class Z: 2/4th ROYAL BERKSHIRE REGT.

ATTESTED ~~Enlisted~~ on the 10th December 1915

CALLED UP FOR SERVICE 24th April 1918

For ROYAL BERKSHIRE REGT. (Here state Regiment or Corps to which first appointed)

Also served in .... TBb

Only Regiments or Corps in which the Soldier served since August 4th, 1914, are to be stated. If inapplicable, this space is to be ruled through in ink and initialled.

†Medals and Decorations awarded during present engagement .... TBb

*Has ~~Has not~~ served Overseas on Active Service.

Place of Rejoining in case of emergency Chiseldon Medical Category A1

Specialist Military qualifications Nil Year of birth 1894

He is* ~~Discharged~~ Transferred to Army Reserve ~~Disembodied~~ ~~Demobilized~~ class Z on 6th August 1919 in consequence of Demobilization.

T. B. Barnes Lt. Signature and Rank.

for Officer i/c Infantry Records. WARWICK (Place).

*Strike out whichever is inapplicable. †The word "Nil" to be inserted when necessary.

N.B.—Any person finding this Certificate is requested to forward it in an unstamped envelope to the Secretary, War Office, London, S.W. 1.

WARNING.—If this Certificate is lost a duplicate cannot be issued. You should therefore on no account part with it or forward it by post when applying for a situation.

(20996). Wt. W 8211—P.P. 2320. 3,000m. 1/19. D & S. (E 1256.)

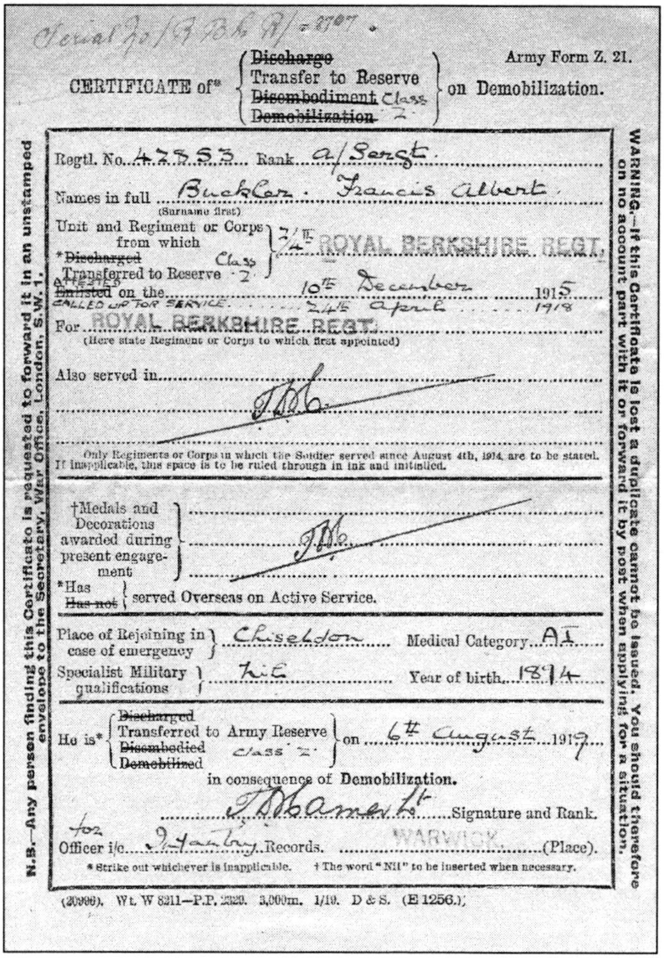

Certificate of Demobilisation

On a global scale the political, cultural and social order environments had changed drastically. Post war the effects of an influenza pandemic were felt with the death toll being several times greater than the war itself. This was undoubtedly responsible for the death of some of the Old Boys, but one of those who managed to fend off the virus was F. Attenborough. He enlisted with the 5th Field Artillery Brigade in the Australian Artillery on the 1st September 1915 having previously been with the Royal Horse Artillery in Warwickshire. He was added to a danger list on the 30th April 1919 suffering from influenza; sufficiently recovering on the 6th May 1919 he was transferred to a hospital ship, finally being discharged on the 16th August 1919 in Australia.

War Memorial Fund

In 1919 the Bablake School memorial fund was launched with this theme: *"In order to perpetuate the memory of the Old Boys of the school who served their king and country in the Great War, it is proposed to erect a memorial tablet in the school bearing the names, with honours gained, of all who served in the forces. The names of those who made the supreme sacrifice will be recorded in a special place of honour"* and an announcement made that *"the war memorial committee would be pleased to receive any information which would tend to make the list more accurate and complete. Such information should be forwarded to any member of the school staff"*.

The chairman of the Committee was Dr. J. N. Frankland, the Honorary Treasurer, Mr. F. W. Humberstone, and the Honorary Secretary Mr. H. T. Suddens of 32 Chester Street, Coventry, to whom all donations were forwarded. The latter was a veteran who had lost his brother Sergeant Major Alfred James Suddens.

As the number of Old Boys who served exceeded 700, it was felt that a generous response to the appeal would be necessary to carry out the scheme in a manner befitting the honour of the school and its Old Boys. At a meeting of the Bablake School memorial fund committee it was decided that copies of the first list of donations should appear in the school magazine and notification would be sent to all who might be interested in the progress of the fund. The amount subscribed up to December 1919 was £149, with a further £51 required to meet the minimum sum required of £200. War memorials started to appear all over the city, and on Sunday July 4th 1920 the cadets attended St. Nicholas Church, Radford, the occasion being the unveiling of a war memorial tablet. The buglers played the last post in the church. After the dedication the headmaster complimented the Corps on their *"bearing both in the church and the street"*.

Twenty four of the Old Boys have a plaque and tree dedicated to them in Coventry's War Memorial Park and we know that for Private Victor Leslie Clarke the costly sum of 25s. was paid by his mother who was distraught at the loss of one of her sons. His family also visited his grave and the picture shows his nephew at his grave in 1930.

Those who made donations were members of staff, Old Boys, spouses and families and friends. The surnames on the list of those who donated were similar to reading the *'Roll of Honour'* and the list of those who served.

The Governors, the Headmaster and Mr. F. W. Humberstone were all quite generous, with donations of £26 5s, £2 2s and £5 respectively. Anonymous donations were made in memory of W. A. Loudon and A. J. Suddens, with the families also donating generously, including Mr. and Mrs. Beacham, Mrs. A. Elliot, Mr. Harris, Mrs. Hawthorne, Mr. H. W. Pails, Mr. Bailey and Mr. and Mrs. Gunn.

On Friday, February 10th 1921, the unveiling and dedication of the war memorial was performed in the school hall; in attendance was a gathering of past and present boys, parents and friends. Mr. O. Rice in an eloquent description of the ceremony in *'The Wheatleyan'* finished his article with the words *"Thus winged with joy and hope shall we go forward, constantly reminded of our duty and encouraged in our efforts by that memorial to the greatest act of devotion to a single cause which Bablake has ever recorded in its annals"*.

The memorial is split into three sections, the main section includes the names of the fallen and those on the left and on the right list 350 names on each side of those who served. The inscription along the top of the memorial reads *"Erected in Honour of Bablake Boys who served in his Majesty's forces during the Great War"*. The list of the names appearing on the fallen section is shown in Appendix B and the list of those who served and appearing on the memorial are shown in bold in Appendix C.
The section of those who served are not recorded in strict alphabetical order and presumably the manufacturers allowed a certain amount of space to inscribe any late additions, this they did until all 700 allotted spaces had been filled.

The Bablake School Memorial

Some Reminiscences

In 1921, *'The Wheatleyan'* published a rare account of the conditions at the front written simply signed A. W. This would have been A. Wilson who started at the school as a master in 1912 and left in 1943. During the war he was Lieutenant A. Wilson, 11th Gordon Highlanders.

" It was exactly three years ago today (March 28th) since the Boches came surging over like a tidal wave on the Arras front. The storm had already burst, just a week before, and the enemy had swung round to such a dangerous extent on our left, that at night we found ourselves gazing, with awful foreboding, at the unusual sight of Verey lights shooting up in our rear. It is only natural that one should become reminiscent on such a day, and call to remembrance other things, both grave and gay, that happened to one during those fateful years.

Curiously enough everyone seems rather reticent about his experiences, and very little has been said or written, since the Armistice, of things that must be extremely interesting to a very large number of people. By common consent the pages have been hastily turned over and gummed together, and the war seems as far away now as if it had been fought fifty years ago. Yet the turbid backwash is still swirling around us. I am afraid there are many ex-soldiers in the country today, who look back regretfully to those strangely unreal, careless days, when they were content with a hard life and poor pay, so long as they could keep their skin whole. Nothing ever seemed to matter, for one might be dead tomorrow; so what was the use of worrying.

And men were always at their best in the Front Line. The further one got back into the safer areas, the more one met with the old spirit of self seeking, petty jealousy, and selfish indulgence. The blustering talkative fool was known for what he was when he came near the firing line; while the quiet unassuming, and apparently easy-going youth, who was generally elbowed out of the way in other walks, came into his own at last, and found some real pleasure in his hazardous life.

Some things one does not care to talk about for various reasons; one can fall back on general impressions. I can remember the first time I entered a Front Line trench. It was a surprisingly pleasant experience; I had been sent up in charge of a working party to dig a new communication trench. It was a glorious evening in June, and the whole place was festooned with scarlet poppies and blue cornflowers – a veritable blaze of colour. There was nothing do to that night and the war didn't seem such a bad thing after all. But coming back at 4.00am in the pouring rain to find every stitch I possessed lying soaking in the open. Two days later I made those trenches my home, when the water was almost waist deep in patches and we lived in a kind of perpetual dampness. I thought I'd never be dry again.

There were trenches and trenches. From Ypres to the Somme you would meet every conceivable sample, depending on geological and geographical conditions. At Armentieres, you couldn't dig and didn't try to. Ergo, it was better to be in the line at Armentieres than at Ypres. But the worst trenches were in the Somme, during the 1916 advance. They were hardly breast high in some places and horribly dangerous.

Talking of the Somme, there were awful death traps on the way up. One was called "The Valley of the Shadow", and led up to the infamous High Wood. I believe the Boche could hit a threepenny bit on that road if he had known where it was lying. I shall never forget bringing a sadly decimated platoon down that valley, when, by a mere stroke of luck we escaped complete annihilation, and had the grim satisfaction of seeing a well timed shell plough up the spot where we should have been but weren't!

Later on you got hardened; the war lost its novelty; you only saw the drudgery, the long weary routine and horror of horrors, you became afraid. There were some things we abhorred more than others and one was the usual night patrol in No Man's Land: it was sometimes done in the most scandalously slipshod manner. The number of fables about the state of the enemy line and as for wiring parties the less said about them the better, I loathe the sight of a barbed wire fence even yet. It required a very strong sense of duty and a very strong minded officer to convince the wiring party that the job must be finished.

But the worst job was the Outpost duty. There you were completely cut off for twenty four hours, and if the Boche took it in his head to raid you, then it was all up. Still you had served the purpose of warning the main line. Away among the marshes in the Valley of the Scarpe was a most hideous outpost called "F Post" the personnel of which had been spirited away on two previous occasions. It was meant to be the work of a man we nicknamed 'Adolf'. He knew the post was visited periodically and sometimes by British Staff officers (I don't think!), so he dressed himself up as an officer and took orders from him. The unsuspecting man turns around and Adolf's revolver covers him, the rest is very easy to imagine. By a cruel irony the officer in charge of the post was overlooked and left sleeping in a hole in the ground. He was eventually court-martialled and narrowly escaped the death penalty.

At first sight the place did not merit its unsavoury reputation and I quite enjoyed the first twenty four hours I spent in the post. But three days later I had another go and we'll I'm glad I'm here to write this article".

Conclusion

Throughout the period of the war, there was a massive effort involved in all those at Bablake, so the school had been less affected than might have been expected. The Old Boys, members of staff and the pupils employed all the resources possible to maintain a patriotic stance. The boys were employed in munitions manufacture, the Cadet Corps provided training for those about to embark on real military careers and the school grounds found multiple purposes including growing produce and cricket matches against wounded soldiers. *'The Wheatleyan'* was published throughout and was an essential medium for communication between the Old Boy network and those currently in the school.

All appeals for donations and assistance were met admirably, despite the hardships occurring at the time. Showing their allegiance to Coventry many of the boys enlisted in the city, having taken up residence and employment in the local industries, whilst others enlisted in the towns and cities where they were studying or employed. Old Boys who had emigrated enlisted locally and provided a notable contingent for the Australian and Canadian forces.

The Bablake Memorial is mounted on the wall at the rear of the assembly hall, where it was erected in 1921 and at the front of the hall the *'Roll of Honour'* is displayed in an unlocked glass box. With over 771 Old Boys serving and 96 of these losing their lives with the Forces, there was a tremendous sense of loss which can be felt even today by reading the names on the Memorial. The names of the fallen are not only commemorated at Bablake but also on other memorials locally as firms and churches dedicated memorials to fallen colleagues or members of the congregation who fell. Memorials which commemorate the Old Boys whether they are *'Rolls of Honour'* or inscriptions can also be found further afield.

The material in this book will no doubt be added to over the coming years as evidence is added of the fallen and those who served; with over 850 Old Boys in His Majesty's forces all aspects of the services were covered with men in the merchant navy, Royal Flying Corps & Royal Naval Air Service (later the RAF), Army and Royal Navy. The true number of Old Boys that served may never be known exactly but the fact remains that Bablake School did indeed *"send its full quota of men"*.

Appendix A

Alphabetical Roll of The Fallen   (96)

Those with no date of death could either not be found or evidence suggests that their names is recorded incorrectly. Those in italics are not fully verified.

Captain Arthur Joseph Adams	30th August 1918
Second Lieutenant Frederick Adams	12th May 1917
Captain Harold Meredyth Adcock	5th July 1916
Private Thomas Herbert Allchurch	2nd April 1918
Sergeant HarryAston	25th November 1914
Private Noel Raymond Averns	19th November 1916
Private Raymond Frederick John Averns	30th July 1918
Corporal Alfred Bailey	25th April 1915
Lance- Corporal Walter Bailey	23rd March 1918
Private David Barber	*26th February 1917*
Private George Norman Barber	*12th March 1917*
Sergeant George Edward Barker	23rd October 1914
Sergeant Henry Barker	23rd October 1914
Private Kenneth Barry	27th July 1916
Private William Charles Beacham	25th April 1918
Private Reginald Thomas Beaufoy	8th November 1918
Corporal George Cyril Biggs	14th July 1916
Gunner Vincent Arthur Bloxham	18th September 1917
Private Harold George Bonham	20th October 1918
Second Lieutenant Harold Masters Brown MC	9th July 1916
Private Edgar Herbert Buckingham	14th April 1918
Private Henry Buckland	2nd October 1917
Sergeant John Weston Burton	26th June 1916
Gunner Frederick Walter Caldicott	9th April 1917
Private Herbert Victor Cantrill	11th October 1918
Gunner Harry Clarke	3rd June 1917
Lance-Corporal Victor Leslie Clarke	3rd July 1918
Private Ambrose John Cole	27th May 1918
Gunner Herbert Charles Collingbourne	4th January 1916
Private James Connolly	7th May 1917
Pioneer Henry Amos Courts	4th August 1917
Private Francis Daulman Cox	26th November 1916
Second Lieutenant Francis Henry Cox	23rd October 1916
Lance- Sergeant Henry Smith Craven	6th March 1916

Lieutenant Frederick Hugh Dodson	27th April 1915
Second Lieutenant Reginald Kenneth Drakeley	11th April 1916
Sergeant Ernest Clifford Elliott	28th April 1918
Gunner Samuel James Elliott	17th May 1915
Boy 1st Class Henry Gordon Farmer	31st May 1916
Private Samuel Husselby Garrett	15th July1915
Able Seaman Frank Kenneth Greening	17th October 1917
Second Lieutenant Walter Ernest Grew	7th October 1917
Second Lieutenant James William Guise	19th August 1917
Private Henry Edwin Gunn	26th June 1918
Second Lieutenant Aubrey Frederick Hall	8th August 1918
Private Alfred Edward Harris	*5th February 1918*
Corporal Frederick Arthur Harris	28th April 1917
Private John Samuel Harris	16th June 1915
Corporal Herbert William Hawthorne	4th July 1918
Second Officer Sydney Charles Hitch	15th May 1917
Acting Captain Percy Hood Hollick	9th May 1917
Bombardier Charles John Hopkins	13th October 1915
Sergeant Joseph Howe MM	29th June 1918
Second Lieutenant Herbert William Hyde	17th May 1915
Second Lieutenant William Arthur Imber	27th August 1917
Gunner Charles John Jones	31st May 1916
Private Leslie Thomas Jones	4th November 1918
Lance Corporal William Percival Kirby	*1st July 1916*
Private Albert Knight	29th September 1918
Private William Alexander Loudon	28th March 1918
Captain Alfred Ernest Mander	9th October 1917
Second Lieutenant Matthew Frank Matts	24th July 1916
Gunner Alfred George Middleton	27th August 1916
Cadet Hubert Arthur Morley	27th October 1918
Private William Hubert Morris	25th September 1915
Second Lieutenant John Claude Murray	9th July 1916
Second Lieutenant Herbert Nelson	19th March 1918
Second Lieutenant Frank Nevey	12th October 1918
Captain Frank Septimus Neville	24th November 1917
Rifleman Hugh Conrad Pails	7th October 1916
Pioneer Herbert Joseph Payne	8th August 1915
Ordinary Seaman Alfred Oswald Peart	15th September 1917
Private Sydney Mornington Pickerill	23rd March 1918
Lieutenant Frederick James Poulton	2nd October 1917
Lance Corporal Leonard Joseph Walker Price	7th October 1916
Second Lieutenant William Alexander Roberts	31st July 1919

Bombardier Harold Eugene Rollason	11th April 1917
Private Joseph Edward Roots	6th October 1918
Private John William Rossiter	27th October 1914
Private Howard Round	25th July 1916
Second Lieutenant William John Salmons MM	22nd April 1918
Lance-Corporal Cecil Sidwell	30th January 1918
Private Wilfred Hibbert Sidwell	25th March 1917
Private John Spencer	2nd August 1918
Sergeant-Major Alfred James Suddens	21st March 1918
Sergeant William Toms	3rd July 1916
Sapper Harry Hassall Underwood	26th September 1915
2nd Lieutenant Frederick Charles Vincent DCM	21st March 1918
Second Lieutenant Bernard Michael Ward	20th November 1917
Private Sydney Frank Ward	25th August 1918
Lance-Sergeant Herbert Ward	19th July 1916
Private Frank William Wells	3rd October 1918
Gunner Arthur Whinfrey	4th October 1917
Sergeant J. A. White	
Private William Wilkins	4th May 1915
A. Wilkinson	
Lieutenant Sidney George Wolfe	22nd October 1917
CSM William Henry Croft Wood	25th July 1916
Second Lieutenant Frank Yardley	7th August 1917

Appendix B

Names of those who fell as they appear on the War Memorial

Adams, A. J.	Cox, F. H.	Nevey, F.
Adams, F.	Craven, H. S.	Neville, F.
Adcock, H. M.	Dodson, F.	Pails, H. C.
Allchurch, T.	Drakeley, R. K.	Payne, H. J.
Aston, H.	Elliott, E. C.	Peart, A. O
Averns, N. R.	Elliott, S. J.	Pickerill, S. M.
Averns, R. F. J	Farmer, H. G.	Poulton, F. J.
Bailey, A.	Garratt, H. S.	Price, L. J. W
Bailey, W. S.	Grew, W. E	Roberts, W. A.
Barber, D.	Guise, J	Rollason, H. E.
Barber, G. N.	Gunn, H. E.	Roots, J. E
Barker, G. E.	Hall, A. F.	Rossiter, J. W.
Barker, H. J.	Harris, F. A.	Round, H.
Barry, K.	Harris, J. S.	Salmons, W. J.
Beacham, W. C.	Hawthorne, H. W.	Sidwell, C.
Beaufoy, R. T.	Hitch, S. C.	Sidwell, W. H.
Biggs, G. C.	Hollick, P. H.	Spencer, J.
Bloxham, V. A.	Hopkins, C. J.	Suddens, A. J.
Bonham, H. G.	Howe, J.	Toms, W.
Brown, H. M.	Hyde, W. H.	Underwood, A.
Buckingham, E. H.	Imber, W. A.	Vincent, F.
Buckland, H.	Jones, C. J.	Ward, B.
Burton, J. W.	Jones, L. T.	Ward, F. S.
Caldicott, F. W.	Knight, A.	Ward, H.
Cantrill, H. V.	Loudon, W. A	Wells, F. W.
Clarke, H.	Mander, A. E	Whinfrey, A.
Clarke, V. L.	Matts, M. F.	White, J. A
Cole, A. J.	Middleton, A. G.	Wilkins, W.
Collingbourne, H. C.	Morley, A	Wilkinson, A.
Connolly, J.	Morris, H. W.	Wolfe, S. G.
Courts, A. H.	Murray, J. C.	Wood, C.
Cox, F. D.	Nelson, Herbert.	Yardley, F.

Appendix C

Those who Served

The following list has been derived from the editions of *'The Wheatleyan'* published from 1914 to 1919 and the names on the War Memorial (those in Bold). The details provided in some cases were minimal. The rank shown reflects that at the point the name appeared on the Roll of those who served and is not necessarily the rank the individual achieved during service. The year shown is the year the individual left Bablake.

1)	**J. Abberley**	1916	Royal Air Force
2)	**E. H. Adams**	1910	Warwickshire Royal Horse Artillery
3)	**H. G. Adams**	1911	Royal Field Artillery
4)	**J. L. Adams**		Westminster Dragoons
5)	**W. G. Adams**	1917	Hampshire Regiment
6)	**1ˢᵗ Officer L. C. Adkins**		Australian Fleet
7)	**C. J. Aldridge**	1910	4ᵗʰ South Midland Howitzer Brigade
8)	**L. H. Aldridge**	1911	4ᵗʰ South Midland Howitzer Brigade
9)	**L.V. Aldridge**		
10)	S. A. Aldridge	1904	Royal Garrison Artillery
11)	**S. Alexander**	1912	
12)	**E. J. Allcoat**	1906	London Territorials
13)	**Sergt. L. Allen MC**		7ᵗʰ Royal Warwicks
14)	**R. Allen**	1910	8ᵗʰ Royal Warwicks
15)	**T. Allit**		
16)	**F. Anderton**	1911	Somerset Light Infantry
17)	**C. Anelay**	1910	Royal Field Artillery
18)	**Gunner F. Anstey**	1909	Royal Horse Artillery
19)	**W. J. Anstey**		
20)	**H.E Archer**		
21)	**Armfield**	1909	Suffolk Regiment
22)	**G. Arnold**		Royal Fusiliers
23)	**W. Arnold**	1903	7ᵗʰ Royal Warwicks
24)	**J. G. Arthur**		
25)	**A. Asbury**		
26)	**J. F. Asbury**		
27)	**C. Ashbourne**		Royal Horse Artillery
28)	**Lt. P. Ashford**	1902	Royal Horse Artillery
29)	**G. H. Askew**	1912	4ᵗʰ South Midland Howitzer Brigade
30)	**H. Atkins**		

31)	**2nd Lt. G. Atkinson**	Staff	Pioneer, Royal Engineers
32)	**F. Attenborough**	1900	Australian Artillery
33)	**R. N. S. Aveline**		7th London Regiment
34)	R. L. Averns	1914	Royal Fusiliers
35)	**T. Bachelor**	1914	1st Somerset Light Infantry
36)	**C. W. Baker DCM**		
37)	**E. H. Ball**	1910	Royal Fusiliers
38)	**C. R. Banning MM**	1916	Royal Lancashire Regiment
39)	**A. C. Bannington**	1887	Royal Field Artillery
40)	**B. Barker**		
41)	**F. W. Barker**	1901	Australians
42)	P. Barker	1910	
43)	**H. Barnacle**	1907	Royal Warwicks
44)	**F. L. Barnett**	1916	Royal Warwicks
45)	**K. Barry**		
46)	**W. Barton**		
47)	**W. H. Batchelor**	1881	7th Royal Warwicks
48)	**J. J. Bates**		
49)	**S. Bayliss**	1907	Royal Engineers
50)	**H. G .Beacham**		Royal Warwicks
51)	**Sgt. G. Bean**		Royal Engineers
52)	**H. W. Beaumont**	1910	10th Warwick Imperial Yeomanry
53)	**L. A. Beaumont**		
54)	**G. Beesley**	1902	55th Battalion Australians
55)	**E. Bell**		
56)	**R. Betts**		
57)	**T. Bickley**	1907	Royal Garrison Artillery
58)	**P. Bidmead**	1901	Middlesex Hussars
59)	**J. H. Biggs**	1909	Royal Engineers
60)	**R. G. Bird**	1905	HMS Weymouth
61)	**A. O. Black**	1904	7th Royal Warwicks
62)	**J. Blackwell**	1901	Royal Naval Air Service
63)	**W. Blackwell**	1901	Royal Naval Air Service
64)	**E. J. Blakemore MC**	1907	7th Royal Warwicks
65)	**J. D. Blakemore**	1910	7th Royal Warwicks
66)	**L. Blakemore**		
67)	**T. Blakemore**	1910	Royal Field Artillery
68)	**Bland**		
69)	**J.H. Blundell**		
70)	**E. Bolton**	1911	7th Royal Warwicks
71)	**A. T. Bonham**		
72)	**A. C. Boon**	1903	Oxford and Bucks Light Infantry

73)	H. Borsley		
74)	A. Bowen		
75)	H. Bowley		
76)	Bromley		
77)	B. Bromwich		Worcester Yeomanry
78)	H. Brook		
79)	G. Brooker		
80)	Brown		
81)	F. H. P. Brown		
82)	J. Brown	1914	Royal Warwicks
83)	W. Brown	1907	Army Service Corps
84)	Lce Corp W. Brown	1917	Gloucester Regiment
85)	B. Browning		
86)	A. Buckland	1894	13th Royal Warwicks
87)	F. A. Buckler		Royal Berkshire Regiment
88)	R. H. Buckley		
89)	C. Burberry		
90)	W. Burdett	1909	Howitzers
91)	R. Burns	1908	Royal Naval Reserve, Mersey Division
92)	S. Burns		
93)	A. Burr	1913	Royal Garrison Artillery
94)	H. W. Bush		Royal Flying Corps
95)	E. Butts	1913	Royal Engineers
96)	F. Butts		
97)	P. G. Campion	1913	7th Royal Warwicks
98)	A. E. Canning		
99)	H. Cantrill		
100)	L. Cantrill	1913	Naval Despatch Rider
101)	M. Carpenter		
102)	G. Carter	1899	Royal Navy
103)	T. Carter	1911	Royal Field Artillery
104)	A. Catlin		
105)	C. W. Chapman	1911	7th Royal Warwicks
106)	A. E. Charleton	1909	Royal Engineers
107)	E. Checkley		
108)	A. Clarke	1911	3rd Oxford and Bucks Light Infantry
109)	A. W. Clarke		HMS Indus V
110)	J. Clarke	1890	HMS Highflyer
111)	W. E. Clarke	1914	Royal Army Medical Corps
112)	W. Clews		
113)	A. G. A. Clowes		Canadian Contingent
114)	W. J. Cole		7th Royal Warwicks

115)	**W. Coleman MC**	1908	Warwickshire Yeomanry
116)	**F. W. Colledge**	1912	3rd Royal Warwicks
117)	**W. Colledge**	1910	Royal Engineers
118)	**W. Collet**	1910	Australian Contingent
119)	**F. Collier**	1908	Royal Fusiliers
120)	**S. Collier**		
121)	**J. H. Collingbourne**	1912	Royal FieldArtillery
122)	**J. Collis**	1912	HM Submarine B.D
123)	**H. Comley**	1909	Royal Army Medical Corps
124)	**L. Comley**		
125)	**R. A. Comley**	1907	Royal Horse Artillery
126)	**R. Coombes DCM**	1911	4th South Midland Howitzer Brigade
127)	**H. H. Cooper**		
128)	**R. Cooper**		
129)	**2nd Lt T. C. Copson**	1898	Royal Naval Air Service
130)	**F. Core MSM**	Staff	Machine Gun Corps
131)	**G. W. Cosby**	1895	Leeds City Battalion
132)	**J. D. Cousins**	1911	Warwickshire Imperial Yeomanry
133)	F. Cox	1907	Artists' Rifles
134)	**H. A. Cox**	1904	Royal Army Medical Corps
135)	**Qrtr Mr Sgt T. E. Cox**		Royal Canadian Garrison Artillery
136)	**G. Coxhill**		Royal Field Artillery
137)	**Crane**		
138)	**H. Cure**	1913	15th Hussars (King's Own)
139)	**A. G. Curtis**	1900	Leicester Yeomanry
140)	**A. W. Curtis**		Royal Garrison Artillery
141)	**F. H. E. Curtis**		Army Service Corps
142)	**H. Darlinson**		
143)	**H. Daulman**		Warwickshire Imperial Yeomanry
144)	**P. Daulman**		Warwickshire Imperial Yeomanry
145)	**E. Davenport**		Warwickshire Imperial Yeomanry
146)	**W. Davenport**		Royal Field Artillery
147)	**F. Davies**	1906	Royal Garrison Artillery
148)	**Percy Davies**		7th Royal Warwicks
149)	**W. L. Davies**	1904	Royal Army Medical Corps
150)	**A. W. Davis**		
151)	**G. Davis**		
152)	**L. Davis**		
153)	H. Day		Royal Warwicks
154)	**W. W. Day**	1900	HMS Woolwich (Yeoman of Signals)
155)	**E. O. Denyer**		
156)	**J. G. Denyer**		

157)	W. T. Denyer		
158)	F. Dewis	1904	Royal Engineers
159)	G. W. W. Dickens	1910	10th Medical Staff Corps
160)	G. E. Docker		
161)	2nd Lt F. J. Doherty	1913	Birmingham City Battalion
162)	T. Dolphin	1910	Royal Army Medical Corps
163)	L. Donald		
164)	W. J. Douglas	1908	Royal Army Medical Corps
165)	A. R. Drakeford		HMS Revenge
166)	P. D. Drinkwater		Royal Horse Artillery
167)	A. F. S. Driver		
168)	T. H. Dunn		
169)	N. C. Eabry		
170)	R. Eames		
171)	E. W. Earby	1908	Grenadiers
172)	H. Eaves	1906	Royal Air Force
173)	N. C. Eborall	1913	Royal Field Artillery
174)	T. Eden		Royal Marine Artillery
175)	C. Elkington		18th Hussars
176)	J. A. Elliot	1899	2nd Company, Coldstream Guards
177)	G. L. Elsey	1913	Royal Army Medical Corps
178)	F. H. Elson		
179)	C. W. Elvis	1910	Royal Horse Artillery
180)	J. Embling		
181)	H. Endicott	1912	Royal Army Medical Corps
182)	G. Ensor		Leicester Light Infantry
183)	T. Enstone		
184)	A. E. Evans		
185)	Lt. S. J. D. Evans		Canadian Light Infantry
186)	W. C. Farndon		Army Pay Corps
187)	QMS E. J. Farren	1897	North Mounted Brigade T.A.S.C
188)	N. C. Farren		Royal Engineers
189)	G. F. Fells	1914	Royal Warwicks
190)	A. W. Fennell	1906	Motor Machine Gun Service
191)	W. G. Fennell	1912	7th Welsh Regiment
192)	A. Fewkes		
193)	G. B. Fewkes		
194)	Lce Cpl R. H. Fish	1909	8th Royal Warwicks
195)	M. B. Fitzgerald MBE	1899	Royal Flying Corps
196)	Cpl C. H. Fletcher	1909	10th Middlesex
197)	C. L. Fletcher	1910	Warwickshire Imperial Yeomanry
198)	Reg. Fletcher	1911	Royal Horse Artillery

199)	**F. L. Flinn**	1909	Royal Engineers
200)	**R. Forster**	1909	15th Hussars
201)	**C. J. Foster**	1903	Royal Field Artillery
202)	**R. Foster**	1907	8th Royal Warwicks
203)	A. Fowkes	1911	Canadian Contingent
204)	C. B. Fowkes	1911	Canadian Contingent
205)	**H. Fox**		New Zealand Expeditionary Force
206)	**J. Fox**		
207)	**F. C. Franklin**	1910	Warwick Royal Horse Artillery
208)	**F. W. Franklin**	1907	Royal Horse Artillery
209)	**E. G. Freeman**	1903	7th Royal Warwicks
210)	**H. Freeman**		
211)	**W. J. French**	1909	Warwickshire Yeomanry
212)	**J. S. Gardener**	1907	Despatch Rider, Machine Gun Section
213)	**H. Garlick**	1907	7th Royal Warwicks
214)	**H. S. Garratt**		Northumberland Fusiliers
215)	**T. Garratt**	1916	Royal Naval Volunteer Reserve
216)	**W. S. Garratt**		
217)	A. Garrett	1910	Oxford and Bucks Light Infantry
218)	**D. Gee MC**		
219)	**W. George**	1914	Motor Machine Gun Section
220)	**Gibson**		Royal Flying Corps
221)	**J. W. Glenn**		7th Royal Warwicks
222)	**W. H. Goddard**	1912	Public School Corps, Royal Fusiliers
223)	**A. G. Goldie**	1906	7th Royal Warwicks
224)	**J. Goldie**		
225)	**A. Gould MC, DSO**	1895	Royal Engineers
226)	**F. A. Goulding**	1908	New Zealand
227)	**J. M. Gourace**	1894	Royal Navy
228)	**C. Gray**	1902	Motor Transport, Army Service Corps
229)	**A. H. Green**		
230)	**J. Green**	1899	Honourable Artillery Company.
231)	**A. Greenway**	1914	Motor Transport, Army Service Corps
232)	**F. Greenway**		Royal Navy
233)	**L. Greenway**		Royal Air Force
234)	**J. W. Greenwood**		
235)	**F. J. Grew**		Engine Room Artificer
236)	**R. R. Grindley**		
237)	**A. Grose**		
238)	J. Guise	1913	4th Royal Warwicks
239)	**Horace Gunn**	1912	HMS Erin
240)	**A. Gunner**	1909	Royal Field Artillery

241)	**G. Hack**		
242)	**R. Haddock**		Engine Room Artificer, Royal Navy
243)	A. Hall	1911	Royal Engineers
244)	**C. Hall**	1910	Naval Brigade
245)	**M. Hall**		
246)	**O. Hall**	1909	
247)	P. Hall	1889	Royal Warwicks
248)	**V. Hall**		
249)	**A. S. Halladay**	1914	Royal Engineers
250)	**P. Halladay**	1887	Army Service Corps
251)	F. Halliwell	1906	Royal Army Medical Corps
252)	**T. Halliwell**		
253)	**V. Hambling**	1913	Royal Army Medical Corps
254)	**B. Hamilton**		Royal Field Artillery
255)	**A. Hammond**	1914	Royal Field Artillery
256)	**D. W. Handow**		
257)	**H. Hands**	1906	Army Service Corps
258)	**P. H. Hanson**		Royal Army Medical Corps
259)	**J. T. Hargreaves**	1901	19th Alberta Dragoons
260)	**S. R. Hargreaves**	1900	Army Service Corps
261)	**2nd Lt G. F. H. Harker**	1916	3rd Manchester Regiment
262)	**C. Harper**		Australian Contingent
263)	**F. Harper**		2nd Australian Contingent
264)	Corpl. A. E Harris	1910	Army Corps
265)	A. E. Harris	1913	Oxford and Bucks Light Infantry
266)	**T. Harris**	1906	Royal Field Artillery
267)	**W. W. Harris**	1915	Royal Naval Air Service
268)	S. B. Hart		Royal Navy
269)	**Hassall**		6th Canadians
270)	E. Haves	1905	21st Surrey Rifles
271)	**H. A. Hawley**		
272)	**H. Hawthorne**		
273)	**F. Hayes**		
274)	**E. Hazeley**	1914	Motor Machine Gun Section
275)	**A. Hazlewood**		11th Hussars
276)	**J. Hazlewood**		Army Service Corps
277)	E. Heape	1910	Royal Engineers
278)	**S. Heape**	1910	Royal Engineers
279)	**A. D. Hegan**	1913	Royal Flying Corps
280)	**F. L. Hegan**	1904	Royal Army Medical Corps
281)	G. Hegan	1917	Royal Flying Corps
282)	**H. Hegan**	1908	Machine Gun Battalion, RFA

283)	**R. Hegan**	1910	7th Battalion Royal Warwicks
284)	**Sgt. W. Hegan**	1900	3rd Royal Warwicks
285)	**W. G. Hegan**		Royal Flying Corps
286)	**A. Hewitt**		
287)	**W. Hewitt**	1910	7th Royal Warwicks
288)	**R. J. Hibbert**	1910	4th South Midland Howitzer Brigade
289)	**F. Hickley**	1910	8th Royal Warwicks
290)	**H. Hickley**	1909	7th Royal Warwicks
291)	**H. E. Hickley**	1910	7th Royal Warwicks
292)	**Wm. Hill**	1913	Royal Fusiliers
293)	**E. A. Hiorns**		HMS Indus V
294)	**E. Hirons**		
295)	**Cpl N. W. Hitchens**	1913	Royal Field Artillery
296)	**R. Hitchcocks**	1911	Royal Army Medical Corps
297)	**Bdr. H. E . H. Hobley**	1907	Royal Horse Artillery
298)	**Sgt. J. W. Hobley**	1904	4th South Midland Howitzer Brigade
299)	**Lt. B. Holden**	1910	Royal Field Artillery
300)	H. Holland		Army Service Corps
301)	**J. Holt**		
302)	**H. G. Horsley**	1917	Royal Flying Corps
303)	**F. C. Horton**	1901	Warwickshire Imperial Yeomanry
304)	H. J. Horton	1896	Canadian Contingent
305)	**J. A. Horton**		
306)	**J. K. Horton**	1910	7th Royal Warwicks
307)	**S. J. Horton**	1898	Canadian Contingent
308)	Hough		
309)	**F. Howe**	1907	8th Royal Warwicks
310)	Jos. Howe	1913	Hussars
311)	**L. A. Hoyle**		Royal Air Force
312)	**C. C. Hoyte**	1912	Warwickshire Imperial Yeomanry
313)	J. Hoyte	1912	Royal Navy
314)	**W. C. Hubbard**		
315)	**J. Hudson**	1914	Royal Garrison Artillery
316)	**L. M. Hudson**		
317)	**N. Hughes**	1909	Royal Horse Artillery
318)	**S. R. Hughes**		23rd London Regiment
319)	**S. F. Huffadine**		
320)	**S. Hulme MC**	1912	4th South Midland Howitzer Brigade
321)	**2 Lt. J. Humberstone**	1895	Royal Field Artillery
322)	**J. P. Humberstone**	1905	3rd Canadians
323)	**T. L. Humberstone**		
324)	**F. Hunt**	1909	Oxford and Bucks Light Infantry

325)	C. Hyde	1907	Army Service Corps
326)	E. Hyde	1901	Army Service Corps
327)	H. Hyde	1911	Royal Field Artillery
328)	H. W. Hyde		
329)	Lce Cpl J. W. Hyde	1905	10th Royal Warwicks
330)	N. A. Imber	1910	Kings Royal Rifles
331)	A. L. Ireson	1913	Royal Field Artillery
332)	C. E. Ireson	1910	Canadian Light Infantry
333)	J. W. Ireson		
334)	Sgt. F. Jackson	1903	Army Corps
335)	Sgt. H. W. Jackson	1897	St. Johns Ambulance Brigade
336)	J. T. Jackson	1917	Grenadier Guards
337)	F. James	1909	4th South Midland Howitzer Brigade
338)	Captain W. J. Jarrad	1893	West Yorks
339)	H. Jarvis		Duke Of Cornwall's Light Infantry
340)	A. R. Jeffrey		7th Royal Warwicks
341)	H. L. Jeffrey	1907	Army Pay Corps
342)	W. Jeffries		
343)	G. A. Johnson	1910	Royal Field Artillery
344)	P. Johnson	1910	
345)	R. M. Johnson		
346)	H. T. Jones	1906	Australian Contingent
347)	L. Jones	1906	Australian Contingent
348)	S. Jones		5th Rifle Brigade
349)	W. Jones	1895	Royal Navy
350)	Art.Engr W. Jones	1896	Royal Navy
351)	W. B. Jones	1911	12th Signal Company, Royal Engineers
352)	Wm. Jones	1915	Royal Air Force
353)	H. Jordan	1910	Grenadier Guards
354)	H. Jordan	1912	Household Battalion
355)	W. Judd		
356)	A. T. Judge		
357)	G. L. Judge		
358)	2nd Lt L. E. Kalker	1908	Royal Warwicks
359)	H. Kelly		
360)	L. J. Kelsey	1910	8th Royal Warwicks
361)	A. Kemp		Royal Army Medical Corps
362)	B. Kemp		Royal Warwicks
363)	G. Kendrick	1914	3rd Royal Warwicks
364)	H. Kenworthy		Canadians
365)	Corp. H. King	1915	Royal Engineers
366)	2nd Lt W. King		Royal Field Artillery

367)	**W. Kings**	1907	Royal Engineers
368)	**Cpl J. H. Kirk**	1907	Warwickshire Imperial Yeomanry
369)	**H. Knight**		
370)	Cpl L. Knight	1910	Canadian Contingent
371)	**Slr C. H. Lawrence**	Staff	Royal Field Artillery
372)	**N. Laxon**		Royal Army Medical Corps
373)	**H. Lee**		Canadian Contingent
374)	**L. Lee**		
375)	**A. E. Leeson**	1909	Warwickshire Yeomanry
376)	**J. Leeson**		Royal Naval Air Service
377)	**D. A. E. Lewin**		
378)	**W. H. Lewis**	1907	R. G. R
379)	**C. B. Liggins**		Army Service Corps
380)	**F. C. Lindon**	1912	11th Hussars
381)	**A. J. Linnett**		3rd Royal Warwicks
382)	**I. J. Linnett**	1913	Motor Machine Gun Section
383)	**N. Linnett**	1910	Royal Army Medical Corps
384)	**A. Lloyd**		
385)	**F. H. Lloyd**	1902	20th Hussars
386)	**H. Lloyd**		
387)	**W. Long**		Royal Army Medical Corps
388)	W. Lord		Army Service Corps
389)	**D. Loudon**		
390)	**Lough**		
391)	**W. J. B. Lowe**	1909	Royal Army Medical Corps
392)	**C. E Lucas**		C. S. Rifles
393)	**G. H. Luckman**		
394)	**W. A. Luckman**		
395)	**W. Lynch**		
396)	**A. J. Macdonald**		
397)	**Corpl S. Makepeace**		Royal Warwicks
398)	**2nd Lt. P. G. Mander**	1896	4th West Riding Regiment
399)	**C. Mann**		
400)	**E. Mann**		
401)	**SM W. J. Marriott**	1907	Royal Field Artillery
402)	**T. F. Marsden**		Warwickshire Imperial Yeomanry
403)	E. Martin	1916	Royal Engineers
404)	**F. Martin**	1901	Army Service Corps
405)	**S. Martin**		
406)	T. Martin	1911	7th Royal Warwicks
407)	**F. Mason**		
408)	L. Mason	1911	4th South Midland Howitzer Brigade

409)	**2nd Lt G. Masters**	1910	14th Sherwood Foresters
410)	**G. Masters**		
411)	**W. L. Masters**		
412)	**E. C. Matthews**		
413)	**F. Mattocks**		
414)	F. R. Matts	1906	7th Royal Warwicks
415)	**J. Mayo**		
416)	**W. Mayo**		
417)	A. McCutchion	1903	Royal West Kent
418)	**H. McCutchion**		
419)	**J. McKennon**	1912	Royal Navy
420)	**W. McKnight**		
421)	**E. McLauchlan**	1912	7th Royal Warwicks
422)	**M. Megainey**		
423)	**2nd Lt. A. A. Miles**	1910	11th Royal Warwicks
424)	**F. Mills MM**	1903	Royal Engineers
425)	**G. Mills**		Royal Field Artillery
426)	**H. Mills**		Royal Army Medical Corps
427)	**S. Mills**		
428)	T. Mills		HMS Indefatigable
429)	F. A. Mole		Royal Flying Corps
430)	**J. Montgomery**	1909	Army Service Corps
431)	**E. Moore**		Royal Field Artillery
432)	**2nd Lt. G. W. Moore**	1910	13th Royal Warwicks
433)	**H. Moore**	1916	Honourable Artillery Company
434)	**L. Moore**		Royal Field Artillery
435)	**2nd Lt. R. E. Moore**	1903	4th South Midland Howitzer Brigade
436)	**Captain F. L. Morgan**	Staff	
437)	2nd Lt. L. Morgan	1908	6th Royal Warwicks
438)	**H. Morley**		
439)	**W. F. Morris**		Kings Royal Rifles
440)	**T. Mortin**	1911	7th Royal Warwicks
441)	**F. Mortlock**	1913	24th Middlesex
442)	**A. H. Moseley**	1911	Royal Field Artillery
443)	**C. C. Mountney**		
444)	**J. C. Mycock**		
445)	R. Nauen	1914	36th Middlesex
446)	**2nd Lt. N. Naylor**	1913	Shropshire Light Infantry
447)	C. Neale	1911	4th South Midland Howitzer Brigade
448)	F. Neale	1910	Army Service Corps
449)	**W. B. Neale**		
450)	**Harry L. Nelson**		

451)	**Horace Nelson**		
452)	**Hugh Nelson**		
453)	**S. L. Nelson**		
454)	**H. Nettleton**	1916	Royal Navy
455)	**J. A. Newbold**		
456)	2ⁿᵈ Lt. John Newman		
457)	**J. E. Newman**	1910	4th Coldstream Guards
458)	**W. H. Newman**	1904	4th Coldstream Guards
459)	**H. B. Nicholls**	1911	Royal Army Medical Corps
460)	**J. W. Nicholls**		Warwickshire Imperial Yeomanry
461)	**T. Nicholls**	1906	4th Coldstream Guards
462)	**Sgt.Major Nixon**	1904	
463)	**F. W. Noble**		
464)	**F. Norbury**		
465)	**W. Norbury**		
466)	**S. T. Norton**	1898	Canadians
467)	**G. Okell**	1910	Royal Field Artillery
468)	**T. Okell**	1909	Royal Garrison Artillery
469)	P. Oldham		
470)	**W. Oldham**		15th London Regiment
471)	**Jas. Oliver**		
472)	**2ⁿᵈ Lt T. Oliver**	1916	Gloucester Regiment
473)	**J. Olorenshaw**	1917	92 Trench Mortar Battery
474)	2ⁿᵈ Lt J. T. Olorenshaw		Royal Flying Corps
475)	**A. Ord**		
476)	**G. A. Ormerod**	1909	Motor Transport Army Service
477)	**R. Ormerod**	1911	4th South Midland Howitzer Brigade,
478)	**G. Orton**	1914	Royal Warwicks
479)	**C. Osborne**		Royal Flying Corps, OTC
480)	**A. J. Oswin**		
481)	**T. Pallett**		Warwickshire Imperial Yeomanry
482)	**A. J. Palmer OBE**		Motor Machine Gun Service, RFA
483)	**B. H. Parker**	1910	Royal Engineers
484)	G. Parker		Royal Navy Volunteer Reserve
485)	**G. Parkes**	1910	Royal Army Medical Corps
486)	G. Parkes		Royal Military Academy, Woolwich
487)	**H. Parnell**		Royal Army Medical Corps
488)	S. Parnell		Royal Garrison Artillery
489)	**J. Parsons MC**	1905	Warwickshire Imperial Yeomanry
490)	**F. Paton**		
491)	**F. Paul**	1903	7th Royal Warwicks
492)	**C. F. W. Payne**	1897	Royal Engineers

493)	E. B. Payne	1905	Royal Engineers
494)	F. Payne	1902	7th Royal Warwicks
495)	K. J. Payne	1900	7th Royal Warwicks
496)	E. F. Peak	1904	Royal Field Artillery
497)	F. W. Pearce	1910	7th Royal Warwicks
498)	G. Pears	1909	3rd Hussars Reserves
499)	Sgt. Maj. A. Pearson	1900	1st Canadians
500)	F. H. Pearson	Staff	Royal Field Artillery
501)	J. Pearson		
502)	R. Pearson		Royal Navy
503)	E. F. Peek	1904	Field Artillery
504)	A. R. Pemberton		
505)	2nd Lt C. C. Penn		Royal Horse Artillery
506)	J. L. Penn	1906	Warwickshire Imperial Yeomanry
507)	L. Pepper	1910	Royal Navy
508)	E. Perkin		
509)	S. C. Perkins		
510)	G. Peters		Royal Army Medical Corps
511)	J. Peters		Royal Naval Air Service
512)	C. W. Phillips	1912	Queen's Westminster
513)	L. Phillips		
514)	R. H. Phillips		
515)	A. A. Pickering	1896	Royal Engineers
516)	Pilkington		
517)	A. A. Pilkington	1914	Royal Field Artillery
518)	H. W. Pilkington	1911	4th South Midland Howitzer Brigade
519)	A. Pinfold	1907	Royal Engineers
520)	A. Pitt	1911	88th Canadians
521)	A. B. Plant		
522)	E. J. Player	1916	Worcester Yeomanry
523)	Sapper F. E. Player		Canadian Engineers
524)	G. Poole	1911	Army Ordnance Corps
525)	G. Poole		Royal Engineers
526)	N. J. Poole		
527)	R. J. Porter		
528)	H. Powell		London Regiment
529)	P. Powney	1913	Royal Army Medical Corps
530)	W. Powney		
531)	A. J. Poxon		
532)	S. Poxon MM		Royal Engineers
533)	C. Pratt	1908	Royal Engineers
534)	S. Pratt	1911	19th Hussars

535)	**2nd Lt E. C. Prattley**	1916	Norfolk Regiment
536)	R. G. Prattley		HMS Indus V
537)	**T. L. Prentice**		
538)	**A. Pritchard**		
539)	H. Pritchard		Army Service Corps
540)	**F. Proctor**	1907	Royal Field Artillery
541)	**H. Proctor**	1910	Royal Navy
542)	**F. Purcell**	1896	East Kent Regiment
543)	**S. L. Purnell**		Royal Army Medical Corps
544)	**F. Putnam**	1908	Royal Engineers
545)	T. Quinney	1906	Royal Engineers
546)	**W. J. Raby**		4th South Midland Howitzer Brigade
547)	**H. A. Randle**	1910	Royal Engineers
548)	**J. H. Ravenhall**		
549)	**F. Reade**		
550)	**Sgt L. Reade**		12th Royal Warwicks
551)	**P. H. Redfern**	1911	7th Royal Warwicks
552)	**H. C. Rees**	1914	Wiltshire Regiment
553)	**P. G. Reeves**	1911	Royal Fusiliers
554)	**A. W. Reid**		
555)	**A. Reynolds**	1910	Warwick Royal Horse Artillery
556)	**R. Reynolds MSM**	1904	Motor Cycle Corps
557)	W. G. Rhodes	1900	Royal Flying Corps
558)	**Sgt R. V. Richards**	1904	Motor Machine Gun Service
559)	**H. Richardson**	1900	Australians
560)	**F. Richmond**		
561)	**Lt C. J. Ridley**	1894	Army Service Corps
562)	A. Rigby		Royal Navy
563)	**H. Rigby**		
564)	**H. Rigby**		
565)	H. Rigley		London Territorials
566)	**F. S. Roberts**	1913	Royal Flying Corps
567)	**J. E. Roberts**		Army Service Corps
568)	**R. Roberts**	1915	Royal Air Force
569)	**G. P. Robertson**	1912	Scots Grey
570)	**G. Robinson**		Scots Grey
571)	**J. E. Roots**		
572)	**E. S. Rose**	1908	4th South Midland Howitzer Brigade
573)	**J. R. Rose**	1904	Royal Fusiliers
574)	**W. G. Rose**		
575)	**A. Rossiter**		7th Royal Warwicks
576)	**F. Round**		

577)	**G. Round**		
578)	**W. P. Rowley**	1903	Army Service Corps
579)	**C. A. Roxburgh**	1915	Gordon Highlanders
580)	**Royle**		
581)	**R. Sadler**	1903	7th Royal Warwicks
582)	**E. Sage**		Royal Warwicks
583)	E. Sage	1914	Royal Air Force
584)	**W. Sage**	1908	Royal Army Medical Corps
585)	**R. Salsbury**		Royal Navy
586)	**H. Sammons**	1910	Warwickshire Royal Horse Artillery
587)	**T. Sammons**	1910	Royal Horse Artillery
588)	**A. Sanders**	1915	Royal Flying Corps
589)	**R. J. Sanders**		
590)	**W. H. Sanders**		
591)	**A. Santy**	1911	Royal Engineers
592)	**2nd Lt H. Scovell**	1914	Royal Flying Corps
593)	**A. Seggie**	1913	Royal Flying Corps
594)	**Corpl. L. E. Sexton**	1901	13th Hussars
595)	**L. Sharlot**	1914	Royal Engineers
596)	**F. W. D. Sharp**	1916	Army Service Corps, Motor Transport
597)	**Corpl J. E. Sharp**	1907	2nd Coldstream Guards
598)	**W. Sharpe**		
599)	**W. E. Sharpe**		
600)	**V. Sharpless**	1911	3rd Worcester Regiment
601)	**Sgt. A. Sheffield**	1897	Warwickshire Imperial Yeomanry
602)	**A. E. Shelley**		Royal Engineers
603)	**H. J. Shelley**		
604)	**2nd Lt. J. Shelley**	1899	
605)	**Wm. Shelley**		Motor Transport
606)	**F. H. Shephard**	1891	7th Cheshire Regiment
607)	**W. Shortridge DCM**	1906	16th Signal Company, Royal Engineers
608)	**A. L. Shuttleworth**		Royal Field Artillery
609)	**W. L. Shuttleworth**		
610)	**A. Sidney**	1909	Naval Despatch Rider
611)	**E. Sidwell**	1909	London Rifles
612)	**F. Sidwell**	1904	Royal Naval Aviation Service
613)	**Srgt. F. W. Simmons**	1903	101st Edmonton Fusiliers
614)	**O. Simmons**		3rd Royal Warwicks
615)	**S. Simmons**		Royal Garrison Artillery
616)	**C. Slade**	1915	7th Royal Warwicks
617)	**L. Slade**		
618)	L. Slater	1907	Royal Horse Artillery

619)	**A. Slinn**		Tanks
620)	**A. H. Smart**	1914	Royal Horse Guards
621)	**A. Smith**		
622)	**C. I. Smith**		
623)	**D. Smith**	1912	9th Royal Warwicks
624)	**F. Smith**	1896	Inns of Court
625)	**F. R. Smith**		
626)	**H. Smith**	1897	Royal Flying Corps
627)	**H. Smith**	1911	Warwickshire Yeomanry
628)	**J. E. Smith**		12th Cheshire
629)	**J. R. Smith**	1912	Royal Navy, Royal Engineers
630)	**2nd Lt. Jas. Smith**		19th Royal Fusiliers
631)	**2nd Lt. Jos. Smith**	1911	3rd Royal Field Artillery
632)	**Reg. Smith**	1905	9th Royal Warwicks
633)	**R. G. A. Smith**	1905	4th South Midland Howitzer Brigade
634)	**R. F. Smith**	1905	9th Royal Warwicks
635)	**Sergt. S. Smith**	1907	4th South Midland Howitzer Brigade
636)	**Sgt. T. Smith**	1907	7th Royal Warwicks
637)	**T. Smout**	1913	Despatch Rider, RNAS
638)	**Eric Smythe**	1912	7th Royal Warwicks
639)	**Ernest Smythe**		
640)	G. Smythe	1911	HMS Empress of Russia
641)	**2nd.Lt S. Snape**		Royal Warwicks
642)	**H. B. Sparkes**	1912	10th Battalion Middlesex Regiment
643)	**F. Spencer**		
644)	**W. H. Spicer**	1906	Warwickshire Imperial Yeomanry
645)	**A. W. Spooner**		
646)	A. E. Stain	1904	St. Johns Ambulance Hospital
647)	**T. H. Stain**	1905	Motor Transport
648)	**Sapper J. Starley**	1909	Royal Engineers
649)	**E. G. Statham**	1908	Royal Horse Artillery
650)	**W. Statham**		
651)	**B. Steane**		
652)	**T. Stevens**		7th Royal Warwicks
653)	A. Stewart	1905	Royal Army Medical Corps
654)	**W. Stewart**		
655)	**H. E. Stockwin**		Royal Naval Air Service
656)	**M. N. Stockwin**		
657)	**H. E. Storer MC**	1905	12th Royal Warwicks
658)	**J. Storer**	1909	7th Royal Warwicks
659)	**W. Storer**	1905	Army Service Corps
660)	**F. Stringer**		Royal Naval Reserve

661)	H. Stringer		Royal Naval Air Service
662)	R. Stringer		Royal Naval Reserve
663)	H. V. C. Such	1911	7th Royal Warwicks
664)	Corpl H. T. Suddens	1910	Oxford and Bucks Light Infantry
665)	W. Sutherland	1913	Oxford and Bucks Light Infantry
666)	C. Swallow	1909	7th Royal Warwicks
667)	W. Swallow		
668)	A. Tatlow		
669)	W. Tatlow		RAMC Australian Contingent
670)	E. Taylor		
671)	G. E. Taylor		HMS Empress of India
672)	S. S. Taylor	1912	Oxford and Bucks Light Infantry
673)	L. G. Tebbutt	1908	7th Royal Warwicks
674)	2nd.Lt V. Tebbutt	1908	7th Royal Warwicks
675)	G. Tee	1914	Oxford and Bucks Light Infantry
676)	C. Teryne		
677)	A. J. Tew		Royal Field Artillery
678)	Guy Thomas	1908	Army Service Corps
679)	W.C.V. Thomas	Staff	12th Welch Regiment
680)	E. Tideswell	1910	Royal Naval Air Service
681)	A. Tipler	1915	29th Royal Fusiliers
682)	Sgt. H. Tomkins	1900	1st Royal Warwicks
683)	C. S. Tongue		
684)	L. Tongue		
685)	F. Townsend	1906	Royal Field Artillery
686)	G. U. W Townsend		
687)	C Pty Off. G. Tozer	1910	Royal Navy
688)	J. Tuck	1918	Royal Naval Reserve, HMS Mercury
689)	N. P. Tuck	1916	Royal Air Force
690)	A. P. Tuckley	1906	Royal Navy
691)	B. C. Tuckley		
692)	H. Tunstall		
693)	E. Tutton	1912	Warwickshire Imperial Yeomanry
694)	W. E. Twamley	1914	Royal Flying Corps
695)	2nd Lt. E. Tyler	1917	Royal Flying Corps
696)	2nd Lt. L. Tyler	1909	Royal Engineers
697)	G. Vanstone	1912	Royal Fusiliers
698)	T. Venn	1916	Royal Air Force
699)	A. S. Vickers	1916	Royal Naval Volunteer Reserve
700)	F. Vince		
701)	F. Voice	Staff	Royal Field Artillery
702)	Sergt. H. Wagstaffe	1907	Motor Machine Gun Section

703)	A. E. Wakefield		
704)	J. M. Wale	1913	Gordon Highlanders
705)	C. Walker	1913	Royal Army Medical Corps
706)	A. A. Walsgrove	1907	4th South Midland Howitzer Brigade
707)	H. A. Walsgrove		
708)	H. N. Walsgrove	1903	Royal Flying Corps
709)	A. J. Wankling		Royal Engineers
710)	H. Wankling		7th Royal Warwicks
711)	H. Ward	1914	Royal Air Force
712)	J. Ward		Gunner, Royal Field Artillery
713)	W. W. Ward		
714)	H. Wareham	1903	7th Royal Warwicks
715)	T. W. Wareham	1901	Birmingham City Bn, Royal Warwicks
716)	L.C Wartnaby		
717)	Watkins	1908	Army Service Corps
718)	C. B. Watkins	1908	Motor Transport
719)	C. Watson		
720)	H. Watts		
721)	A. Webb	1913	Warwickshire Imperial Yeomanry
722)	H. J. Webb	1906	1st King Liverpool
723)	W. Welch	1894	East Africa Expeditionary Force
724)	A. J. Welton	1911	Royal Army Medical Corps
725)	L. Welton	1912	Royal Field Artillery
726)	H. G. West		
727)	W. J. Weston	1908	7th Royal Warwicks
728)	W. Wetton		
729)	L. Wheatley	1911	Royal Engineers
730)	E. J. Wheeler	1904	Army Service Corps
731)	C. Whinfrey		
732)	F. W. Whinfrey	1911	Royal Horse Artillery
733)	A. J. White		
734)	C. White	1914	3rd Gordons
735)	J. A. White		Royal Field Artillery
736)	N. White		
737)	S. H. Whitehouse	1899	7th Royal Warwicks
738)	F. B. Wilcox	1908	Warwickshire Imperial Yeomanry
739)	L. Wilday		
740)	F. J. Wilding	1914	Royal Navy
741)	Wilkins		
742)	J. Wilkinson		
743)	J. Wilks		
744)	Williams		

745)	A. J. Williams	1903	Royal Garrison Artillery
746)	J. Williams		
747)	Lt G. W. Willigg	1900	Royal Naval Reserve, HMS Otranto
748)	Lt A. Wilson	Staff	11th Gordons
749)	A. E. Wilson	1904	Royal Field Artillery
750)	A. G. Wilson	1911	Northumberland Fusiliers
751)	H. Wilson		Training Reserve Battalion
752)	R. S. Wilson	1911	26th Royal Fusiliers
753)	W. S. Wilson	1909	Highland Light Infantry
754)	A. Windridge	1917	Royal Flying Corps, OTC
755)	L. A. Windridge	1912	King's Royal Rifles
756)	W. Windridge		
757)	Captain C. Winfrey		
758)	W. Winsor	1916	Royal Air Force
759)	A. G. H. Witherick	1904	Royal Engineers
760)	J. Witherick	1906	Warwickshire Imperial Yeomanry
761)	S. Witherick	1904	Warwickshire Imperial Yeomanry
762)	E. Wood		Army Service Corps
763)	F. Wood		
764)	H. C. Woodward		Royal Naval Air Service
765)	T. N. Woodward		
766)	F. T. Woof		Royal Army Medical Corps
767)	K. T. Wootton MC	Staff	3/10th London Regiment
768)	R. Wormell	1905	Warwickshire Imperial Yeomanry
769)	A. Worster	1910	
770)	W. A. Wragg	1913	Royal Field Artillery
771)	R. Wright		Warwickshire Imperial Yeomanry

Appendix D

Military Terminology

Able seaman: Merchant Navy seaman, certified to carry out routine duties at sea. This rank is higher than an Ordinary Seaman

Adjutant: Officer acting as an administrative assistant

Army: Commanded by a General with approximately 250,000 to 300,000 troops, sub-divided into 3 – 4 Corps

Bar: Small emblem on a military decoration showing a further award of this medal

Battalion: Army unit comprised of approximately 1,000 men, commanded by a Colonel or Lieutenant-Colonel; divided into four companies.

Brigade: Commanded by a Brigadier-General, comprised of approximately 4,000 – 5,000 troops sub-divided into 3-4 Battalions.

Captain: In the army, an officer who commands a company, troop, or battery; in the navy, an officer ranking above a Commander and below a Commodore

Casualty Clearing Station: The first stage on the route back from the front for the wounded, normally located about 1.5 miles from the front line.

Clasp: Metal bar or similar, clasped to the ribbon of a military decoration. Clasps were awarded according to the individual's deed or service. A Clasp could also be a further award of the same medal

Commander: The chief commissioned officer of a military unit whatever their rank

Company: Sub-unit of a Battalion, commanded by a Major or Captain comprised of approximately 200 men divided into four platoons.

Corporal: in the army, a non-commissioned rank below Sergeant and above Lance-Corporal.

Corps: A component of the army forming a unit comprised of approximately 80,000 men divided into 4 – 6 divisions, commanded by Lieutenant-General.

Derby Scheme: Named after Lord Edward Derby, all eligible males were asked to express their willingness to serve. The scheme lasted for 5 months from July 1915 to December 1915 and provided less then 350,000 troops.

Division: Largest tactical unit of the British Army (beneath Corps). Commanded by a Major-General, with approximately 15,000 – 20,000 troops split into 3 brigades.

Enfilading Fire: Fire which is directed from the side rather then the front

Gazetted: Officer's promotions and awards were posted in the London gazette.

Hindenburg line: A vast system of defence constructed during the winter of 1916-1917 under the guidance of General Paul von Hindenburg

Leading Seaman: A non-commissioned rank in the navy, above Able Seaman and Ordinary Seaman

Lieutenant: In the army, a commissioned officer below a Captain; in the navy, a commissioned officer below a Commander

Mentioned in Despatches: The award of a Mentioned in Despatches (MID) was the lowest form of recognition for services during the war, and was announced in the London Gazette

Merchant Navy: Term used for civilian seafaring personnel, the military used merchant ships and their crew during wartime

Minenwerfer: Translates into Mine Launcher, a class of short range mortars used to target obstacles including trenches and barbed wire

Non-Commissioned Officer: a position above private and below Officer

Ordinary Seaman: Lowest grade of crew member

Other Ranks: Soldiers, as opposed to Officers

Parados: Barricade at the rear of the trench to stop shrapnel getting into the trench.

Platoon: approximately 50 men, commanded by a Lieutenant or 2nd Lieutenant sub-divided into 4 sections

Rank: Level of authority held by an officer or soldier

Regiment: A large body of troops, organised under the command of a superior officer, and forming a definite unit of an army or military force; the specific name of the largest permanent unit of the cavalry, infantry, and foot-guards of the British Army.

Salient: A battlefield feature that projects into enemy territory. The salient was typically surrounded by the enemy on three sides making the salient vulnerable.

Section: Approximately 12 men commanded by a NCO

Sergeant: In the army, an NCO next in rank above a Corporal.

Sunken Road: A well worn road that over time had become sunken below its original level.

Yeoman of the Signals: Petty Officer who specialised in the handling and conducting of flag signals in the communications departments of a naval vessel.

Zero Hour: The time at which the military operations were planned to start

Appendix E

Military Abbreviations

Anzacs: Australian and New Zealand Armed Corps
ASC: Army Service Corps
BEF: British Expeditionary Force
BWM: British War Medal
CASC: Canadian Army Service Corps
CCS: Casualty Clearing Station
CEF: Canadian Expeditionary Force
CO: Commanding Officer
CSM: Company Sergeant Major
CWGC: Commonwealth War Grave Commission
DCLI: Duke of Cornwall's Light Infantry
DCM: Distinguished Conduct Medal
DOW: Died Of Wounds
DSO: Distinguished Service Order
GHQ: General Headquarters
GOC: General Officer Commanding
HAC: Honourable Artillery Company
HMT: His Majesty's Transport
KIA: Killed In Action
KOSB: King's Own Scottish Borderers
KRR: King's Royal Rifles
KSLI: King's Shropshire Light Infantry
MC: Military Cross
MGC: Machine Gun Corps
MIC: Medal Index Card
MID: Mentioned in Despatches
MM: Military Medal
MMGS: Motor Machine Gun Service
MSM: Meritorious Service Medal
NCO: Non-Commissioned Officer
NZEF: New Zealand Expeditionary Force
OBE: Order of the British Empire
OBLI: Oxfordshire and Buckinghamshire Light Infantry
OR: Other Ranks
OTC: Officer Training Corps
POW: Prisoner Of War
RAMC: Royal Army Medical Corps

RAF: Royal Air Force
RAMC: Royal Army Medical Corps
RE: Royal Engineers
RFA: Royal Field Artillery
RFC: Royal Flying Corps
RGA: Royal Garrison Artillery
RHA: Royal Horse Artillery
RNAS: Royal Naval Air Service
RNVR: Royal Navy Volunteer Reserve
RWR: Royal Warwickshire Regiment
SWB: South Wales Borderers
TMB: Trench Mortar Battery
VC: Victoria Cross

Appendix F

Cemeteries and Memorials

This section details the Country and Locality of the Cemeteries and War Memorials where the Bablake Fallen are commemorated. Exact location information, visiting information and historical information can be found on the Commonwealth War Grave Commission website www.cwgc.org or by phoning 01628 507200.

Belgium

Comines-Warneton, Hainaut

Ploegsteert Memorial and Cemetery:	Sergeant George Edward Barker
	Sergeant Henry Barker
	Private Edgar Hebert Buckingham
	Private John William Rossiter

Heuvelland, West-Vlaanderen

La Clytte Military Cemetery:	Private John Spencer
Oosttaverne Wood Cemetery:	2nd Lieutenant Frederick Adams

Ieper, West-Vlaanderen

Brandhoek New Military Cemetery:	2nd Lieutenant James William Guise
Buffs Road Cemetery:	Gunner Arthur Whinfrey
Ypres (Menin Gate) Memorial:	2nd Lieutenant Frank Yardley
Menin Road South Military Cemetery:	Sapper Harry Hassall Underwood
Vlamertinghe Military Cemetery:	Gunner Harry Clarke

Poperinge, West-Vlaanderen

Dozinghem Military Cemetery:	Captain Frank Septimus Neville
Mendinghem Military Cemetery:	Pioneer Henry Amos Courts

Zonnebeke, West-Vlaanderen

Tyne Cot Cemetery and Memorial:	2nd Lieutenant Walter Ernest Grew
	2nd Lieutenant William Arthur Imber
	Captain Alfred Ernest Mander
	Lieutenant Sidney George Wolfe

Egypt

Chatby Memorial:	Private Ambrose John Cole

France

Aisne

Premont British Cemetery:	Sergeant Major Alfred James Suddens

Beaurains

Beaurains Road Cemetery:	Gunner Frederick Walter Caldicott

Nord

Bachant Communal Cemetery:	Private Reginald Thomas Beaufoy
Conde-sur-l'Escaut:	Private Raymond Frederick John Averns
Glageon Communal Cemetery:	Private Frank William Wells
Landrecies British Cemetery:	Private Leslie Thomas Jones
Laventie Military Cemetery:	Sergeant William Toms
	Lance Sergeant Herbert Ward
Meteren Military Cemetery:	Private Henry Buckland
Selridge British Cemetery, Montay:	2nd Lieutenant Frank Nevey
Tannay British Cemetery, Thiennes:	Sergeant Joseph Howe MM

Pas de Calais

Aire Communal Cemetery:	Lance Corporal Victor Leslie Clarke
	Corporal Herbert William Hawthorne
Arras Communal Cemetery and Memorial	
	Lance Corporal Walter S. Bailey
	Acting Captain Percy Hood Hollick
	Private William Alexander Loudon
Chocques Military Cemetery:	Sergeant Ernest Clifford Elliott
Croisilles British Cemetery:	2nd Lieutenant Bernard Michael Ward
Etaples Military Cemetery:	Private Francis Daulman Cox
	Private Wilfred Hibbert Sidwell
Grevillers British Cemetery:	Private Albert Knight
Guards Cemetery, Cuinchy:	Private William Hubert Morris
Hebuterne Military Cemetery:	Sergeant John Weston Burton
Le Touret Memorial:	2nd Lieutenant Herbert William Hyde
Longuenesse (St. Omer) Cemetery:	Gunner Herbert Charles Collingbourne
Loos Memorial:	Lance Sergeant Henry Smith Craven
	Bombardier Charles John Hopkins
Tilloy British Cemetery, Tilloy-les-Mofflaines	
	Bombardier Harold Eugene Rollason
Vimy Memorial:	Private John Samuel Harris
Vis-En-Artois British Cemetery and Memorial	
	2nd Lieutenant Arthur Joseph Adams
	Private Joseph Edward Roots

Wimereux Communal Cemetery: Gunner Vincent Arthur Bloxham
    Private William Wilkins

Seine Maritime
Ste. Marie Cemetery, Le Havre: Private Harold George Bonham
St. Sever Cemetery Extension, Rouen: Private Noel Raymond Averns

Somme
Adelaide Cemetery, Villers-Bretonneux: Private William Charles Beacham
Aveluy Communal Cemetery Extension: Gunner Alfred George Middleton
Franvillers Communal Cemetery Extension:
    2nd Lieutenant Aubrey Frederick Hall
Heilly Station Cemetery, Mericourt-l'Abbe
    CSM William Henry Croft Wood
Pozières Cemetery and Memorial:

    Private Thomas Herbert Allchurch
    2nd Lieutenant Matthew Frank Matts
    Private Sydney Mornington Pickerill
    2nd Lieutenant Frederick Charles Vincent
Thiepval Memorial: Captain Harold Meredith Adcock
    Private Kenneth Barry
    Corporal George Cyril Biggs
    2nd Lieutenant Francis Henry Cox
    Corporal Frederick Harris
    Lance Corporal William Percival Kirby
    2nd Lieutenant John Claude Murray
    Rifleman Hugh Conrad Pails
    Lnce Corpl Leonard Joseph Walker Price
    Private Howard Round

Iraq
Amara War Cemetery: 2nd Lieutenant Reginald Kenneth Drakeley

Israel
Gaza War Cemetery: Lieutenant Frederick James Poulton

Italy
Montecchio Precalcino Cemetery: Private Henry Edwin Gunn

Turkey
Helles Memorial: Gunner Samuel James Elliott
Lone Pine Memorial: Corporal Alfred Bailey
    Lieutenant Frederick Hugh Dodson

Appendix G

Cemeteries in the UK

This section details where the Bablake Fallen are buried and commemorated in the UK. Exact location information, visiting information and historical information can be found on the Commonwealth War Grave Commission website www.cwgc.org or by phoning 01628 507200.

Coventry

London Road Cemetery: Sergeant Harry Aston
                        Private James Connolly
                        2nd Lieutenant Herbert Nelson
                        2nd Lieutenant William John Salmons MM
                        Lance Corporal Cecil Sidwell

Windmill Road, Cemetery: Private Herbert Victor Cantrill

Other UK

Bath (Locksbrook) Cemetery: Cadet Hubert Arthur Morley

Chatham Naval Memorial: Able Seaman Frank Kenneth Greening

Plymouth Naval Memorial: Ordinary Seaman Alfred Oswald Peart
                           Boy 1st Class Henry Gordon Farmer

Portsmouth Naval Memorial: Gunner Charles John Jones

Shirebrook Cemetery, Mansfield: 2nd Lieutenant William Alexander Roberts

Tower Hill Memorial, London: 2nd Officer Sydney Charles Hitch

Appendix H

Grave Locations In London Road Cemetery

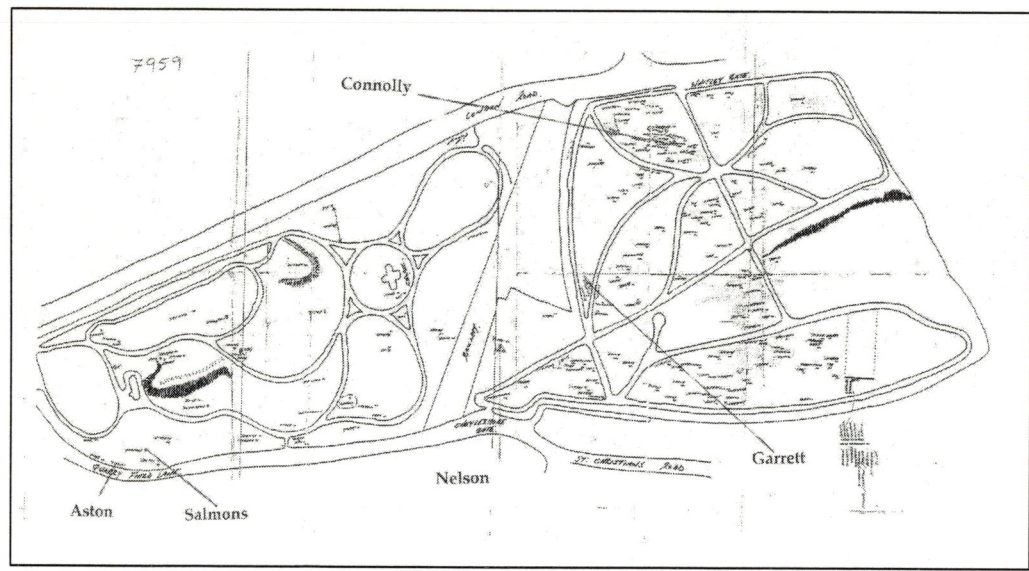

Sergeant Harry Aston, 9th Lancers died 25th November 1914

Private Samuel Husselby Garrett, 2/7th Battalion Royal Warwickshire Regiment died 15th July 1915.

Private James Connolly, 20th Battalion Royal Fusiliers died 7th May 1917

Lance Corporal Cecil Sidwell, 1/1st Warwickshire Yeomanry died 30th January 1918. Grave location not known

Second Lieutenant Herbert Nelson, Royal Flying Corps died 19th March 1918

Second Lieutenant William John Salmons MM, 65th Squadron Royal Air Force died 22nd April 1918

Appendix I

War Memorials in Coventry

<u>British Thompson Houston Memorial</u>: This memorial is dedicated to those who fell from the firm British Thompson Houston Company and can be found in the Royal Warwicks club, Tower Street, Coventry.

<u>Central Methodist Church</u>: This memorial can be found at the top of the staircase in the church and records the names from the congregation who fell during the Great War.

<u>Coventry Corporation Memorial</u>: Each department from Coventry Corporation had a memorial to those that served and those that fell. These are located throughout the Council House.

<u>Earlsdon Working Mens Club</u>: Now known as the Albany Club, shows the name of five Fallen members situated behind the bar.

<u>Holy Trinity Church</u>: This incorporates three panels showing the names of members of the congregation who fell.

<u>Iliffe Works Memorial</u>: The location of this memorial is not known, but a picture of it was found during research

<u>Post Office:</u> Wall-mounted in the main Post Office; bears the names of those who fell.

<u>Queen's Road Church:</u> Stained glass panels showing the names of the fallen from the congregation.

<u>Radford Memorial</u>: A free standing memorial next to St. Nicholas's church showing the names of 112 members of the Radford community who either fell or served during the Great War.

<u>St. Barbara's Church</u>: A brass plaque at the rear of the church, showing the names of members of the congregation who fell during the Great War. The majority of whom lived in the Earlsdon district.

<u>St. John's Church</u>: Stained glass panels that show the names of the fallen and located near to the old school in Hill Street in the City centre.

<u>St. Michael's Church</u>: A stone tablet with the names of the fallen inscribed, mounted in the front porch of the church in Stoke.

<u>Triumph and Gloria Memorial</u>: A free standing memorial in the grounds of Coventry cemetery dedicated to the employees of the firm who died.

<u>Walsgrave Memorial</u>: A free standing memorial located on the Walsgrave Road dedicated to those who fell from the community.

<u>War Memorial Park</u>: The park was paid for by public subscription and opened in 1921, relatives of the fallen were offered the opportunity to purchase a plaque and tree as a memorial.

Meet The Author

Trevor Harkin lives in Earlsdon, Coventry with his wife and two children. After leaving Secondary School, he furthered his education at Coventry University initially achieving a Batchelor of Engineering and furthered this with an MBA in Management and an MSc in Automotive and Automotive Component Manufacture. He then wrote several articles on Knowledge Management and performance metrics which appeared in Engineering periodicals.

Having completed his studies, he began researching his family tree and found on his Mother's side that his Grandmother lost three uncles in the Great War and on his Father's side his Great grandfather served all the way through the war, although he never spoke about his experiences.

On a visit to Coventry's War Memorial Park he noticed the plaques dedicated to those who fell during WW1 and WW2 and set about researching the plaques and started a web page www.warmemorialpark.co.uk. Following a local appeal for information an article was shown in an assembly at Bablake School at which his nephew, Alex Hoare was in attendance. This started a dialogue with Bablake School and he promptly added the names of the Bablake fallen to his list of men to research. Trevor has contributed articles to a local magazine *'The Earlsdon Echo'* and a number of his articles have featured in local newspapers, *'The Coventry Telegraph'* and *'Coventry Observer'*.

Where time permits he has also assisted relatives of the Fallen and those who have expressed an interest in soldiers from Coventry. This is his first book and further work is nearing completion on Coventry's War Memorial Park.

Index

Adams, Arthur Joseph 36, 58, 128, 129

Adams, Frederick 57-59, 128, 146

Adcock, Harold Meredyth 19, 20, 25-27, 86-88

Adelaide Cemetery 121

Aire Cemetery 124, 126

Allchurch, Thomas Herbert 120

Allen, L. 142

Allsopp, H. L. 10, 11

Amara War Cemetery 66

Anzacs 61, 63, 93, 94

Argyll and Sutherland 18, 117

Armentieres 70, 157

Armistice 46, 47, 72, 77, 83, 121, 128, 132, 149, 150

Arras 101, 102, 103, 115-117, 129, 156

Arras Memorial 105, 117, 119

Aston, Harry 38-40

Atkinson, Gerald 24, 26, 27, 151

Attenborough, F. 153

Australian Contingent 24, 30, 36, 37, 61, 62, 84, 121, 135, 153, 158

Aveluy Cemetery 95, 96

Averns, Noel Raymond Francis 98, 99

Averns, Raymond Frederick John 126

Bachant Cemetery 134

Bailey, Alfred 30, 61, 62

Bailey, Walter 117

Baker, C. W. 139, 141

Bancrofts School 6, 7, 8

Banning, C. R. 27, 145

Bannington, A. C. 28

Barber, D. 135

Barber, G. N. 135

Barker, Frederick William 30

Barker, George Edward 32, 69, 70

Barker, Henry 32, 69, 70

Barry, Kenneth 95

Batchelor, W. H. 7, 28

Bates, Joseph Innis 7, 8, 149, 150

Bates, J. 151

Beacham, William Charles 121, 155

Beaufoy, Reginald Thomas 133, 134

Beaumont, S. A. 29

Beaurains Road Cemetery 102

Beesley, George Arthur 37

Biggs, George Cyril 91

Birt, M. D. 11

Blakemore, E. J. 142

Bloxham, Vincent Arthur 109, 110

Bonham, Harold George 132

Bouzincourt 91, 93

Brandhoek Cemetery 108

British Thompson Houston 40

Brown, Harold Masters 88-90, 141

Buckingham, Edgar Herbert 120, 121

Buckland, Henry 110, 111

Buckler, Francis Albert 147, 152

Buffs Road Cemetery 111

Burton, John Weston 29, 30, 83

Cadet Corps 10, 20-25, 88, 111, 115, 158

Caldicott, Frederick Walter 101

Cambrai 102, 106, 114, 116

Canadian 30, 31, 46, 57, 73, 74, 129, 135, 158

Cantrill, Harry 46

Cantrill, Herbert Victor 30, 46, 119

Carter, Alfred 13, 151

Chatby Memorial 56

Chatham Memorial 55

Chocques Cemetery 122

Christs College 86

Clarke, Harry 105

Clarke, Victor Leslie 123-125, 154

Core Frank 20, 22, 24, 26, 145, 151, 166

Council House 84, 85, 101, 106, 117, 149

Courts, Henry Amos 106

Cox, Francis Daulman 57, 58

Cox, Francis Henry 96-98, 100

Cox, Thomas Edwin 31

Crampers Field 7

Craven, Henry Smith 19, 81, 82

Croisilles Cemetery 115

Croydon, Richard Hunt 78, 79

Dardanelles 24, 43, 53, 60

Daulman, H. 137, 138

Day, W. W. 37

Debating Society 13, 87

Despatches 37, 44, 61, 105, 146

Distinguished Conduct Medal (DCM) 10, 117, 139-141, 143

Distinguished Service Order (DSO) 139, 140, 142

Dodson, Frederick Hugh 61-63

Dozinghem Cemetery 115, 116

Drakeley, Reginald Kenneth 65, 66

Duke Of Cornwall 110

Earlsdon 24, 42, 56, 62, 63, 77, 92, 98, 99, 101, 109, 110, 113, 114, 121, 130, 131, 133, 139

Earlsdon Club 94

East Kent Regiment 81

Elkington, C. H. 35

Elliott, Ernest Clifford 64, 122

Elliott, Samuel James 63, 64

Engleton Road Memorial 124, 127

Etaples Cemetery 57, 90, 100, 135

Farmer, Henry Gordon 48-50

Festubert 72

Fillongley War Memorial 70

Fitzgerald, B. M. 58, 59, 146

Fletcher, Chas 28

Fletcher, Claude 28

Fletcher, C. H. 28

Fletcher, Reginald 28, 29, 78, 79

Frankland, Dr. J. N. 13, 151, 152

Franvillers Cemetery 127

Gallipoli 60-65, 146

Garrett, Samuel Husselby 40, 41

Gee, D. 143

Glageon Cemetery 130

Godiva pageant 150

Gould, Arthur Ernest 139

Greening, Frank Kenneth 53-55, 136

Grevillers Cemetery 129

Grew, Walter Ernest 27, 111, 112

Guards Cemetery 75

Guise, James William 107, 108

Gunn, Henry Edwin 68, 155

Haig, Sir Douglas 48, 105, 106, 146

Hall, Aubrey Frederick 127

Hanson, P. E. 11, 15

Harper, Charles 36

Harris, A. E. 135, 136

Harris, Albert 135, 139, 144, 145

Harris, Frederick Arthur 101-103

Harris, John Samuel 30, 73, 74, 81

Hattrell, J. A. 29

Haucourt Cemetery 129

Hawthorne, Herbert William 126, 155

Hazebrouck Cemetery 71, 72

Hebuterne Cemetery 83

Hegan, Harold 15, 16

Hegan, Reginald 15, 16

Heilly Station Cemetery 94

Helles Memorial 63

Herbert, Alfred 11, 62, 77, 92, 139

Highland Light Infantry 24

Hill Street 6

Hindenburg Line 101, 102

Hitch, Sydney Charles 52

HMS Malaya 49, 50

HMS Queen Mary 49-51

HMS Strongbow 53-55

Hodson, Frederick 8, 13, 21, 26

Hollick, Percy Hood 103-105, 146

Holy Trinity 29

Hopkins, Charles John 77, 81

Howe, Joseph 122, 123, 143

Hulme, Stanley 143

Humberstone, Francis William 6-8, 22, 31, 79, 150, 151, 154, 155

Humberstone, John Percival 31

Hyde, Herbert William 71, 72

Hyslop, Reverend A. R. F, 13

Imber, William Arthur 36, 42, 109

Italy 56, 68

Jones, Charles John 48, 50, 51

Jones, Leonard 24

Jones, Leslie Thomas 132

Jutland, Battle of 48-51

Kelsey, Luther James 141

Kenilworth 34, 103

King Henry VIII 29, 34, 78, 79, 91

King's College 6, 8, 89, 131, 132

King's Liverpool Regiment 128, 129

King's Own Scottish Borderers 104, 119

King's Royal Rifles 27, 35, 64, 117, 119, 122

King's Shropshire Light Infantry 69, 70

Kirby, W. 135, 136

Kut-el-Amara 65, 66

Knight, Albert 129

La Boisselle 89, 91, 93, 94

La Clytte Cemetery 127

Labour Corps 122, 132

Lancashire Fusiliers 10, 27, 70, 86, 87, 105, 113, 143, 145

Lancers, 9th 39, 40

Landrecies Cemetery 133

Langemarck 107

Laventie Cemetery 83, 84

Lawrence, C. H. 26, 152

Le Touret 73

Locksbrook Cemetery 47

London Regiment 27, 41, 57, 96, 98, 132, 143, 151

London Road Cemetery 38-45, 96, 108

Lone Pine Memorial 63

Loos 73, 74, 102, 128, 145

Loos Memorial 77, 81

Loudon, William Alexander 46, 119, 155

Loveitt, Lieutenant 94

Machine Gun Corps 26, 106, 107, 127, 130, 145, 151

Mander, Alfred Ernest 19, 36, 112, 113

Mander, Henry 6

Mander, P. G. 15, 17, 19, 112, 113

Mason, A. E. W. 9

Matts, Matthew Frank 29, 30, 92, 93, 94

Memorial Plaque 147, 148

Mendinghem Cemetery 106, 115

Menin Gate Memorial 107

Menin Road Cemetery 77

Meritorious Service Medal 137, 139, 144, 145

Mesopotamia 15, 65

Messines 58, 105, 116

Meteren Cemetery 111

Methodist Central Hall 45, 61, 117

Middlesex Regiment 28

Middleton, Alfred George 95

Military Cross (MC) 68, 88, 90, 139, 141, 142, 151

Military Medal(MM) 44, 45, 122, 123, 139, 143-145

Mills, F. 36, 143

Montecchio Precalcino Cemetery 68

Morgan, Frank Leslie 11, 16, 36, 82, 143, 144, 151

Morley, Hubert Arthur 38, 47

Morris, Hubert William 74-77, 148

Motor Machine Gun Service (MMGS) 15, 16

Munitions 10, 11, 15, 142, 158

Murray, John Claude 90, 91
Nelson, Herbert 38, 42 – 44, 57, 61
Nelson, Horace 44
Nelson, Hugh 43, 61, 146
Nevey, Frank 131, 132
Neville, Frank Septimus 115, 116
Norfolk Regiment 27, 36, 112, 133, 134
Northamptonshire Regiment 115
Northumberland Fusiliers 120
Nottinghamshire & Derby 24
Olorenshaw, John 27, 37
Oosttaverne Wood Cemetery 59, 107
Ovillers 89, 94
Oxfordshire and Buckinghamshire 74, 75, 83, 94, 102, 107, 108, 116, 117, 135, 136, 148
Pails, Hugh Conrad 96, 155
Palestine 67
Palmer, A. 146
Pargetter, A. 7
Parsons, Jack 9, 143
Passchendaele 19, 105-107, 112, 114, 116
Patrick, D. H. 10, 32, 33
Payne, F. W. 35
Payne, Herbert Joseph 63, 64
Pearson, Frank H. 32, 37, 151, 152
Pearson, H. 29
Peart, Alfred Oswald 52
Peirson, E. J. 30
Pickerill, Sydney Mornington 118, 119
Pickering, A. A. 145
Player, Francis Edwin 31
Ploegsteert Memorial 70 – 72, 121
Plymouth Naval Memorial 52
Portsmouth Naval Memorial 51
Post Office Memorial 79
Poulton, Frederick Joseph 67
Poxon, Silas 145
Pozieres 88, 92 – 94

Pozieres Cemetery 94
Pozieres Memorial 117, 119, 120
Prattley, E. 10, 27
Premont Cemetery 116
Price, Leonard Joseph Walker 96, 97
Queens Road Church 101, 120
Redfern, P. 29, 30
Reynolds, J. 145
Roberts, William Alexander 27, 38, 47
Rollason, Harold Eugene 101, 102
Roll of Honour 32 – 34
Roll of the Fallen 100, 107, 127, 135-137
Roots, Joseph Edward 130
Rossiter, Alexander 72
Rossiter, John William 32, 71, 72, 107
Round, Howard 92, 94
Royal Air Force 44, 46, 47, 57, 146, 158
Royal Army Medical Corps 15, 36, 90, 112
Royal Berkshire Regiment 88, 89, 93, 121, 147
Royal Dublin Fusiliers 27, 97, 98, 114, 115
Royal Engineers 36, 57, 64, 71, 77, 106, 127, 133, 139, 142, 143, 145, 151
Royal Field Artillery 26, 40, 77, 95, 123, 137, 139, 144, 146
Royal Flying Corps 42, 44, 45, 57, 59
Royal Fusiliers 36, 41, 44, 94, 95, 96, 97, 98, 100, 126
Royal Garrsion Artillery 63, 105
Royal Horse Artillery 28, 78, 79
Royal Inniskilling Fusiliers 72, 73
Royal Naval Air Service 33, 36, 43, 57, 61
Royal Sussex Regiment 72, 73, 111, 129
Royal Warwicks Club 40

Royal Warwickshire Regiment 16, 26, 45, 68, 92, 98, 107, 110, 118, 121, 127, 128, 129, 131, 141, 143

1st Battalion 22, 72, 97, 128

2nd Battalion 28, 71

3rd Battalion 30, 103

4th Battalion 108

2/6th Battalion 121

7th Battalion 15, 28, 72, 74, 109

1/7th Battalion 35, 68, 83, 91, 109, 113

2/7th Battalion 40, 84, 118, 120, 123

8th Battalion 109

1/8th Battalion 132, 136

9th Battalion 65

13th Battalion 128

14th Battalion 122

15th Battalion 126

16th Battalion 105, 111

Royal West Kent 126

Rudge 42, 43, 123

Salmons, William John 44, 45, 57, 143

School Magazine 15 – 19

Selridge Cemetery 132

Selwyn College 126

Shirebrook Cemetery 47

Shortridge, W. L. 139, 143

Siddeley Deasy 19

Sidwell, Cecil 42, 101

Sidwell, Wilfred Hibbert 42, 100, 101

Smith, F. R. 29

Somme, Battle of 36, 57, 83 – 90, 95, 99 – 102, 113, 117, 118, 124, 127 – 130, 136, 145, 157

Southam, Richard 6

South Wales Borderers 90

Southampton 38, 42, 69

Spencer, John 127

SS Polymnia 52

SS Ravensworth 52

St. Barbaras Church 99, 114, 121, 130, 133

St. Johns Church 45, 47, 88, 89, 97, 111, 112, 127

St. Michaels Church 50, 94

St. Omer Cemetery 79

St. Sever Cemetery 99

Ste. Marie Cemetery 132

Storer, H. E. 142

Storer, Joseph 35

Suddens, Alfred James 116, 117, 154, 155

Suddens, H. T. 117, 154

Tannay Cemetery 123

Thiepval Memorial 88, 91, 94, 95, 96, 102, 136

Tilloy-les-Mofflaines 102

Tipler, Alfred Frederick 20, 35

Toms, William 83

Tower Hill Memorial 52

Trinity College 113

Triumph & Gloria Memorial 95

Underwood, Harry Hassall 77

Victoria Cross 39, 50, 142

Vimy Ridge 74

Vincent, Frederick Charles 117, 139

Vis-En-Artois Memorial 128, 131

Vlamertinghe Cemetery 105, 108

Walsgrave Memorial 117

Ward, Bernard Michael 114, 115

Ward, Herbert 83, 84

Ward, Sydney Frank 128, 129

War Memorial Fund 127, 154, 155

War Memorial Park 47, 51, 57, 64, 79, 81, 84, 93, 96, 99, 109, 110, 111, 113, 115, 119, 121, 124, 130, 132, 133, 134, 154

Warwickshire Yeomanry 26, 28, 30, 42, 56, 101, 126, 130, 135, 137, 138, 143

Well Street Church 84, 85, 92

Wells, Frank William 129, 130

Wesleyan Methodist Church 61

West Riding Regiment 15, 112, 113,
   131, 132, 135
Wheatleyan 15 – 19
Wheatley, Thomas 6
Whinfrey, Arthur 111
White, J. A. 137, 145
White & Poppe 10
Wilkins, William 72, 110
Wilkinson, A. 135
Wilson, A. 8, 21, 26, 151, 156

Wilson, William Smith 24
Wimereux Cemetery 72, 110
Windmill Road Cemetery 38, 46
Wolfe, Sydney George 113, 114
Wolston 74, 77, 143, 145
Wood, William Henry Croft 92, 94
Woodward, Harry Collins 33
Wootton, Kenneth 37, 143, 151
Wyley, Colonel 8, 22
Yardley, Frank 106, 107